AT THE POINT OF NEED

Teaching Basic and ESL Writers

MARIE WILSON NELSON

With a Foreword by
NANCY MARTIN

Boynton/Cook Publishers
HEINEMANN
Portsmouth, NH

Boynton/Cook Publishers, Inc.
A Subsidiary of
Heinemann Educational Books, Inc.
361 Hanover Street, Portsmouth, NH 03801-3959
Offices and agents throughout the world

Library of Congress Cataloging-in-Publication Data
Nelson, Marie Wilson.
    At the point of need : teaching basic and ESL writers / Marie
    Wilson Nelson.
        p.   cm.
    Includes bibliographical references (p.) and index.
    ISBN 0-86709-265-3
    1. English language—Composition and exercises—Study and
teaching.   2. English language—Study and teaching—Foreign
speakers.   I. Title.
PE1404.N45   1990   90-44002
808' .042'07—dc20   CIP

Editing, design, and production: G & H Soho, Ltd.
Cover design by Wladislaw Finne.

Printed in the United States of America.
91   92   93   94   95   10   9   8   7   6   5   4   3   2   1

Dedication

This book is for the students I didn't know how to teach because they didn't grow up speaking standard English at home. Its roots stretch back to my first job in the South Carolina upcountry where I taught two whole classes of Lesters and Rays and Ems from the cotton mill village near the proud new suburban high school. Em had to drop out of school that year to "get marred and have this baby" because in those days pregnant teens were not allowed in school. But at nineteen Lester and Ray, who towered above my small frame, had more influence in my eleventh grade classroom than I ever did. Though their files contained scant evidence of intellect, these two outwitted time and again my efforts to teach them to write. Then in early spring they dropped by my apartment to ask for help, and before long I was seeing them on Saturday afternoons. Lester said he and Ray needed "good English" to "get good jobs," but according to Em, she "just came to keep them company." Two or three weeks after school let out, Em showed up in tears with the news. The boys had run Lester's daddy's Harley up under the back of a semi on a winding mountain road one moonless Saturday night.

This book is also for Lotty, a sixth grader in Atlanta, whose family left their holler in the mountains of North Georgia after the haint that lived in the barn moved into the house. "Hit wasn't me was afraid," she said, "but Ma got downright jumpy." The suburban students in my sixth/seventh grade combination understood long before I did that Lotty would fail my class.

And it's for Jimmy Sunday, at Savannah State College, a bright young man who—though he spelled his name three ways that term—brought Malcolm X, E. Franklin Frazier, and John Hope Franklin for me to read and then hung around my office until I discussed them with him. Jimy (as he spelled it once) went home to Jacksonville soon after midterm, but like the others, he had a strong impact on me. Each activated my search for ways to help nonstandard speakers master the written dialect of mainstream society. Thanks to them, I now know more about how that can be done.

Contents

Foreword

Nancy Martin

This is a book about qualitative research, about how teaching improves when teachers look closely at what they are doing and how their students respond. More specifically, it is a book about basic and English as a second language (ESL) writers writing, about observing how they learn. It shows how five successive teams of tutors over five years used teacher-research to teach themselves to teach the kinds of students that have baffled educators for years. Professor Nelson says, "From the beginning our goal has been that of reflective teaching. Each year we tested the assumptions on which our program was based—assumptions about how writers work and how writing is learned."

The project was a five-year program set up for native and nonnative (40 percent) speakers of English who scored below a cut-off point on a test of standard written English. The program was established in the context of a new university tutorial center in which the tutors were graduate assistants selected and trained by Professor Nelson, who designed the program and settled certification. The students were scheduled for two hours a week of study in small workshop groups of four or five led by a graduate assistant. In addition, Professor Nelson held a weekly seminar for tutors for continuous review, modification, and analysis.

The book is not a conventional research report. Rather, it calls to mind famous scientific journals. Observation is a large part of it, as well as skepticism about established educational procedures—almost everything that happens is a matter for inquiry. The outstanding features of the study are the continuous restructuring of the procedures in the light of the reflective writing and discussion that was a basic thread in the structure, together with the unexpected power that the small workshop groups generated to affect students' learning, attitudes, and confidence.

Much of the book consists of case studies of individual students based on excerpts from their writings at various stages of drafting, on transcripts of small-group discussions, and on descriptive quotations from students' and tutors' logs. Alongside and interwoven with the student case studies are comparable case studies of the tutors culled from similar sources and accompanied by a running commentary by Professor Nelson on their perception of their progress as fellow learners with the students, as well as on the progress of the whole endeavor. Of course, the program generated an enormous amount of writing and recorded talk. From this corpus, Professor Nelson selected items that, on the one hand, supported her two starting hypotheses based on her previous research and that, on the other hand, revealed the discoveries she and her teams made in the process of their work—discoveries that operated consistently enough for them to be described as principles.

The starting hypotheses were that regardless of courses or students, the most confident and successful teachers differed in two ways from teachers who felt frustrated, defeated, or ambivalent about teaching: (1) in the degree to which their own writing experience shaped their teaching and (2) in the degree to which they listened to students describing the kind of help they needed. The teams never needed to revise these starting hypotheses—though they questioned them continually—and the second one gradually came to underpin the whole program.

It is a great narrative as we follow the tutors, the students, and their director interacting with each other and as we gradually begin to perceive what is happening and become explicit about it—the analysis always following the continuously shifting events. The teams' chief discoveries relate to the gradual taking of responsibility by the students for their own work. The observed dependence–interdependence–independence syndrome illustrates this process. Professor Nelson writes, "Dependence was the entering condition of our Writing Center students—afraid to take risks and unwilling to take responsibility, they cowered in the shadow of evaluation." So evaluation was put aside until the end of the course, the word "Sanctuary" was written over the entrance of the Writing Center, and all writing was brought to the small-group seminars for advice and support. It took perhaps four years of observation and analysis to reveal this consistent pattern of dependence, interdependence, and independence and to relate it to the features of the context that had produced it—and the comparable changes in reverse of the tutors, from a highly directive stance to one of adviser, if required.

It is a complex, and in some ways, a mysterious story because it is far from some of the most deeply held ideas we as teachers have inherited. For example, foward planning looms large in a teacher's work—and life; yet this writing program was set up on a dynamic of retrospective planning. Its policy was "Wait and see" and "What do you see?" Traditional procedures, experiences, and expectations were—mostly—put on ice. For example, one tutor, at the top of a journal entry, scrawled, "Hindsight, insight, foresight." Below she had written,

> It's from my logs that I'm learning how to teach. . . . While I write, I look back on what we did each day, and that's where I figure out what's going on with students. Without the insights I get from studying what we've done, I'd have no way to figure out what my students need next.

Another focus for analysis was the phenomenon of "breakthrough." In documenting the points of breakthrough in students' writing, together with their regressions and final success, the tutors found that planned, direct teaching failed to be remembered and used. The breakthroughs were somehow achieved by other means. Marie Nelson puts forward a theory to account for breakthrough: The tutors found that the most acceptable and effective teaching was to give the help the students asked for *when they asked for it*—that is, as the students perceived the need. In addition, the tutors taught new points about grammar, structure, and punctuation as the need became apparent from a number of students' essays.

The transfer from self-initiated writing to academic essays on assigned topics was a matter of anxiety for both students and tutors, with the tutors being prepared to renege on their practice hitherto and do some direct, planned teaching. But academic writing did not prove the hurdle they had expected. The students asked similar questions and sought the kind of advice they had become accustomed to, and the tutors had the confidence to remain within their chosen pattern of procedure. Excerpts from logs trace a transition from a focus on individual involvement in a self-chosen topic to one of examining the views of a group of workmates toward academic writing. A student saw this evolution as an advance and wrote, "Not only do we more thoroughly (in writing) examine our own thoughts and understand them better, but we are also able to consider and question those of others."

I have selected these examples of tangential learning to introduce *At the Point of Need* because this kind of learning is the special strength of the project. The concept of teaching only at the students' perceived points of need, and as they arise, presents a different view of learning from that of planned and sequenced series of lessons. The former view depends on recognition of the power of a person's intention as the operating dynamic in writing—and in learning.

It would be a mistake, I believe, to see this program as specifically linked to similar programs of writing for basic and ESL students at the university level. This study is a rich quarry for ideas and practice for writing teachers. The study is so rich and has so many facets that could be incorporated into student programs, not only in colleges but in high schools. Such programs might have a very different overall shape, or special features might form part of a more traditional format. Consider, for example, the postponement of grades until the end of the term. This decision transformed the initial attitudes of Professor Nelson's students. Or take the use of small peer groups as a continuous sounding board for receiving and giving help. Perhaps most closely related to the views of learning presented here would be the practice of relying increasingly on students' control of and responsibility for their own work (choice of topic and genre, revising, and editing).

A further strength of this study is its scope and length. A five-year span, a new team of teachers each year, some ninety groups of students studied in detail, extremely rich and varied documentation, extensive field testing, and a considerable amount of comparison with other programs and other institutions: All of these ingredients reflect an innovative and extensive study of considerable weight in the field of English research and research into learning. As such, the study has as much to say about general learning as it has about learning to write.

And this is perhaps where this truly innovative research finds common ground with some of the directions in contemporary thinking about language and about learning: It catches some of the directions observable in subjects other than English; it uses research techniques drawn from the social sciences; it sought ways of making institutional learning as much like natural learning as possible; and it found ways, within a narrative mode, of documenting its experiments, observations, procedures, and analyses.

How This Book
Came to Be—And Why

Eight years ago, I set sail with a small group of explorers to investigate whether or not the earth was actually flat, whether or not by venturing past long-respected horizons we might improve the help we were offering basic writers and nonnative writers—those who spoke English as a second language (ESL). For each of the next five years a small group of teaching assistants and I examined our tacit theories about how writing develops as those theories shaped instruction in a small-group tutorial center. This book presents what we learned from working with hundreds of college students through the diverse processes of collaborative teacher-research, processes by which our thinking grew more rigorous and our problem-solving more systematic than they otherwise would have been.

Tracing the cumulative findings of five successive teams, I have tried to portray—and critique as best I can—changes in teaching methods that resulted from what we learned. *At the Point of Need* is, therefore, in part a report on reflective teaching. It's about how writing improved when we adapted methods in response to what we learned about how students responded to them. At the same time, it's a story about newly successful writers, about layers of untapped potential we never expected to find.

Our story offers hope, I think, for burned-out and burning-out teachers who experience failure and frustration in their work. I hope it will interest those who teach nontraditional students, those who educate teachers, and those attracted to the way teacher-research empowers teachers by providing self-assessment tools, by putting them in charge of evaluating their own work, and by providing tools they need for improving it.

Though the tutors and I would be gratified if our findings prove useful, our purpose is not to suggest that others mimic our teaching. (In fact, our approach—which changed repeatedly during the study's five years, growing more effective as the years went by—would need adaptation for use in other settings.) Instead, we want to share what we learned about basic and ESL writers and describe our experience with the teacher-as-learner stance—to step you through rather ordinary data-collection techniques to the not-so-ordinary insights these approaches produced—so you can see what, if anything, reflective teaching offers you.

With student guidance we reshaped our program a bit at a time, and this book records in detail the evolution of our endeavor. Retracing the steps by which we teased out findings, one by one, from the tangle of variables that emerged, *At the Point of Need* records our struggle to integrate and reconcile late-breaking patterns with the more tentative early "findings" that preceded them. These understandings derive from three main layers of perception:

1. The first-level testimony of basic and ESL writers who describe their experience writing and growing as writers firsthand

2. Five successive teams of tutors' second-level perceptions—from tapes, logs, phone calls, videotapes, discussions, portfolios, and research reports

3. My still emerging third-level meta-analysis/metasynthesis of patterns spanning the work of successive tutor-research teams

One of the more endearing aspects of teacher-research, we found, was its holistic, solve-any-problem flexibility. Because neither formal theory nor prefabricated design limited what we viewed as data or how we analyzed it, we solved some classroom problems with surprising speed, as when tutors first balked at (but within two weeks accepted) my plan to offer whole-to-part language instruction to nonnative writers (Chapter 2). By contrast, we traced other themes and patterns for years, as when we determined a workable size and makeup for Center groups (Chapter 3). Still other patterns reshaped the program from the start but were not recognized consciously until long afterward (Chapter 3). Open-ended designs helped us understand student attitudes (Chapter 4), describe their behaviors (Chapters 4 and 5), and trace related features in their writing (Chapters 2 and 5). Longitudinal case studies were instructive too, as when Maria, Dianna, and I traced the progress of the "slowest of the slow" basic writers for a full year (Chapter 8). We confirmed the benefits of taking the long view when we found Kamal, who reconstructed what he'd learned during five years in Center groups (see quotations from Kamal scattered throughout the text). We also followed developments taking place outside the Center, as when we assessed the influence of our program on academic writing across the curriculum (Chapters 7 and 8) or described the constraining impact, on student and tutor success, of hierarchical structures within our institution, in the high schools our students came from, and in society at large (Chapter 8).

The insights in these chapters did not arrive full-blown. They developed unevenly, by fits and starts, engaging us in a constant struggle to make sense of experience. Relying largely on open-ended (emergent) research designs to collect naturalistic (qualitative, holistic) data, we shifted our primary focus from induction to deduction—from exploration to confirmation, in other words. In the process we cycled, time and again, from question-posing and data-collection, to tentative analysis and confirmatory work, and then back to refocusing earlier hypotheses. Eight years into the project, with publication deadlines approaching, many emerging hypothetical stones remain unturned.

In fact, I have to remind myself that though there's still much to learn, it's time to cut short the analysis and get this book into print, that still-emerging insights can be saved for future work (Chapter 9). What this book contains, then, is a cross-section of my thinking, my current best-guess synthesis of what tutors, students, and I understood (or thought we did) when we penned (or uttered) these words.

Instead of offering a map of an already charted island, I therefore offer a travelogue, a personal case history of excursions into the little-understood culture of basic writers. Reporting new insights sequentially, much as they occurred to shape and reshape our thinking about student development, I trace changes in our methods, spell out the logic that shaped them, and give samples of the evidence on which that logic was based. Of necessity, I've been selective, focusing on more central findings, leaving out dead-end excursions, and reducing the data (in places as much as a thousandfold) while illustrating the theoretical framework that emerged.

The goal has been to demonstrate how insights built layer by layer, first assimilating patterns abstracted from like events, then recognizing the differences by which they refined themselves. This theme-and-variations structure is consciously repetitious: After all, it was repetition that drove the patterns home to us. The point, then, is to step you through our learning processes so you can understand and evaluate our methods and our results and adopt a teacher-as-learner stance if you so desire.

To capture the cyclical processes of the emergent design, I've combined a narrative style with what Bob Boynton, my editor, tells me Rosemary Deen and Marie Ponsot call, in *Beat Not the Poor Desk*, "the art of incremental repetition." While agreeing that the text was still repetitious at points, Bob told me to avoid further cutting and tightening, insisting that the book's incremental repetition illustrated patterns of analytic induction that are rarely spelled out in research reports. The important thing was, he said, that I *demonstrate* for readers the gradual process of successive approximation by which student knowledge and know-how—not to mention our own—emerged.

We hope you'll find our insights and illustrations useful. Most of them emerged from repeated interactions among the forty or so researchers who worked on the project. Some chapters have had more recent input from tutors (and students) than others, however. So, while the analysis was in large part collaborative, I alone am responsible for any analytic oversights, inconsistencies, and loose ends that remain.

Acknowledgments

This book reflects a collective understanding of events that, though they ended some time ago, survive in imagination, etched there in vivid detail by the writing of all five teams. A few teammates were teachers or future teachers doing internships in order to understand firsthand how basic and ESL writers learn. The majority were first-year master's degree-seeking students who had been offered English Department teaching assistantships. Three were experienced tutor-researchers on research assistantships; the rest, most of whom were pursuing doctorates, had joined the team to obtain qualitative research experience.

To help readers keep our large cast of characters straight, I've introduced only a subset of Center tutors in the text, but all of those listed below (and hundreds of their students) contributed to the data base from which our findings emerged. And all of them contributed to these analyses. In a concrete sense, then, this book is more theirs than mine; certainly without their efforts this work could not have been done:

Julie Baka Holland	Judith Friedman
Kay Benton	Maria Greig
Karen Berger	Beverly Heneghen
Linda Blair	Daniela Hoefer
Andy Blanchard	Miki Jackson
Jody Bolčik	Soon-Ja Kim
Jody Brady	Frieda Kulish
Sandra Brew	Lorry Lawrence
Kathy Briggs	Jane Lofts Thomas
Juanita Clemmer	Geri Madigan
Andy Cooper	Bonnie Martin Orzolek
Lois Cucullu	Martha Merz
Susan Davis	Dianna Poodiack
Kathy Eckhardt	Todd Post
Yitna Firdyiwek	Jan Schrader
Ruth Fischer	Linda Topper
Ruth Furr	Kathy Trump

<table>
<tr><td>Dung Vo</td><td>Kim White</td></tr>
<tr><td>Taejung Kim Welsh</td><td>Ashley Williams</td></tr>
<tr><td>Kai Wheatley</td><td>Louise Wynn</td></tr>
</table>

Tutors who questioned aspects of the Center program deserve special appreciation for the role they played. Disagreeing openly and assertively, especially at the start of each year when the program was still new to them, they pushed us all to examine our data and our assumptions with more rigor than we would otherwise have done. Special benefits also resulted from those who taught traditionally, retrofitting the program wherever they saw fit. By providing comparison groups that were taught in traditional ways, they gave us negative cases we otherwise would not have had. Though these tutors rarely led the most highly successful groups, their data greatly informed and strengthened the analysis.

Just as important as the graduate students who worked on the project were the hundreds of undergraduates that the tutors and I taught, both in the Center and in regular classes. As we experimented with a new teaching paradigm, these students provided feedback on our methods, theories, and drafts, thus helping us reshape small-group and classroom instruction in effective ways. Tutors, I'm sure, would credit dozens of students. I myself owe particular thanks to two: Jeff Alderman (who read and commented on this manuscript) and Mohamad Amir Moh'd Yusoh.

Colleagues at my own and other universities responded to the manuscript, or to pieces of it, in one or more of its ever-changing drafts. I cannot name all who helped me refine the book's content and style, but I'd like to single out Lilly Bridwell Bowles, David Dillon, Marcia Farr, Judith Harris Kravitz, Margaret Holland, Ken Kantor, Dan Kirby, Nancy Martin, Bill Smith, Barbara Spector, Chris Thaiss, and Mike Williamson, all of whom offered support and thoughtful responses at various points. Night after night, year after year, Charlene Hurt listened, playing devil's advocate as the ideas emerged and contributing more than she will ever know.

With unlimited patience and good humor, editors Nancy Sheridan at Heinemann-Boynton/Cook and Fran Bartlett at G&H Soho shepherded the manuscript through the production process, deciphering dozens of hand-written scrawls that even I am often unable to read.

By providing a safety net, of which he is probably unaware, my publisher, Bob Boynton, of Heinemann-Boynton/Cook, made it possible for this project to become what it wanted to be—a book of rigorously conducted research written for teachers to read in the hope of supporting them in their efforts for change. Bob's professional integrity, clear to all who know his firm, convinced me not to succumb to pressures to rush the book into print, modify my vision to fit opportunist goals, break the whole into bits and pieces for quicker publication, edit out personal voices, rewrite with "a more formal research tone," or change my audience from teachers to "Capital R" researchers. I'm grateful to Bob for being, in a highly competitive market, a publisher in whose values teachers and researchers can trust.

Unlike tutors, students, colleagues, and publishers—who joined the project briefly before moving on to other pursuits—Nomi and Josh Nelson lived with this book from its infancy, and for several months each year adapted their lives to its rhythms. I am especially grateful for their tolerance and support.

1

A Golden Opportunity
to Study How Basic Writers Learn

*Whenever you run onto something interesting, drop everything else
and study it.*

—B. F. Skinner (1956)

Several years ago at Central Atlantic University (the pseudonym by which I
refer to the institution where this research was done) I agreed to set up a
program for native and nonnative speakers who scored below a cutoff point on
the Test of Standard Written English, a subtest of the SAT. In addition to
designing the program, I would prepare graduate students to teach in CAU's
new Writing Tutorial Center, soon to be known by all involved as "the
WTC." In many ways the outlines of the program were ideal. Students would
study two hours a week in small classes of four, and I could design the
instructional plan and train the tutors myself. I would also influence the
context in which basic writers would work. In addition to materials and
methods, for example, I was responsible for scheduling and certifying students
and (as part of a committee) for choosing the teaching assistants who would
lead the small workshop groups. In effect, the position allowed me to set up
my ideal basic writing program and, if anything went wrong, to experiment to
find out why.

Given these factors, I looked forward to building the program, for it would
pull together all of my training and experience—my background as a writing
specialist and teacher educator, my work with second-dialect and second-
language writers, my training in languages and developmental linguistics, my
research on how writers teach writing, and my experience writing in several
languages.

Years of teaching writing to open-admissions students had taught me that
writing tends to improve when basic writers relax and focus on content while
drafting, postponing correctness concerns until later drafts. I'd also seen how
practicing writing strategies and techniques led more surely to improvement
than did memorization and drill. And I knew that though many basic writers
wrote in nonschool settings—composing songs, keeping journals, writing
letters, jingles, and poems—most avoided academic writing out of fear.

Through the years I'd come to understand students' fears—fears of correction, of harsh evaluation, of being told their ideas were illogical and their style

1

immature. Most could easily list ten ways their grammar was "not good," but few I'd taught knew where their writing was strong, perhaps because their strengths had rarely been pointed out. As a result, though my basic writers dreaded criticism, they ironically tended to give stinging responses to peers. Their attitudes and behavior were reminiscent in many ways of the nonnative writers I'd taught for several years in Japan, so I decided to schedule basic and ESL writers into tutorial groups together rather than isolating nonnative students from native speakers of the language they needed to learn.

My Tentative Plan

By summer I knew in general what I wanted for the program. First, I'd create a homey atmosphere in the center, to contrast with the classrooms basic writers associate with failure. To offset the cold school tables and walls of concrete block, I'd find a hooked rug, a coffeepot, floor lamps, and an overstuffed chair. I'd teach tutors to reduce anxiety by eliminating first-draft grading and encourage them to abandon grades on individual papers. And because basic writers so often avoid failure by avoiding, forgetting, losing, or plagiarizing assignments, there would be no homework in the required, noncredit groups. Looking over what their students had done at the end of each session, tutors could base plans for the next session on the writing students added to their portfolios.

Tutors would work with groups of four (a number determined by economics before I took over the program) in regularly scheduled writing workshops two days a week for a semester. To help build students' confidence that they could learn to write well, to help them learn to recognize what in their writing was strong, and to keep them from revising the good parts out, we would begin each semester by reinforcing strengths rather than focusing at first on writing deficiencies. In this relaxed environment, students would work each day on topics and in genres of their choosing. Revising and editing draft after draft to their own and their groupmates' content, they would study whatever grammatical, mechanical, and organizational strategies they needed to improve their pieces. To tap their natural desire to communicate, the semester would begin with writing they chose to do. Then, as the students grew more fluent with language, topics, and genres, tutors would help them meet the demands of academic assignments using strategies the students had practiced on self-selected work.

The groups would help each other revise and edit their papers, and tutors would post the best ones on colorful bulletin boards. The center would print weekly *WTC Excerpts*—at first freewritten, later edited—dittoed handouts of the strongest passages of the week (see pp. 4–6). And near the end of each semester, to reward those who'd worked hard, we'd publish a collection of the best work students had done and hold a publication celebration honoring them. (Figures 1–1 and 1–2 show examples of student-designed covers of two editions of this WTC book.) Based on portfolio and process assessments by pairs of tutors, certification would depend less on memorizing rules than on demonstrating competence using rules and on the tutors' sense that students were confident and independent enough to continue to improve on their own. These were factors we could evaluate by noting

- The number and kinds of pieces students drafted
- The diversity of strategies they used
- Their ability to recognize strengths and weaknesses in their work
- Demonstrated willingness to revise and edit as needed
- Whether or not they sought and applied advice from peers, tutors, and references
- The degree of independence with which they pursued their work, including whether they identified features they needed to study further and worked without prompting to refine their knowledge of conventions

The Rationale

Linguistic Research and Theory. For fifteen years the winds of change had been sweeping through writing instruction, bringing new developments in theory and research (Emig, 1981; Hairston, 1982; Young, 1978). Based on new understandings of how writers actually write, on studies of texts that undermined many traditional composition rules, and on growing evidence from psycholinguistic research, process-based methods such as those I proposed were no longer uncommon in native language instruction (Macrorie, 1968; Murray, 1968; Elbow, 1973; Kirby & Liner, 1981), and I had used them for several years with open-admissions students. I'd also spent two years researching, in middle and secondary schools, outstanding teachers—themselves writers—whose very successful teaching was consistent with emerging theory. In short, I knew firsthand that small-group workshops could succeed—at least for standard English and minority-dialect speakers.

I stood on less firm ground, however, when it came to the ESL students who would make up 40 percent of the center's clientele; even though I'd taught writing years before in Japan, at that time I had not known about process-based methods. When the WTC opened in 1981, native and ESL composition texts were very different. Though interest in process-based writing instruction would soon burst on the ESL scene (Allen, 1982; Krashen, 1984; Zamel, 1982, 1983), little awareness of its methods seemed to have

WTC
EXCERPTS✻

FALL SEMESTER   **OCTOBER 10, 1984**

---

*This is "Writing in Progress" and not to be confused with the final drafts. If you think these excerpts are something, try to imagine how good the final versions will be!

I think WTC is a very helpful period. I feel it has great benefits for the student. One reason is because we don't have to pay for it. Some tutor sessions can cost up to $15-20 an hour. I think the WTC class is a great motivator. It only asks us to write what we want to write, therefore I think people are more inclined to write outside of class. If we are writing what we want in class, then we should want to write it outside class too. - N. L.

At first I was a little insulted by the class. I didn't like the idea to be required to take this class. I thought only on the negative aspect that I couldn't write. But I kept trying to tell myself to look on the positive side. If you can't write then this is a great place to get help. If you can write then use this time to write and quit complaining. - M.S.

I will probably continue going to WTC even if I get certified. I like small groups and I like being tutored. I feel the tutor is more interested in my work than a regular teacher is. Besides I need help in writing & I want to be good at it because I enjoy writing. - Tami

Once all of the organs were removed from the body. The body looked like a tub. The blood had settled towards the back of the body. The pathologist gathered all the organs and put them in a large black plastic bag and stuffed the bag in the body, then began sewing the body up. I asked the Doctor if I could stich the body. I felt that this would be a good experience for me, because if I decide to work in the operating room, the nurse must know how to suture for the doctor. He

was kind enough to show me step by step how the procedure was to be
done. He handed to me what looked like a fishing hook, I took the metal
object in my hand, and I could feel myself shake. I steadied my hand
and made the first puncture through the skin, it was tough and I had to
force the needle hard to get through the skin. - Patti

Before New Year about one month, we have a fair on every city.
The fair has many sections. Each section has its specifics: Fruit
section will has all kinds of fruit such as apple, grape, pear, mango,
orange, watermelon, banana, etc. Candies section has the special kinds
which you can not find them in the normal days. Clothes section, shoes
section, wines section...
    Especially the best section is the flowers section. They have all
kinds of flowers with good smell, good color such as roses, carnation,
cherry, special flower (in my country that it just blossom only in New
Year)...If you walk in the flower sections then you will feel exciting,
good; where you can breath with good smell, fresh air; where you can
find the crowded people - Chi

It was about 5:00 o'clock. I was sitting on the window with a
warm cup of coffee. Outside, wind was blowing the rain all over the
place. It was foggy. There is no pedestrian. I could not see far
because of the fog. I wrapped a blanket around me and took a sip of
coffee. That afternoon brought back lots of my memories. I was
thinking of my own future. Why am I struggling with my life so much? I
was thinking when I will finish my study and become a engineer. Then I
can depend on my self and help my parents. - Mahmoud

I feel like I'm learning something from the WTC program. The
first day I came to class I thought that this program was a waste of
time. But the weeks have pasted since then and I feel that I am
learning a little at a time. I had the concept that this class was
going to teach you grammar and organization of an essay. But this is
not really the case. To me its like a therapy session. The program is
trying to break down your mental blockness when it comes to writing.
When I think about that, its true. It is hard to do this but in the long
run I hope to accomplish this. Organization I learned comes after all

your ideas are freely expressed on paper. So far I have attended six sessions. And I have learned that writing can be divided into 3 groups. Freewriting your ideas, organization, and finally grammar.

There will be more concepts that I will probably learn from this class in the future. But the question that was asked, "Have you learned anything from this WTC program?" my answer would have been "yes." - Ted

If you have ever seen a frustrated fly you would know what I mean. My wings would go bizurk leaving me with no control of the direction I was heading. Awkwardly, I would land on a table in clear view of the people I was trying so hard to hide from. Out of the corner of my eye I could see a book, a thick heavy book ready to flatten me into nothing but squashed fly. I spread my wings, as if I was an airplane ready to take off down a runway. - Polly

Rang, Rang, Rang... The alarm clock was ringing. I got up and still. Then I sat back on my bed. I looked at the clock. It was only 5:00 a.m. I mumbled myself that this was too early to get up. I still felt so sleepy. I looked at the clock again and began to lie down on my bed. My eyes were close but my brain was not. I was thinking to make a choice for myself. Either I got up and studied for my math's quiz or went back to sleep and got bad grade for not studying. God, I hated myself. I should have studied for it last night and didn't have to worry about it this early in the morning. I got to do it, I knew. - KTN

Sundays are always busy at Erol's.Lines longer than a telephone pole. Checking in movies, checking out movies, filing the new movies, and checking people for cards.

As I was filing the tapes back on the shelf, in the drama section, someone came up from behind me and covered my eyes. I could smell something sweet and pretty almost as if I were in a garden. The deep voice said "guess who." By the sound and tone, I could tell it was Tommy. He's an old friend of mine. I haven't seen him since he left for college at the University of North Carolina. I was so surprised to see him. And as I turned around he handed me a rose and said "hello."

- Lori

Figure 1–1   Cover of *The Drafted Writers* (Vol. I, No. 1, Fall 1983)

affected practice. This was my dilemma regarding ESL instruction: Should I train tutors to teach ESL and native writers alike, applying the findings of recent studies about how writing is learned? Or should I accept the assump-

The Write Connection

Figure 1–2 Cover of *The Drafted Writers* (Vol. I, No. 2, Spring 1984)

tion that second-language writers are different and have tutors prescribe the vocabulary, grammar, and rhetoric drills that then dominated available ESL texts?

Fortunately, I found two articles (Taylor, 1981; Zamel, 1976) suggesting that ESL writers needed process-based teaching approaches. And while most theory focused on oral language teaching, developmental approaches that tapped student motivation had for some time been advocated by ESL theorists (Dulay & Burt, 1978; Gardner & Lambert, 1972; Gingras, 1978; Krashen, 1978, 1981; Schumann, 1978; Stevick, 1980; Taylor, 1974; Terrell, 1977). These scholars' conclusions were consistent with research-based findings on first-language acquisition (Brown, 1973; Dale, 1976; DeVilliers & DeVilliers, 1979; Slobin, 1971) and lent support to the idea of teaching all students alike.

My Research on Writers Who Teach. My own two-year study of writers who teach full-time at the middle school and secondary levels (Nelson, 1982a, 1982b, 1983b) lent further support to my tentative conviction that ESL writers would benefit little from separate tutorial groups. Let me explain what I learned from that study, for its findings provided both methods and a rationale for the WTC program and will be referred to occasionally in the chapters that follow. After screening a hundred writers who teach, interviewing twenty-three, and observing for one or two days in the classrooms of eight, I'd spent a year observing each of the three most successful (of those available) three days a week for a twelve-week academic term. Comparing what I learned by watching a few master teachers at work with what the other ninety-seven reported about their teaching, I discovered that regardless of the courses or students they taught, the most confident and successful differed in two ways from writers who felt frustrated, defeated, or ambivalent about teaching. One was the degree to which writing experience shaped their teaching, even when it conflicted with "what English teachers are *supposed* to do." The other was the degree to which these most successful teachers trusted what students (regardless of grade or ability level) told them about the kinds of support they needed in order to write.

The findings from the study of writers who teach were unambiguous: The writers who taught more successfully did so intuitively, guided by personal writing experience rather than by traditional composition experts and texts. In fact, though some had started as traditional English teachers, they'd abandoned accepted methods when conflict arose. The more successful the teachers, the more they empathized with student writers, set aside class time to talk about writing problems and successes, transferred responsibility for learning to their students, offered real-world rewards for writing well (publication, varied audiences, status, praise, peer attention, and so on), and put students in charge of decisions about their own work. For example, they might let students decide what topics and genres to work on, who would read their writing, which revisions to make (or not make), and what sorts of errors they were ready to work on next. As one writer, Morty, said when I asked why he gave such autonomy to seventh and eighth graders, "How else would I know how to help them, Marie? You gotta follow the kid. You see, what's missing in the writing is in the student—it's not in me!"

If this study of writer-teachers taught me anything, it was that to teach successfully, writers should do two things—trust personal writing experience as a guide and learn to "follow the kid."

My Experience as a Writer. To evaluate process-based methods for second-language learners, I therefore examined my experience writing in several languages, only to find that I approached all writing similarly. Though I got stumped more often in languages I knew less well, the problems I ran into were strikingly similar, and I could usually solve them by using similar strategies:

- Drafting and redrafting repeatedly
- Backing up and circumventing the problem
- Consulting a dictionary or thesaurus
- Referring to a grammar text
  or (and this was a frequent one)
- Asking someone for help

All of these were natural language-learning strategies that I hoped WTC students would learn to use.

In many years of teaching, I had also learned to examine my own experience as a learner for likely insights into how others learn. I knew from my varied experience speaking and writing—in English, Latin, French, Spanish, and Japanese—that I learn language best (1) in context, (2) when I have some reason to, (3) when there are people I want to speak or write to, and (4) when honest responses quickly follow my attempts. I remember, for example, as a high-school graduate, writing excitedly to a college roommate I'd not yet met. Though we arrived at school believing ourselves devoted "friends," we were disappointed to find how little we had in common. Isolated from the contexts of each other's lives, we had tried too hard to control, in writing and in responding, the images we projected of ourselves. From that experience I learned that our not-quite-honest writing had served me and my roommate rather poorly in the end.

Some years later, in Japan, I remember two frustrating days confusing *nomu* and *yomu* in dialogue and pattern drills only to have the distinction stamped indelibly in memory by the unguarded laughter of a bookseller in an arcade. "Have you drunk this book?" I had cautiously inquired.

The contrast between my fluency after six years of school French and a year and a half of in-country Japanese study left no doubt in my mind as to which led to more fluency, spontaneity, and accuracy in my speech. All of these experiences shaped my thinking as I planned how the tutorial program would be run.

Experience teaching and learning and observing learners and teachers convinced me that rapid language growth is fueled by real-world demands and that we fail as teachers when we ignore that fact. I therefore decided to replicate, as best I could, nonschool learning conditions in the tutorial Center. I also decided to set up the best writing program I could, let tutors begin the semester teaching ESL and native students alike, and adapt the approach when necessary as we went along.

Preparing the Tutors to Use Process-Based Approaches

Deciding to use new approaches posed another problem, however—how to prepare tutors to use methods they'd never seen used. (Note: From this point on, for purposes of clarity, I will distinguish between the terms *tutor* and *student*. *Tutor(s)* will refer to graduate teaching assistants and to graduate students who did internships in the center. The term *student(s)* will refer to undergraduates required to attend the program and to both graduate and undergraduate students who joined tutorial groups voluntarily.) Fortunately, ample time had been set aside for this purpose. Teaching assistants (TAs) would attend, in addition to a three-credit graduate course in the teaching of writing, a ten-day seminar in August, just before classes began. Informed by what I'd learned about success from writers who teach, I tried to teach tutors to act like the best writer-teachers I'd found—confident enough to rely on writing experience as a guide and willing to empathize with students, to "follow the kid." More of these beginning tutors would succeed, I reasoned, if they knew about writers' successful behaviors and attitudes.

I designed the program for tutors with these goals in mind. To increase TAs' awareness of their own writing processes, to build confidence in their experience as writers, and to demonstrate methods they could use in the groups, we would spend class time thinking about our writing processes, evaluating past experiences with writing teachers, and working in small writing groups like those the Center students would join. Consciously modeling the kinds of methods I hoped they would try, I would give tutors practice in many kinds of writing and have them read widely in writing theory and research.

Teacher-research would provide the means to my other goal—helping inexperienced teachers learn to "follow the kid." Teacher-research is a reflective process by which classroom teachers, without extensive formal training in theory or research, look closely at how their teaching affects student learning with the goal of improving how they teach. Relying for the most part on qualitative techniques supplemented by numerical counts and simple statistics, teacher-researchers make conscious and systematic use of learning strategies normal people use in conducting their daily lives: familiar strategies, in other words, for recording, analyzing, and evaluating. The major difference we found between out-of-school learning and teacher-research, in fact, was that in the Center teacher-researchers collaborated, under the guidance of a trained researcher, to make their analyses more systematic than most of them would otherwise have been.

Early studies by teacher-researchers (see, for example, Sandra Worsham's [1980] report on developing a program for basic writers at the high-school level and Anne Miller Wotring's [1981] study of "writing to think" in high-school chemistry) had convinced me that teacher-research can provide important insights that improve teaching. Relying on log-writing as a way of learning (Emig, 1977; Martin et al., 1976), I decided to teach tutors strategies used in participant observation, naturalistic data collection, and qualitative analysis. Each week I would respond to their logs, praise what was strong, make suggestions, and answer questions they asked. In class we would talk about teaching, share our failures and successes, and search our collective experience for explanations to the problems tutors had. Returning to the tutorial program better informed, we would collectively test each other's hypotheses, looking for reasons to refine, extend, confirm, or reject the approach.

The Assumptions on Which the Program Rested

On the assumption that first- and second-language writers develop similarly, I scheduled ESL and basic writers into groups and trained the graduate assistants to teach all students alike, dealing with differences (and problems) incidentally, as they occurred. This was an assumption tutors and I accepted tentatively, though I held it more confidently than they, because there was almost nothing in the literature to indicate that ESL specialists agreed. It was the first of many assumptions we systematically tested. Other assumptions underlying the program that first year were these:

1. Writing, like speaking, is natural. Just as everyone learns to speak, so everyone can learn to write. This includes ESL-, dialect-, and standard-speaking writers.

2. Language isn't mastered in isolation. We learn to write as we learn to speak—by interacting with others. That's why it helps student writers to have a number of live readers.

3. When beginners who neither know nor care about their topics are taught to focus on structure before developing their ideas, they have a hard time using what language resources they possess.

4. Anxiety interferes with learning and with effective expression. As a result, beginners need to work in a safe atmosphere where errors aren't penalized, so they can learn by making mistakes.

5. Writing ability expands naturally when writers themselves control what they write—that is, skills develop faster with real rather than with practice writing.

6. In addition to its artistic and informative functions, writing can be a way of learning and directing activities (Emig, 1977; Martin et al., 1976; Wotring, 1981).

7. Writing experience is a dependable guide for writing students and teachers; if what a text or teacher prescribes doesn't match how they write, writers are wise to question its validity for them (Hearn, 1920; Murray, 1968; Nelson, 1982b).

8. ESL and native writers use similar strategies, and their writing abilities develop similarly.

9. Teachers take new approaches to teaching seriously when they help develop and implement them.

Another assumption, a finding from my study of writers who teach, was also subject to testing during Year 1:

10. Writing teachers who empathize with student writers and adapt their teaching to "follow the kid" tend to be more successful than those who do not.

These, then, were the major assumptions on which the program was based. They were also the working hypotheses I was hoping to test. Using these assumptions as points of entry into the research, the tutors and I began to examine our dealings with students for data to confirm, refute, or refine them empirically.

Beginning that fall, tutors offered dozens of small-group writing workshops, used qualitative research to evaluate individual and collective findings, and took risks with new approaches when problems occurred. Not only did each of us learn to "follow the kid," we monitored our success, identified methods and policies that weren't working very well, and in time evaluated the adaptations we made. Primarily, then, the tutorial Center was not an ESL program, though hundreds of ESL writers would enroll over the years, and most of them had some input on the findings reported here.

The Kinds of Data We Collected

For five years after the Center opened, teams of tutor/researchers gathered many kinds of data, some quantitative, most qualitative in nature. To validate observation logs that tutors kept on some ninety-odd groups, we audio- and videotaped sessions, transcribing many of these. At the beginning and end of each semester we gave entry and exit essays, the Writing Apprehension Test (WAT), and Center-developed questionnaires. We did planned and impromptu interviews with students and their writing professors to compare others' perspectives on the progress students made. We saved and examined the students' writing, keeping all drafts in folders, and compared their progress with us to their grades in writing classes. We kept copies of Center publications—the weekly *WTC Excerpts* and twice-yearly *Drafted Writers*—and had students "thinkwrite" in process logs on their writing progress and problems. Many of these things we would have done, even without the research, as part of the process-based teaching we did, but after seeing how these activities helped both students and tutors, we began to rely on them more systematically.

In addition to leading the small-group workshops, we tested similar methods in CAU's drop-in writing center, in required writing classes, and in courses for writing majors. And in the process we documented many perspectives—from students, tutors, teaching interns, outside researchers, and faculty. Four bilingual and four ESL-speaking graduate students joined the project as tutors, teachers, or researchers (see, for example, Lofts Thomas, 1988 and Welsh, 1988) and shared the dual perspectives they brought as second-language writers. We also studied the progress of ESL and native students in a variety of writing classes and collected reports from ESL specialists teaching at several levels, including courses in CAU's English Language Institute, in a Korean university, and in community college programs. Several area teachers also contributed their experience adapting the WTC approach with adults and middle-school writers. And one doctoral student conducted WTC-model writing groups for students enrolled in a doctoral program at CAU. In other words, the methods described in this book have been field tested extensively—on basic and ESL college writers, at CAU, in adult education, and in public schools.

The Analytic Approach

Like our methods of collecting data, our analytic approaches were not esoteric (Wolcott, 1988), though among researchers some go by impressive names. Instead of using existing theory to shape data collection and analysis, we used existing theory only as a starting point, a tentative framework to disprove, discard, or refine. We therefore began by casting our nets wide, using open-ended and inclusive data collection, then shifting to increasingly focused, in-depth techniques.

In general, we followed a principle of selectivity in which interest and emergent opportunity take priority over random selection (Schatzman &

Strauss, 1973). During Year 1 my assumptions (as embodied in the program) served as tentative hypotheses, and this book traces the process by which we abandoned or revised them. But we also tested tutors' beliefs about writing, and dozens of hunches and hypotheses that emerged. Once the importance of a variable emerged, confirmatory data collection grew increasingly focused as we examined supporting and discrepant cases closely, doing case studies (Stake, 1988) on those that seemed most illustrative. At every stage, as preliminary lines of analysis developed, we chose times, places, products, people, and events from among the range of feasible alternatives according to their perceived productivity for the research. Using the constant comparisons method, analytic induction, typological analysis, and microethnography, successive teams of graduate students discovered, shaped, and refined the theoretical framework I present in this book through case studies, comparisons, and thematic analyses.

Researchers often use special terms to describe their methods so they can talk with precision about their procedures. I've worked hard to make our analytic processes clear by tracing the steps we went through without using much jargon, however. When possible, I've referred to procedures without using technical terms. For those who would like some background on analytic technique, however, let me describe briefly the theoretical context from which our analytic approach derived.

Two Research Traditions That Influenced Our Work

This study has roots in two qualitative traditions—the symbolic interactionism of field sociology and the microethnography of sociolinguistics. When applied in educational contexts, symbolic interactionism "provides models for studying how individuals interpret objects, events and people in their lives and for studying how this process of interpretation leads to behavior in specific situations" (Jacob, 1987, p. 31). Guided by the assumptions and methods of this tradition (Blumer, 1969; Glaser & Strauss, 1967; Schatzman & Strauss, 1973), we examined the perspectives of those we studied, the processes by which those perspectives were socially constructed, and the way the perspectives shaped specific interactions.

Unlike researchers in positivist traditions, where the primary goal is to test or verify existing theory, symbolic interactionists develop new theory to account for the behavior patterns they observe (Jacob, 1987). During the exploratory phases of the research they compare data taken from contrasting sites, look for conceptual categories, describe the categories' characteristics, and develop hypotheses about how the categories interrelate (Glaser & Strauss, 1967). They see theory as emerging from and grounded in their data (Glaser & Strauss, 1967), which they gather using a range of collection techniques—participant observation, life histories, case studies, pieces of writing, autobiographies, and open interviews (Meltzer, Petras, & Reynolds, 1975)—depending on the direction in which their analyses lead (Schatzman & Strauss, 1973). The goal is to "identify themes and construct hypotheses (ideas) as they are suggested by the data" and, in the confirmatory stages of the research, to marshal support for those themes and ideas (Bogdan & Taylor, 1975, pp. 79–80).

In short, research designs in this tradition are emergent (Blumer, 1969; Schatzman & Strauss, 1973), with data collection and analysis being recursive processes. During the course of a study, researchers shift increasingly from an exploratory to a confirmatory stance, cycling from data collection to analysis and back again. After using tentative preliminary findings to refocus and reshape their designs, they then use the refocused designs to test findings that have emerged, going through this process time and time again until the return on their efforts decreases significantly (Becker, 1970; Schatzman & Strauss, 1973; Bogdan & Biklen, 1982). In addition to using writing throughout this cyclic process both to document events and to reflect on them (Schatzman & Strauss, 1973), symbolic interactionists use "sympathetic introspection" to interpret informants' experience (Meltzer et al., 1975).

Rooted in the assumptions and methods of symbolic interactionism, our study also incorporates microethnography, also known as "ethnography of communication." Assuming that "interpersonal communication is culturally patterned" (Phillips, 1983, p. 4, as cited by Jacob, 1987), researchers in this tradition (Erickson, 1977, 1986; Gumperz, 1968; Hymes, 1972, 1974) document "processes of face-to-face communication," combining participant observation ("direct, continuous observation and reflection, recorded in running fieldnotes") with microanalysis of film and of audio- and videotapes (Erickson & Wilson, 1982, p. 43). Here again, studies are progressively focused, shifting gradually "from a more general participant-observation phase to a more focused phase in which detailed data on social interaction patterns are collected" (Jacob, 1987). In our project, for example, we did fine-grained analyses of the "micro" processes of face-to-face interactions (see, for example, Welsh, 1988). Parts of this report also show (see Chapter 8) how such patterns related to the "macro" patterns of academia and of U.S. culture as a whole (Erickson & Mohatt, 1982; Erickson & Wilson, 1982).

The Research Design

While individual tutors and teams used a range of research designs, depending on the directions in which their investigations evolved, an overarching design for this study soon became clear. This design both shaped and was shaped by the program's evolution, and the rigor of the analytic framework that emerged seems to be largely attributable to three traits—the design's recursive, collaborative, and cumulative nature.

Let's look first at collaboration, which took at least two forms. Without consciously following any particular plan, we practiced what I now call "same-time" and "cross-time" collaboration. With same-time collaboration, team-mates (including myself) talked with each other, with their students, and at times with other faculty to develop, test, abandon, refine, and confirm hypotheses. In cross-time collaboration, successive teams of tutors took the collective analysis of the preceding team as hypotheses for testing. Team 2, for example, tested the findings of Team 1. (Team 1, with no preceding team, tested—by acting as if they were true—the findings of my earlier work in the classrooms of writers who teach.) In the former sense, *collaboration* takes on its everyday meaning. In the latter, it also takes on a cumulative effect. It was this latter process, through which earlier, tentative findings were tested and re-tested by successive teams who had little or no investment in prior teams' results, that confirmed the reliability of our results.

All of these design issues can be diagrammed. I diagram the two types of collaboration horizontally and vertically, with same-time collaboration taking place within blocks and cross-time collaboration taking place in the spaces between (see Figure 1–3). An interaction between same-time and cross-time collaboration led to a gradual shift from exploration to confirmation, adding yet another dimension to the design (see Figure 1–4). But even this sketch fails to capture the design's complexity. Though they are more reflective of my process than that of tutors, the straight-line diagonal arrows oversimplify what went on. While my understandings increased fairly steadily, tutor analyses were interrupted every summer, with an inexperienced team beginning, from scratch, each fall. (Though many tutors elected to work in the Center a second year, they did not take part in the second year's seminar and were therefore largely excluded from that analysis.)

The result was that as my confidence in our cumulative findings grew, I progressed rather directly from exploration to confirmation. By contrast, each fall a new group of tutors began their work skeptically, testing every feature of the tutorial program anew, documenting and hypothesizing in their logs, and honing their analyses both together, through group discussion, and alone, while writing their research reports. Later teams must have been influenced by my growing confidence—and with time it grew harder and harder for me to withdraw so they could rediscover what I had already learned. In short, in addition to the overarching progression of Figure 1–4, each team cycled recursively from tentative tests of their own assumptions to increasingly focused, confirmatory work (see Figure 1–5).

Findings of the Study

I use words about *research findings* with some misgivings, for as commonly used in our society, they imply certainty and permanence I don't think

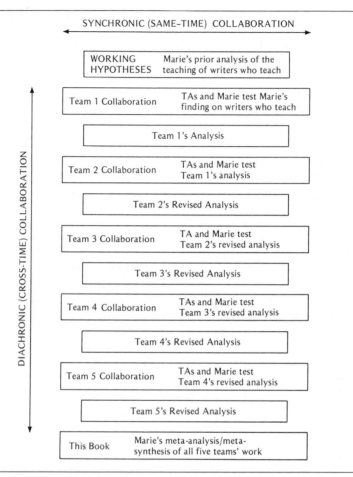

Figure 1-3 **Design Diagram I. Two Types of Collaboration That Shaped the Emergent Design: (A) Synchronic (same-time) collaboration among members of a single team; (B) diachronic (cross-time) collaboration in which analysis is in large part a test of the findings of a prior person or team**

findings can have. As used, the words imply the discovery of *facts* or *patterns* that are somehow imbued with a significant dose of *truth*. *Perspectives* or *interpretations* might be more accurate substitutes, but given the conventions of research reporting and the *fact* that others present their *interpretations* as *findings*, using those terms might undermine confidence in our *results* in a way I do not believe they deserve.

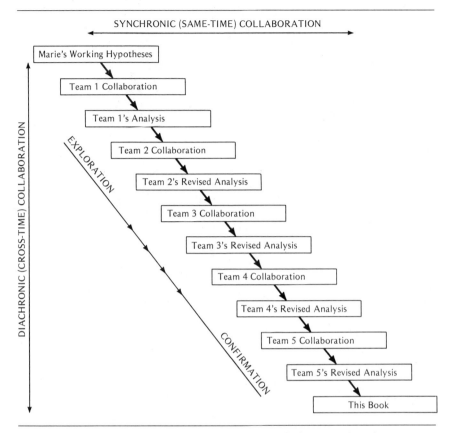

Figure 1–4 **Design Diagram II. The Gradual Shift from Exploration to Confirmation That Is Produced by the Interaction of Same-Time and Cross-Time Collaboration**

As my own shifting, emerging, evolving *perspective* reveals, *truths* derived from empirical evidence can be unstable. I would neither claim that these *findings* would hold *true* across time, for example, nor that they would hold *true* under alternative conditions. We discovered early in the program's first year (see Chapter 2) that *findings* (*interpretations*, *perspectives*) not only change in response to changing external conditions, they also change with the mindset of the *finder/interpreter*. We had only to change the lens through which we viewed students' writing to change our *interpretation* of their achievement, which in turn changed downward spirals of failure and frustration into dramatic upward spirals of increasing success. In other words, an observer's mindset or paradigm is a powerful determiner of what she will *find*.

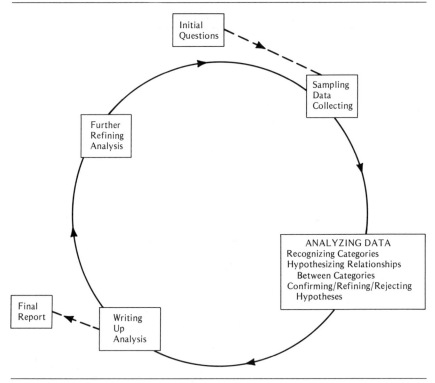

Figure 1–5 **The Recursive Nature of the Research Process**

For these reasons, I describe our *findings* with ambivalence. Despite reservations, however, and despite an awareness that the books various tutors would have written would all be different, I hope the perspective emerging in this, my account of our project, will be of interest to others in the field.

Some of our most important insights took place when we recognized patterns we'd been vaguely aware of but had not thought much about. Once we took note of these patterns, debated what we'd seen, considered others' opinions, and examined discrepant cases, we found some of our assumptions false or only partly true and ended up abandoning quite a few of our former beliefs. In other words, much of our analysis involved teasing out patterns we had been vaguely aware of but had not fully understood. Much of this process took place during writing—while tutors kept logs, while they drafted individual research reports, and while I drafted and redrafted the chapters of this book.

The chapters that follow illustrate several categories of "findings" about how basic writers learn. They also trace the emergence, refinement, and confirmation of the "findings" and show how each helped shape the tutorial program that evolved. These are the primary areas into which our "findings" fall:

1. Similarities and differences between basic and ESL writing development

2. The existence of basic skills students have but do not use

3. How awareness, attitudes, and behavior affect student texts

4. Relationships among freedom, goals, and responsibility

5. The role of small peer groups in facilitating independence by developing reading, writing, listening, speaking, and critical thinking skills

6. The inverse relationship between teacher control and student independence

7. The relationship between incidental teaching at the point of need and students' ability to apply the conventions of standard written English

8. The similarity between slow learners and other students

9. The central role of risk taking in writing development

10. The power of premature summative evaluation to reverse upward spirals of increasing confidence and success

11. The mechanisms by which different kinds of evaluation set up different expectations in teachers and in students, which in turn determined writers' failure or success

12. The degree to which resistance, in both tutors and students, was related to unfamiliarity with the new methods and to fear of failure with the new approach

I uncovered another finding while watching successive teams of tutors struggle to shift from familiar, traditional composition approaches to process-based methods of teaching incidentally, at the point of need:

13. The more experience tutors had being taught by the new approaches, the less resistance they felt and the easier time they had making the new methods work.

For tutors who had never been taught by whole-language approaches—and fortunately their numbers decreased every year—changing one part of the system threw the rest of it out of kilter. For example, when we decided we would not give grades, shocked tutors had to find new ways to motivate hard work. They also had to learn—as I'll show in a later chapter—to wait patiently when motivation took time to develop. In other words, a writing classroom is a complex system, and when one aspect of a teaching approach is changed, what's left of the system must also change to accommodate the first change—

otherwise, remnants of the old paradigm will undermine efforts to implement the new.

This book results from our efforts to adapt teaching methods our own teachers had used when we were in school to meet the needs of the basic and ESL writers we taught. In it I show how dozens of variables—such as type of assignment, attitude, student ability level, grading procedure, motivation level, number and types of errors, improvement, direct or incidental instruction, regression (backsliding), grammar, freewriting, monitoring, and locus of control—gradually realigned themselves until the new approach, which even at first worked better than had the traditions in which *we'd* been taught, was largely free of the problems that had plagued us at the start. No longer did tutors worry about lack of motivation once we saw that students did better in the long run when we waited patiently for commitment to develop. No longer did tutors have tugs of war with hostile students once we found successful ways to defuse negativity. No longer did students resist freewriting once tutors assured them we'd help them learn to correct their mistakes—*after* they found a topic they wouldn't mind taking through several drafts.

The goal is to illustrate what we learned from basic and ESL writers. The small workshop size simplified that task, because tutors were able to document, in lifelike detail, just how students responded to the old and new methods they used. The following chapters show five successive teams of tutors using teacher-research to teach themselves to teach the kinds of students that have baffled educators for years.

2

Putting the Program to the Test

*The vast majority of people have enormous potentialities of thinking,
far beyond anything ordinarily suspected; but so seldom do the right
circumstances by chance surround them to require their actualiza-
tion that the vast majority die without realizing more than a
fraction of their powers. Born millionaires, they live and die in
poverty for the lack of favourable circumstances which would have
compelled them to convert their credit into cash.*

—A. R. Orage (1930)

How Basic and ESL Writers Converted Their Credit into Cash

Just as people generally take for granted that they know how to think,
English teachers tend to take for granted that they can teach writing. Accepting a body of traditional wisdom from other teachers and popular texts—
wisdom that has been debunked by recent writing research and theory—they
remain unaware that more effective methods of teaching have been evolving
over the past few years. Part of my job, therefore, was to help new tutors
examine their assumptions about how writing is learned and to help them see
how their assumptions affected learning.

Two weeks before fall semester started, when the teaching-of-writing seminar began, I was pleased by Team 1's responses to the writing—academic,
creative, and exploratory—I suggested they do. To experience writing as a way
of learning so they could teach basic writers to "thinkwrite," they reflected in
learning logs on the assigned readings, on the content of class discussions, on
their teaching methods, and on writing as they experienced it in my course.
To inform intuitions on which to draw while teaching, I encouraged as much
self-selected writing as they could do and modeled unfamiliar process-based
teaching approaches. They responded positively to this phase of the training
and to the theories of teaching discussed in the seminar.

I monitored TAs' progress by reading what they wrote. As they relaxed and
wrote more freely, I began to see references in their learning logs to increased
motivation, productivity, and risk taking. Writing now flowed more easily,
they were more confident, and they felt motivated after sharing with others,
they said. They all worked on favorite pieces, taking them through many
drafts, and grew more thoughtful and probing in what they wrote about.
Soon Andy was bringing in poetry and Kay revised travelogs, while Ruth

worked at sorting out feelings and Kathy wrote family tales. Once fall semester started, the group met weekly rather than daily, so lunch became a favorite time for reading each other's work. I received help with my essay on teaching poetry (Nelson, 1983a), and Linda received support on a paper one of her professors had harshly criticized.

Together we struggled to get our work ready—for our children, spouses, groupmates, lovers, teachers, and editors—to read. In her journal, Ruth Fischer described our growing reliance on each other:

> To paraphrase an old Beatles song, we get by with a little help from our friends, listening to our writing, praising the good, constructively criticizing the not-so-good, asking questions to fill in the gaps, and generally serving as sounding boards for testing the effectiveness of what we are trying to communicate.

Little did we realize during that first fall semester that the interdependence we'd come to value in our group of seven would become a predictable outcome of writing tutorial groups and that future tutors would spend months figuring out how it developed, showing how it bridged the gap between dependence and independence, and determining which of our methods best fostered it.

Research Team 1, however, was aware of few such concerns. At this stage the only problems they reported having were unaccustomed bottlenecks of as-yet-unwritten ideas: There simply wasn't time, they said, to write all they wanted to. One tutor told classmates that she'd dreamed of being a writer but had been blocked for years by fear that no one would like what she wrote. In the safety of our group, with harsh criticism forbidden, she'd found an attentive audience, and the words were flowing again. When I walked in one morning a day or two after she told us this, I met a brightly lettered sign on the center door:

SANCTUARY

(Safe Writing Done Here)

In large block letters of Carter green, Ruth Fischer had posted a message for incoming basic and ESL writers to see.

The Emergence of Tutor Resistance

The positive way TAs responded to my teaching left me unprepared for the resistance that surfaced three days before school opened. Suddenly the sign-making tutor and her closest TA friend began to express ambivalence about applying the new approach. Both were ESL teachers returning to graduate school to get master's degrees in linguistics and earn TESL certification.

"It's not that the method's not sound, Marie," said Ruth Fischer, who'd made the sign. "After being in your class and doing a lot of writing, I've been wishing I'd been taught like this when I was in school. And I really want my children to learn to write this way. In fact, I've offered to help their teachers teach writing for a few weeks. So it's not that the method isn't sound. It's just that—well . . . ESL is *different*, you know."

"I agree," said her friend Kathy, who had recently invited me to talk about teaching writing to her children's PTA. "I feel more sure of my writing than I've ever felt before. In fact, I'm thinking of writing a book on my life as the mother of twins. So you see, it's not that I don't think the process method works. It's just that . . . well . . . Marie, we just don't *do* this in ESL!"

I could see my "ideal program" swirling down the drain, but I could also empathize with Kathy and Ruth's resistance to the new teaching paradigm. After all, I myself was as yet uncertain whether or not the program would work for ESL students, though I thought it more likely to work than traditional approaches. Having spent two years studying writers who teach, however, I'd known dozens of writers who burned out or became frustrated teaching because they dared not challenge what "English teachers are supposed to do," and I didn't want the tutors I trained to run into that dead end.

It wasn't hard to figure out what was going on. These resistant tutors and I had different theories of learning—they believed that ESL students learn differently from native speakers; I believed that ESL writing would develop similarly. Fortunately, these theories were something we could test, for I'd incorporated follow-the-kid research into the graduate seminar to ensure our success with trying a new teaching paradigm.

Hoping tutors would agree to give process-based teaching a chance, I thought for a moment, held my breath, and plucked a time frame from the air. "Let's give the program two good weeks," I said. "That's only four hours of tutoring per group. Let's start with process-based teaching and look closely at what students write. If we don't find similar patterns among ESL and native writers, after the two weeks we'll try other methods that the data suggest. We can always fall back on traditional methods if the new ones don't work. Let's give our students a chance to try them first."

My Early Hypotheses and Tutors' Tentative Findings

I made a few suggestions for the first days of school. I suggested that tutors open their groups as I had opened the seminar, reducing anxiety by not assigning grades on early drafts and responding aloud to ideas before correcting form. Begin by encouraging students to write freely without monitoring for structural correctness, I said, and tell them they need not read aloud if a piece gets personal. Show them how to write quickly and freely by writing along with each group, and offer to read your messy, unrevised freewriting first. If they worry about grammar, say you'll teach them to fix errors later, *after* they've drafted a piece they care strongly about.

Instead of marking errors for the first few weeks, I suggested, the challenge would be to find some strengths in every student's work, even if all one could say was that the writer had "tried something new" or "worked hard." Phony praise, however, was as bad as harsh correction: Both were unbalanced responses that confused beginning writers rather than informing their intuitions objectively. If there really wasn't much to praise in a piece, tutors might ask groupmates to help the writer find a topic she cared more about before she began writing again. It was through ideas the students *wanted* to communicate, I advised them, recounting what I'd learned from open-admission dialect speakers, that basic writers would break away from inhibiting concern for form. Later, we drafted and ran off for students in the Center copies of the letter shown in Figure 2–1, which served as our "syllabus":

Together those first six tutors (Kay Benton, Linda Blair, Andy Cooper, Ruth Fischer, Ruth Furr, Kathy Trump) and I planned a two-week evaluation. Every day as groups dispersed, informal research began, with tutors noting changes in behavior and attitude and examining every piece of writing their students did. They then compared pieces done under our "sanctuary" conditions with the more formal test essays we'd rated a few days before. Light enrollments that first semester left us plenty of time to look very carefully at the writing students did, and what we learned about writing during those first two weeks contained the roots of all five teams' subsequent analyses.

Hypotheses Tutors Tested

Given the two-week time frame I'd agreed to for testing the program, we couldn't hope to test the final results of process-based teaching. All we could

Central Atlantic University

WRITING TUTORIAL CENTER

Welcome to the WTC,

Here you will join a writers' group and trade writing strategies with each other. An experienced writer will get you started and serve as a resource person.

Writing well means finding good topics, drafting, revising, and editing. It sounds hard if you haven't had much practice or have lost your confidence. BUT WRITING, LIKE TALKING, IS NATURAL. Follow your group's advice, and you'll improve rapidly.

Our system has lots of advantages--no grades, no homework, no assigned topics for writing, no grammar and punctuation drills. To be certified in a semester, however, there are several things you'll need to do:

1. CHOOSE TOPICS THAT INTEREST YOU AND YOUR GROUP.

2. FREEWRITE WITHOUT WORRYING ABOUT CORRECTNESS ON THE FIRST DRAFT.

3. REVISE YOUR FREEWRITES. Your group will help you. Strunk and White's <u>Elements of Style</u> will help you too. Please buy it and bring it to group.

4. LEARN TO COPY-EDIT YOUR WRITING FOR PUBLICATION. We publish a WTC book, post work on four bulletin boards, send letters to friends, foes, and editors, and print weekly <u>WTC Excerpts.</u> We have dictionaries and handbooks for you to refer to. Please buy V. Hopper's laminated summary of English grammar and punctuation, available in the bookstore.

Most students are able to earn WTC certification in a single semester. You should understand, however, that your success in the WTC depends on

1. PARTICIPATING ACTIVELY. Choose topics you like, read to your group, try their suggestions to see if they improve your writing, and respond helpfully to what others write. YOUR PROGRESS IS UP TO YOU.

2. ATTENDING REGULARLY. Tardies and absences interfere with learning. If you must miss, schedule a makeup session with your tutor at the next session. Continued absence can delay your certification for another semester and prevent early registration.

3. BEING SUPPORTIVE OF OTHERS IN YOUR GROUP. Writing is difficult, especially for people without experience. In the WTC we begin by looking for each others' strengths and commenting on what's good in the writing. Later we make suggestions for improvement, always in a constructive way. Be careful not to undermine another writer's confidence by giving unkind criticism. If you do so unnecessarily, you may be asked to leave the group, thereby jeopardizing your certification until the following semester.

Marie W. Nelson

MARIE W. NELSON, DIRECTOR
Writing Tutorial Center

Figure 2-1   "Syllabus" given to students entering the WTC program

do was examine a few hypotheses about how ESL writing would respond when tutors *untaught* what researcher Mike Rose (1980) has called "rigid rules and inflexible plans" and set up a sanctuary in which making mistakes felt safe.

I suspected that ESL writing would change in a safe atmosphere, just as I'd seen native writing change when the new methods were used. I guessed that writing would become more fluent and engaging as students began to find topics they cared about. I also suspected that students' work would lose the stiffness so typical of beginning attempts at academic prose. When attention shifted from stucture to meaning, I imagined, students would write more as they spoke, producing more natural rhythms, fewer direct translations, and less-garbled sentences.

I also suggested that tutors watch for increased imagery, detail, and length and look for fewer flashy but incorrectly used words. I thought they might see better logic and more developed ideas as well as *increases* in some kinds of errors on freewritten drafts. Such regression errors were no cause for concern, I told them, for students should be able to correct them while editing. These were some of the changes I myself expected to see, and though I was fairly certain at least some would show up, I felt unsure which ones we would see and how long they would take to occur. Four class periods wasn't much time for measuring improvement. All I could do was sit back and wait for the data to come in.

It wasn't long in coming. The second day of the term, the two skeptical tutors—Ruth and Kathy—appeared in my office to say that some ESL students had responded well to their invitation to write freely about a person they cared about. Others had acted dubious about the value of personal writing, however, and one Korean student announced that grammar was *all* he needed to learn. Soon, though, tutors began to suspect that there were more differences between the writing of those who resisted and those who welcomed the new approaches than there were between the writing of natives and that of ESL speakers. As students discovered their voices and began to write as they spoke, a change I had *not* predicted also began to show up: When ESL students became deeply involved in their content, their article, preposition, and idiomatic problems decreased. In short, process-based teaching led to changes—mostly improvements—in the writing of those ESL and native writers who were willing to try freewriting early on. This finding, which we came to call *the principle of similarity*, would become the foundation of all five teams' analyses:

THE PRINCIPLE OF SIMILARITY: Given the kinds of process-based teaching practiced in the Center, the range and kinds of early changes in writing characteristics (including writing attitudes, be-

havior, and products) are similar across groups of students, including native and ESL categories.

Evidence for the Similarity Principle

Let's look at a few comparisons between entry essays and early freewriting to see the kinds of changes that took place in those first two weeks. Of course, it's important to realize that given the short time span, these changes were probably due to *unteaching* inhibiting rules as much as to any new learning that went on in groups. Screening essays provided most of the base-line data we used, and directions for these essays typically read:

> Write an essay in which you explain how some past experience has influenced you and helped make you the person you are now. In recent years, students have chosen to write about such things as their lives in other countries, past work experiences, and specific events or people who have affected their lives. Include concrete details.

Despite the request for a personal essay, students often attempted a stiffly formal style that came out rigid and jumbled. Yongsook (names of all students have been changed) was no exception. Though she wrote with feeling about a former teacher, Yongsook's apparent confusion about grammar made Linda Blair (who originally drafted the material on Yongsook) wonder where to begin:

> I worked hard with chemicals and equipments instead of play or sleep. I did not mine been in lab at night or hot summer. She was so please with me and so I was. At the last day of high school I told her I want to be a good chemistest and she blessed me with all her heart.
> Here I am trying to achieve my goal and keep that promise with her. My high school life is mostely effected me the person I am now.*

Though she'd studied English in Korea and had attended high school in this country, Yongsook omitted articles, misused prepositions, made agreement errors, confused word classes, and jumbled English word order. She also appeared confused about how to use mass/count nouns and about how the active/passive distinction is commonly made. But her willingness to try new approaches changed her writing: On her very first day in the Center Yongsook wrote more freely, with less monitoring: "Biology book is too big and heavy

---

*Student writing is reproduced as written with all errors and changes (except undetectable erasures) preserved. In-process insertions are marked by carets (^. . .^), between-draft insertions by double carets (^^. . .^^), spelling uncertainties by (*sp*) after the word, and deletions by striking through (~~the~~).

for me. The professor talks so fast I can't even take a note. This was my seconde day of school. My first day I don't recall anything. I guess I got lost.''

Once Linda removed pressure to produce a perfect first draft, Yongsook relaxed and aspects of her work improved. While shorter than those in the diagnostic essay, these sentences are precise, the word order better reflecting the rhythms of English prose. Yongsook did switch tenses, but her subjects and verbs agree, and the one indefinite pronoun is correctly chosen and placed. All but one of the articles are present and correctly used, and articles are a feature that gives ESL students much trouble.

Many similar changes show up in the following pairs of excerpts, the first taken from an essay (left) and an early "freewriting" (right) drafted by a Cambodian student named Voan. In the freewriting, preposition and grammatical problems largely disappear, and when read aloud the paragraph flows almost like native English:

VOAN—CAMBODIAN, MALE

ENTRY ESSAY

On the past twenty years, I've been in three different countries. On the first ten years, I enjoyed living in my native country which I had all my families around, as time progressed, my families started scattered from one place to another. The cause of my family is migration was caused by the war. In 1975 the communist took over my country and I experienced the bitterness of that regime and after three or four years I and a few cousin fled the country. . . .

FREEWRITING

We were the middle-class family or maybe a little higher than middle class. My parents were the nicest persons to me. Especially, my dad, he loved me more than my other two brothers and I loved him so much too because he used to take me with him where ever he was going. He was a very intelligent and generous man. He was elected as a congressman in 1973 and he lived most of the time in Phnom Penh (the capital city of Cambodia). We had three houses in three different provinces. In one particular house, my dad opened a restaurant on the first floor. . . .

For two weeks tutors examined every piece of student writing, showing the more dramatic changes—which they called "breakthroughs"—to me and discussing attitude and behavior changes in the seminar: Instead of sitting sullen and resistant, staring from behind clasped hands, sighing and shifting and erasing one word for every two they wrote, ESL and native students increasingly came in smiling, joking with each other, and staying late to chat. One Bolivian girl always wrote curled up in the ragged old overstuffed chair that tutor Andy Cooper found for five dollars at Goodwill. Others would drop in at the Center hoping a table would be free for writing or would hang around to examine Andy's photographs on the wall. "I just really love this room," said one American boy on first seeing Kathy Trump's geraniums in the window. "It sorta feels like home."

For many students, writing behavior changed almost overnight. Jorge, an Argentinian graduate student who heard about the Center and attended as a "volunteer," had not been required to take the entry essay. Kay Benton described Jorge's first-day drafting.

> I couldn't help but observe the painful path he took to get his words on paper. He would write one word, then two, go back, erase a word, pause, write another word, talk to himself in Spanish, erase some more, rub his forehead, look at his paper, write a word, and so on. It was as if he analyzed exactly the words he might choose and then analyzed how he was going to put them in a sentence. It took him half an hour to write four sentences.

Changes in behavior and fluency showed up immediately:

> Jorge wrote nearly a full page in a half hour. Although I could tell the process was still painful for him, I observed that he made fewer erasures, spent less time on single words, and actually wrote five or six words between pauses to think. He seemed pleased that he wrote as much as he had. I told him the important thing was to get the words out and down on paper—he could always fix them up later or toss out whatever parts he didn't want to use further.

Kay's promise that Jorge could improve his papers was not an empty one. Some time later she wrote in her research report: "Most of Jorge's writing problems centered on subject/verb and pronoun agreement, but even in our few sessions (eight) he began to find his own errors as he read his papers aloud."

Jorge's first language was Spanish rather than English, but inhibited drafting behavior was not unique to ESL students, as tutor Ashley Williams documented three years later:

> Terry is a worry for me. He's the one native speaker in the group. He's correct, formal, nervous, inhibited, jumpy. He wrote 6 sentences in his tiny, neat handwriting about the roads in W. VA. He used "these roads" 5 times in those sentences. . . . He looks so uncomfortable when he writes, gripping the pen all the way down at the tip, stopping and starting frequently, looking up, staring at the wall, moving his lips as he writes, hunching his shoulders forward, and then shifting back in his seat as if trying to get a better perspective on the paper in front of him.

Like Jorge's, Terry's writing improved once he relaxed a bit:

> Terry, who has been writing very stiffly, grabbing each time for the dictionary, wrote (at my direction) a stream of conscious sort of piece. I said,

"Terry, let's try something—Don't use any punctuation. Don't worry about verbs or spelling." He wrote, "Stuck unsure uncertain frewriting feels strange weird blue pen," etc. . . . (The piece incidentally went into the *Excerpts* and has gotten several student responses.) [*Note:*When the *Excerpts* come out each week, the students each receive a copy and may take a few minutes to write responses to authors of their favorite pieces.]

In his response (to perhaps the most lyric and descriptive piece in the *Excerpts*), Terry wrote:

> I could almost see the lake and hear the crickets and the frogs.

I was so pleased with that relaxed sentence. . . . I feel he may be beginning to loosen up a bit.

Tutors were startled by the similarities between ESL and native writers. Likenesses not apparent when grammar or idioms were compared showed up in attitudes and behaviors that affected writing in other ways. We also noticed that though individual ESL and native papers might exhibit different structural traits, when we compared *sequences* of writing, underlying patterns of development were similar. One trait both groups exhibited often during those two weeks was overmonitoring while drafting, probably due to fear of making mistakes. For both groups, unmonitored drafting led to regression errors—such as omitted words, misspellings (especially homonyms), dropped inflections, and failure to paragraph. Another trait we saw was the "censoring" of personal content—"screening" or "filtering" tutors sometimes called it. Students told us they had been taught to write impersonal prose, but their efforts to produce formal, objective pieces were accompanied by linguistic inhibition and distortion, logical convolutions, and little concrete detail. When either group stopped *avoiding* personal content, however, their writing grew more vivid, detailed, and logical.

The next excerpts, by a standard English-speaking minority student, show differences between an overmonitored essay and an early freewritten piece not unlike the differences we saw in ESL writing. Though Dolly does not censor personal content much in this essay, wordiness and self-conscious concern with verb endings diminish as soon as she adopts a conversational tone. Though Dolly spoke standard English, it was interesting to see that she overcorrected past tense endings when monitoring and dropped them when freewriting—both patterns typical of ESL and dialect speakers and both features she could fix easily on a later draft.

DOLLY—STANDARD ENGLISH SPEAKER, BLACK FEMALE

Entry Essay	Freewriting
Monitored/Uncensored	*Less Monitored/Uncensored*
On Oct 7, 1979 at 5:10 P.M. my life changed. After the incendent took	We went to the canal. The canal was far enough in the woods that kids

placed nothing much matter in my life. I didn't care if I lived or died.

It started out as an overcast day. Nothing was unuseal. I got up & got dressed. I was getting ready to go out to Milton Hershey Boys school to see my boyfriend.

After I was ready, I went over to Trudy's house to pick her up. Trudy was my best friend at time. We went everywhere to gether. Together we then went to Hershey to see our boys.

We had a group at Milton Hershey we pal around with. . . .

could go and drink there and not get caught by the cops. . . . Most of the time we would get a case of beer and drive around all night until we get drunk then we would drive home. Sometimes, we would go to the mountains a have a party then drive home on bumpy, windy mountain roads. That was the social norm. People were concern about drinking and driving but noone thought about getting caught or the consequences involve.

Sometimes I wish I grew up where the drinking age was lower. Half of the trill of drinking in Pennsylvania was sneaking around. When I move to Virginia, I was legal. The trill of drinking was gone. I didn't have to sneak into a bar anymore. It was fun in Pennsylvania getting a fake I.D., going up to the doorman and sliding by the doorman. In Virginia I hardly go to bars anymore. I prefer to go over to a friends house. . . .

This entry essay is atypical in that, though Dolly overmonitored for correctness, it has a strong voice and a number of vivid details. Despite these strengths, her freewriting has better-developed paragraphs and smoother transitions between ideas than her test essay does. Like much writing that is not heavily censored for personal content, it also has potential for development, and a serious expository essay could be developed from these ideas if Dolly so chose.

The following excerpts from Giao, a male Vietnamese student, show changes between a monitored, censored (highly impersonal) entry essay and an early but more freely written piece.

GIAO—VIETNAMESE, MALE

  life as a human being must conquers some of the problems and complexed enviroment. We always

I got to know her when we were in our first day of freshman class. Well, I didn't have the guts to ask her out

ENTRY ESSAY

Monitored/Uncensored

learned from the past and the experience that had influenced us. For instant, one single event that have dominated my life was the arrival into united states. Just imagine a individual doesn't speak the language and not accustoms to the culture, the enviroments and the atomspheres. Those problems have to be solve within one's honesty, willing to struggle and having dignity to survive at the lowest point of life in a New World. My biggest problem is the language difficult. . . .

FREEWRITING

Less Monitored/Uncensored

until the second year. May be I didn't know how to drive yet. So I decided not to embrasss myself. The first time we got to talk to each other was in ~~library~~ ^the class^ where she sat next to me. First we just are friends and nothing special. As days past by, our relationship intensified. A week before the date, she asked me if I have anything to do on weekend. ~~I ansed~~ I replied with a soft tone and said "my research papers are due on Monday and I have to finish it." Too bad we couldn't go. . . .

On examining students' freewriting, tutors often marveled at how often spelling and capitalization improved, how syntax straightened out, how meanings became clearer, how misused idioms and hypercorrections disappeared. Though ESL monitoring tended to focus on syntax and vocabulary, whereas native speakers monitored more at the whole-text and paragraph levels, both styles of structural monitoring inhibited fluency, and both turned out to have been instruction-induced. For ESL students, for example, most past instruction in English had emphasized grammar and vocabulary study, whereas native speakers had more often been drilled on topic sentences and essay structures, thus accounting for the different problems they had. Both groups were also similar in their resentment and frustration with school writing, in their lack of confidence, and in the underdeveloped, self-conscious nature of their heavily monitored drafts.

Excerpts from another native speaker reveal a different pattern from the one Dolly exhibits. With Chuck, text-level monitoring and attempts at a formal tone are accompanied by (or perhaps produce) a reduction in meaningful content. Notice the empty formality of Chuck's entry essay, with its Latinate vocabulary and all-or-nothing generalities almost entirely unsupported by concrete detail.

CHUCK—STANDARD ENGLISH SPEAKER, WHITE MALE

ENTRY ESSAY

Monitored at Text Level/Partly Censored

There are many things that influenced me to be the person I am today. Many of which are strong influences. There are many people in my life that encourage me to my highest expectations.

For example, my parent encourage me and push me to my best potential.

They seem to know what is right and what is wrong, and they are correct. As far as my education goes they have encouraged me to push myself to the limit, and that is what I intend to do. I really think that they are the biggest reason why I am the person I am today.

In addition to my parents my coaches I have had in the past in football and baseball. They are the people that aide in my good sportsmanship and character. When ever it seemed I was going to lose my cool, they would step in to correct my behavior. Having the good sportsmanship would always bring out my character. . . .

Though the essay is ostensibly personal, Chuck oversimplified ideas, constructing an empty thesis and the three parallel topic sentences required by essay formulas. He also sacrificed punctuation in the process: His only sentence fragments occur in the memorized essay format. In the more freely written childhood memory, by contrast, better-developed paragraphs and in-process revision that focused on meaning rather than on form confirm that for this piece Chuck's attention has shifted from tone to content. Unlike his entry essay, the memory is rich with detail, its sentences flowing more smoothly, with natural transitions between.

FREEWRITING

Unmonitored/Much Less Censored

As I was running around and throwing rocks and bottles, I looked down at my feet for a split second and as I did I saw a money clip with money in it. In an instant I picked up the clip of money and ran to the house. I was so excited about the money that my mind lost interest in playing. When I arrived at the house, I told my grand father about the money. ~~He said that~~ I was ready for him to say that it was mine to keep, but instead he said we would have to put an ad in the paper to see if anyone would claim it. When he told me that, my heart fell to the floor. I thought I would be able to buy some candy and some toys. . . .

Because both of Chuck's topics have similar potential for personal involvement, he may not have been consciously censoring for personal content in his entry essay. More likely, I think, its vacuous prose sprang from efforts to achieve a formal tone and conform to a rigid structural format while drafting the piece. It was not faulty grammar and mechanics that had made tutors decide not to pass his entry essay. It was his generalities, garbles, clichés, and fragments—though not one of these features appears in his memory piece. Like most of our students, Chuck came to us with implicit knowledge that he could not tap while monitoring for structural features, and that his test essay therefore failed to reveal. The freewriting shows how easily he was able to tap this knowledge once he knew that he could revise and edit through several drafts, systematically separating and sequencing the writing tasks that he had tried, in the test essay, to handle all at once. Had he had such information a week or two before, his freely written memory piece might well have become the kind of focused essay tutors would have passed.

Native speakers were not the only ones to write with empty formality. One of the "skeptical" tutors, Kathy, reported an ESL case in which early censoring and monitoring made content and fluency break down:

> Khaled taught me not to be fooled by what appeared to be fluent writing . . . [but] on closer examination turned out to be meaningless and dishonest. He . . . always tried to say what the teacher wanted to hear. When he was forced into writing . . . beyond his abilities, his writing disintegrated into a jumbled mess. He was writing only for "looks" and never really worried about meaning. . . . He needed to work on fluency more than any of my other students.

Once students stopped trying to write in this "meaningless and dishonest" way, underlying problems in their writing often cleared up—as shown in the following excerpts from native speaker Dale. Gracelessly adhering to a rigid five-paragraph formula, his entry essay contains a meaningless contradiction ("life is not all it turns out to be"). This standard speaker also made three other kinds of errors that are more common in the writing of ESL or dialect speakers. One was hypercorrection in subject-verb agreement (e.g., "The past experiences I have had, ~~have~~ ^has^ made me the person I am now"); another a wrong preposition ("the respect to others"); the third the faulty construction of a common word (*courtesly*).

DALE—STANDARD ENGLISH SPEAKER, WHITE MALE

ENTRY ESSAY
Overmonitored for Text-Level and Surface-Level Structure
   The past experiences I have had, ~~have~~ ^has^ made me the person I am now. These experiences have should me the meanings of life, the respect to others, and the kindness and courtesly toward others. These will ~~shoul~~ shown in this essay.
   My first experience was the meaning of life. I found out ~~this~~ ^that^ life is not all it turns out to be. When I was young, I got what ever I liked by asking my parents. but as ^I^ ~~gou~~ grew ~~up~~ ^older^, the demand became bigger and the ~~response~~ ^responce^ became smaller. then I realized that you have to work for what you want. Nothing is given to you unless you work for it. This I felt is the meaning of life. . . .

Unlike the changes students made when focusing on content, in-process revisions (verb agreement, spelling) confirm Dale's correctness concern, while the formulaic first sentence defines a rigid five-paragraph theme. By contrast, though his freewriting (below) tends to ramble and is all one paragraph, it's more focused than the essay and could easily be organized around its central point—the frustrations Dale was experiencing in his calculus class. Perhaps the most obvious changes, however, are better spelling, fewer hypercorrections, and increased specificity. And as with the ESL-type errors, the self-conscious "stuttering" (that is, "as ^I^ ~~gou~~ grew ~~up~~ ^older^, the demand became" and "the ~~response~~ ^responce^ became") of the entry essay is almost completely gone:

> Well right now I'm worrying about Calculus. I have a test tomorrow and Im not having the easiest of times. I can't understand how they can let a teacher teach, when he can hardly speak english. I should not even show up for the class. I go home and read the book that night to learn what is to be learned. . . . He writes the Theorems on the board, and does an example, which does not make sense, and then gives the homework. This I feel is not fair. Calculus is a hard class as it is. I paid a good deal of money to learn calculus and I can't even understand the teacher. I tryed to switch out of the class to another, and there is no more room in the other classes. I always liked math, but know its just frustrating to go to class. Also the room is small & crowded and the air condition does not work. Plus they have construction workers outside the window. The smell of tar and the yelling of the workers add to the frustration. This situation could not be worse. . . . Calculus is not a breeze threw class, and it needs to be explained clearly. I don't mean to be mean, he is a nice guy as a teacher but he can't explain what Im asking, and if he does, I can't understand him. . . .

This piece has its problems but, less censored and less monitored, it's more vivid, coherent, logical, organized, and developed than the entry essay. Observing such changes confirmed Team 1's increasingly strong conviction that ebb-and-flow patterns of improvement and regression, of risk taking and mistakes, were similar for ESL, standard English, and dialect speakers. For all groups, regression errors occurring with the monitor turned down proved to be only slips of the pen that students could later correct by turning the monitor up again while reworking subsequent drafts. This finding is confirmed by Lydia, whose speech had black dialect features. Though many surface-level problems appear in her writing, for an entering Center student, her revising was sophisticated, and her entry essay speaks with uncommon authority. Self-conscious stops and starts when focusing on correctness, however, reveal some insecurity about its acceptability.

LYDIA—NATIVE SPEAKER WITH
SOME BLACK DIALECT FEATURES

ENTRY ESSAY

~~I believe the~~

To alleviate confusion, people must communicate. ~~To communicate, feelings~~ When there is communication, attitudes & beliefs are brought

FREEWRITING

My father could have cared less if we went to school or not. I have 2 brother & 2 sister. ~~They~~ ^We^ all would have dropped out of school if it hadn't been for my mother. She was determined to have educated

ENTRY ESSAY

out. ~~to the~~ ~~There~~ ~~is~~ ~~no~~ Once conflicts ~~are~~ have started, no one wants to communicate, thinking one side won't listen to the other anyway.

For the problem of the Germans indiscriminately killing turkish people in Germany. I believe their is no real happy solution. The Turkish can leave the country to avoid being killed. ~~the~~ ^or^ They could stay a fight a long bitter battle to help change ~~the~~ ^curl^ conditions. . . .

FREEWRITING

kids because education was something that was lacking in her life. My mom ~~was~~ ^and her siblings^ were punished for going to school when ^they^ ~~was~~ ^were^ young. Her father believed working the farm was more important than learning how to read & write. My grandmother ~~would~~ ~~tell~~ ~~told~~ wanted her children to attended school but was afraid to let them go ~~in~~ ^out of^ fear of physical abuse from her husband. My mother did finish the 9th grade. My father never went to school in his life.

I think my ^mother^ made an accomplishment. ~~All~~ ~~of~~ She has fulfilled her goal. All her kids have ~~or~~ completed high school. All have been to or are attending college. ~~One~~ I ^have a brother^ who is a lawyer, brother who's an engineering asst, a sister who's a teacher, an a sister who is attending a police academy. . . .

At the start of the entry essay Lydia abandons the first-person pronoun, then forgets this decision in a later paragraph. By contrast, her early freewriting reveals unusual competence. Notice the increase in concrete detail when she chooses a topic she knows more intimately. She also monitors verb agreement and revises *during drafting*. Apparently, for Lydia, some revising and editing skills were in the process of becoming automatic and, for some features, were already integrated into drafting. In other words, Lydia entered the WTC program with some skills other Center students took a term or more to reach. Though her writing processes were more developed at entry than those of some other students would be after weeks in the Center, what she wrote under test conditions was relatively weak.

Lydia illustrates the potential, which I'll document later, of assigning students heterogeneously to writing groups. Despite the occasional intrusion of nonstandard features in her prose, she provided a strong role model for standard speakers where voice, revising, and topic choice were concerned. While freewriting, she found a topic she wanted to take further, a topic she could write on with authority, a topic she could have developed into several kinds of formal essays—persuasive, comparison and contrast, or personal narrative. Apparently she also cared a lot about this piece, for in addition to this draft (of September 13) her folder contained fourteen handwritten pages of changes and additions, plus a three-page, typewritten version that she prepared while editing her piece for inclusion in the book that the WTC students published every semester.

Though overcensoring sometimes decreased as rapidly as overmonitoring did, more often it disappeared gradually, as trust levels rose among students in the groups. To reduce the monitor, students needed only to trust the tutors who evaluated their work. But to write about topics close to their hearts, they had to feel safe with their peers. Lydia's improvements accompanied a shift to more personal material, a shift that often occurred in the sanctuary, a shift followed by more engaged and engaging, more committed and authoritative writing.

Certainly, students must learn to handle teacher-assigned topics. They must also be able to pull new information together into formal reports. Tutors and I had a strong commitment to the students' success, and how they learned to accomplish such tasks is the focus of this book. But for diagnostic purposes early in the term, and until they were confident with revising and editing, letting them write about topics they already knew and cared about provided a quicker, more accurate way to assess their basic skills. For until we offered free choice in topic and genre, we had no way to tell what students could do on their own.

Letting students choose what to write about offered another advantage: It motivated them to work hard enough to improve. I should note in passing, however, lest any misunderstand, that Center policy was *never* to assign personal writing. That would have been an egregious invasion of privacy and would have usurped students' control of decisions about their work. Instead, we encouraged students to write whatever they chose and maintained an atmosphere in which that could be comfortably done. What we found was that, given control and a sanctuary atmosphere, most of the basic and ESL writers who enrolled in our program *chose* to begin their writing careers by writing about their lives. Later, as they grew more confident, many gravitated to less personal topics. Only after we spotted this tendency, however, did two other important variables come into focus—the existence of the content censoring (which I've documented) and its inhibiting influence on basic writers' logic and form.

I could give scores of examples of how student writing changed rapidly when monitoring form and censoring content were postponed until later drafts. Not all students improved right away, however. Yung, for example, was a Cantonese speaker who resisted for some time the quiet insistence of Year 2 tutor, Judith Friedman, that freewriting was worth a try. In Yung's garbled entry essay, tense sequence shifted repeatedly, but it was the global errors that made Judith despair:

YUNG—CANTONESE SPEAKER, MALE

ENTRY ESSAY

Monitored at Text Level, Not Noticeably Censored

When the time that I was a little kid, I didn't ~~ha~~ know anything. I always believed people and did what they had said. But everything was change when ~~it~~ I worked in the [resturant] the first time. All the people is different from what I think. Most the waiters in the resturant cared their tips very hard. I was a busboy in there. But they are nice to me. *There has anything that I dose not realize before in the position different.* I need to say all the good words before the employers for keeping them to angry. If I make a word to inspire them angry, I will end up to lose my job. [italics mine]

The thing about this excerpt that startled me most was the almost completely unintelligible sentence I've italicized. Though it took Yung a while to relax and trust his tutor, the following piece (done September 18), shows that once again freewriting helped reduce errors and straighten out garbled prose. Here syntax and idiom are becoming more natural, and this time the most surprising segments, at least to me, are those that are *perfect* syntactically. Though the opening sentence remains self-consciously awkward, Yung quickly warmed to his subject, and his syntax began to flow:

ENTRY ESSAY

Monitored at Text Level, Not Noticeably Censored

One Friday, when the time my friend or my former teacher drove me down along the George Washington Parkway, a sudden storm came up at nowhere. *The storm came up very fast and blew down a tree branch on the parkway. The car in front of us was hit by it. Then my teacher started to sing a holy song.* She said that when you had fear it was the time for praying. Then she drove slowly around the following branch and said that God was showing mercy so our car didn't hit by the branch. She talked so nice and gentle. [italics mine]

With writing as with speaking, when concern for correctness dominated, powerful affective barriers inhibited fluency. By contrast, when they began to separate and sequence writing tasks, students tapped stores of tacit knowledge, orally and visually acquired, and many problems disappeared in early drafts. When they later returned to those drafts with monitor and censor running, students found they could retrieve rules they'd memorized in the past but had so far been unable to apply. In short, WTC students converted their credit into cash by activating hidden writing abilities. They were thus rewarded for the risks freewriting entailed by being able, for the first time in most of their lives, to apply to their writing two kinds of knowledge they all had—grammatical and mechanical rules they'd been taught in school and intuitive linguistic know-how picked up in the course of their day-to-day lives. As working terminology for these two types of knowledge, Team 2 found Krashen's (1982) distinction between *learned* and *acquired* knowledge useful. These terms also distinguished two types of written features—those for which "errors" increased and decreased respectively depending on whether the writer was drafting freely or monitoring for form.

The risks students took when freewriting also aided tutors and me by helping us separate rules students knew from rules they still needed to study. By unmasking monitor interference parading as deficiencies, drafting freely helped tutors distinguish apparent from actual knowledge and apparent from actual knowledge gaps. Once Yung finally freewrote a draft, for example, his competencies could be seen, and his tutor could at last identify correctly what help he needed in order to improve. Until Yung wrote freely, however, his tutor had felt overwhelmed by what appeared on the surface to be another "hopeless case," but was merely evidence of overmonitoring.

In short, freely written pieces improved in content and in form, forcing tutors and me to reexamine our assumptions about what students "errors" actually meant. Perhaps Yongsook and Yung were not "hopeless," as their tutors had feared. Perhaps Chuck was not doomed to draft vacuous clichés forever; maybe he didn't even *like* writing that way. Perhaps, instead of revealing deficiencies in structural knowledge, entry essays had been distorted by error-avoidance strategies, inexperience with revising and editing, and the test anxiety most students said they felt. Observations like these confirmed the practice—advocated by theorists (Elbow, 1973; Macrorie, 1968, 1970; Murray, 1968) and observed among writers who teach (Nelson, 1982a, 1982b, 1983b)—of separating and sequencing writing tasks, and they confirmed it for ESL, standard English, and dialect speakers.

Basic Skills or Hidden Skills?

They Knew More Than We Thought They Did

The existence of hidden abilities released by separating and sequencing tasks was the second most important finding of the two-week testing period. Since then we've checked and double-checked this discovery against both student and English faculty perspectives and against follow-up data collected by all five teams. At the end of the term, for example, having presented supporting data, Kathy Trump concluded that premature structural monitoring was preventing three female students from writing as well as they otherwise might:

> Sharon and Anna were both competent writers when they came to the WTC. They were also completely blocked by the word *paper* with a capital "P." Anna was unable to write even simple assignments. . . . I asked her to

freewrite and saw her skills as a writer for myself, but form was being imposed on her so heavily [by another teacher] that she couldn't write.

Sharon was also unable to write effectively because she was trying too hard to write in . . . academic style. Her thoughts got lost in this stilted style. . . . Simply teaching [these students] to get their ideas down first and then go back and worry about form later helped both become better writers in a very short time.

An ESL student named Tatiana was also struggling with five-paragraph themes, and it hurt to watch her throw out good ideas because they wouldn't fit the mold. Unlike Sharon, she was able to handle the restrictions on form but needed more help with mechanical errors.

By the end of fall semester, Kathy had come to believe that overmonitoring produced these blocks and inhibitions and kept her three female students from applying writing strategies and rules they already knew:

Actually, they were already good writers—what I showed them was how to put their good writing into the form the teacher wanted.

Ruth Fischer reached a similar conclusion about Phong. Like many students with writing anxiety, he'd begun by making excuses for writing he hadn't done:

When Phong first came, he didn't know what to write and didn't seem to care about writing. During our early discussions, I mentioned it was all right to write things with mistakes while the ideas and feelings were coming. I said the ideas were of primary importance—the mistakes could be dealt with later. Phong had spent that session telling me how his English was poor and that he thought in Vietnamese or in pictures.

Excuse-making ended when Phong got permission to relax, and motivation mushroomed when he tapped his fluency. Taking a risk (in the safety of his home), he abandoned censoring and monitoring at once, discovered something he *wanted* to write, and tapped a store of stylistic skills that built his confidence:

At the next session Phong presented me with a six-page freewrite with some allusions to his final days in Vietnam. (These were to be taking-off points for further powerful writing.) Phong said that my telling him it was all right to write down mistakes let him keep writing. He had images and feelings he was ready to share, so my few words served as the catalyst to unblock his writing.

Andy Cooper also found "hidden skills" that students "already had":

In four weeks, Minh has already taught me a lot. The useful points I got from him were things he brought to the WTC, hidden skills he already had. His mechanical skills were worse than other students', but his images and use of metaphor were better by far. He wrote the best freewrite I have ever seen. It had errors in every sentence, but it was full of emotion and some rather sophisticated images. He comes up with a good image, usually several, in every piece of writing, while most other students have to relax first.

Though weak in several areas, Minh's writing struck Andy favorably because Minh had special talents to share with the rest of his group:

> I found style already present in his work. He already has a strong voice, while their style takes awhile to appear. In his first freewrite Minh wrote of feeling alone in the U.S. after leaving Vietnam during the war: "like a kitten under the big paws of a big lion." I also thought this use of repetition was strangely moving: "I was afraid, afraid of everything."

Tutors also documented student perspectives that confirmed the interpretation presented here. In addition to interviews and anecdotes noted in tutors' logs, almost all students did process "thinkwriting" and self-evaluations that revealed their perceptions of changes in their work. Mai was a female student from Vietnam who found that trying to monitor while drafting reduced fluency. Andy quoted her in his research report:

> Mai's lasting improvements came from recognizing her own errors. She was frustrated with grammar rules. I feel sure that the rules kept her from implementing the very concepts they were designed to teach, for as Mai said herself, "Sometimes those grammar rules ruin my thoughts and writing."

After she learned to separate and sequence writing tasks, Mai actually began to *like* editing. Andy reported that later in the semester, "Mai eagerly corrected all the grammar she could."

The excitement students expressed at their newly found "hidden skills" soon became a recurrent theme of the analysis, as did the fact that new feelings of competence boosted confidence, motivation, and the desire to work hard. When Kay Benton did summer follow-up interviews with ten fall semester students, surprise and pride—"Oh, *geez*! I can *write*!" as Yun Jeung expressed it—was common. WTC students had been unaware of their potential until reducing the monitor helped them to discover strengths:

> Before I went to [the Center], I was so afraid to be asked to write something, but after I practiced writing and went there once a week, I regretted that I couldn't go twice a week because of my schedule. Now I feel I am very able to write something.
>
> Before I went to WTC I stopped and stopped when I wrote—it just wouldn't come to my mind. I didn't notice when I had changed, but later I realized after I write something: "Oh, *geez*! I can *write*!" After practicing, it just comes out, so I wrote it down and I read it loudly— I find I pick up some wrong stuffs that way.

> Now, my paper isn't going to be *that* good, but better than before. I think I am not as good as the natives maybe still, but at least if someone asks me to write, I can write. Also, I can write what I *want* to write, and I am very glad with that.

This young Korean girl's professor seemed to agree: She gave Yun Jeung a "B" in English 101. Yun Jeung reported:

> My friends were amazed when I got a *B* in my English class. They said, "You had to go to the WTC, but you got this kind of grade?"
> I said, "*Well*, that's *why*! If you want to get good grades, go to the WTC."

By these kinds of testimony, we confirmed that students grew increasingly confident and aware of the processes by which good writing develops. Once convinced that we would postpone summative evaluation, they quickly began to convert their credit into cash, drawing on tacit knowledge many had not known they had and applying rules they knew but had not been able to use.

The Passing of Tutor Resistance

Just like basic writers, ESL students at CAU entered the WTC with unrecognized basic skills they were able to use only after tutors gave them permission to separate and sequence writing tasks. This discovery gave comfort to Ruth Fischer and Kathy Trump, who now saw the continuity between their experience writing for my Teaching of Writing seminar and that of the ESL students attending their groups. Neither woman lost any time revising her assumptions about how ESL writing abilities develop. For example, on her midterm, Ruth restated the question with which Team 1's research had begun:

> Earlier this semester I became intrigued with the response of my ESL students to the process-oriented method of teaching writing as compared to the response of native speakers. Since teaching English to speakers of other languages is my special area of interest, I found myself trying to *understand* the differences rather than simply noting them. Would the processes we were using—that had been used successfully with native speakers—be as effective with ESL students?

In less than three months this ESL teacher, who once felt resistant to process-based teaching approaches, referred to herself as a "convert" to the kind of writing instruction that Team 2 tutor Jane Lofts Thomas (1988) would label "flexible and oblique approaches."

> My personal interaction with [this] approach began in skepticism until I realized that I had been writing "their" way for a long time. Until I

thought it through, I had my doubts as to how [process-based teaching] would work with students. But it makes such sense and we have had some breakthroughs in the WTC. Besides, whatever its shortcomings—and they are admittedly hard to find—it outdistances the traditional method by at least a mile!

For Ruth, the problem of how to teach grammar had finally been solved:

> Grammar is finally put in its rightful place. Brought down from the lofty heights to which English comp teachers have placed it, grammar is not seen as an end in itself but as a means of clarifying, in a conventionally accepted manner, what the message is, as a means of putting the acceptable code of punctuation and spelling on our message so that its improper use won't get in the way of the message. By postponing the search for comma splices, usage errors, and the like until the last draft before the final copy, we save ourselves in our own writing—and our students in theirs—the busywork of correcting surface-level mistakes that might not even show up in the final copy.
> That's energy conservation I can live with!

Ruth's "conversion" was confirmed when she observed a "traditional" ESL teacher teaching "composition." Shortly before midterm, as part of her assistantship, Ruth was asked to grade papers for a 101-equivalent course that CAU called "Composition for Foreign Students":

> I did not realize the depth of my "conversion" until I recently became involved with correcting English Composition papers that were products of a more traditional ESL approach. I found I didn't want to be involved at all in evaluating papers assigned in such a way that form was raised to a level above content. [In the class where I assisted], grammar and mechanics were again on their old pedestal, while the revision process was totally ignored.
> I could see from the attitude and comments of English 100 students I taught in the WTC that this traditional approach produced anxiety, stifled creativity and dichotomized writing into "school" writing and real writing.

Attitude and behavior changes Ruth experienced as a writer foreshadowed similar changes her students would soon go through:

> My attitudes are changing with respect to my personal writing, too. Until this semester I was a functional writer; I wrote when the need arose. I was a transactional writer, daughter of a transactional writer. Then changes started happening.
> As I wrote—in response to a teacher saying "Write!"—I found all I had to do was start. . . . Also I began looking at people and experiences differently. I got so excited about our court being paved early one morning that I wrote about it (though my first entry of the day was about how much I didn't want to write). Then I worked it up into a finished piece for the local community newsletter.

No longer did Ruth write merely for a grade. Publication had become a goal, and motivation grew when she wrote what she chose, experimenting and noticing which strategies worked for her:

> My latest adventures have been attempts to turn my non-prose into poetry, something that earlier in this course I said I didn't care to do. I also have pieces that have not worked out or that I return to in spare minutes. These may or may not ever reach completion; however, I know it's okay to let them sit. Also, I have recognized an important incubation step in my process without which what I write is incomplete, and I feel more comfortable writing in a less formal style without the predetermined need for third person and *Thesaurus* vocabulary.

Exhibiting both of the traits I'd found in my study of writers who teach to distinguish more successful from less successful teachers, Ruth's words convinced me she was on her way to becoming a talented teacher. First, she'd stopped adhering to what English teachers "ought to do" whenever it conflicted with her writing experience. Second, she'd shifted from traditional evaluation focused on the surface-level problems in students' prose toward a more holistic approach to judging writing that included students' behavior and attitudes. No longer did Ruth believe that ESL "deficiencies" should be assessed for use in organizing instruction. Instead, emerging empathy for basic and ESL writers organized her teaching so as to build on writers' strengths. In addition, Ruth no longer saw her role as that of a writing authority dispensing knowledge. Teacher-research had helped her shift to a fellow-learner stance:

> Now, how does all this personal history relate to me as writing teacher? Having grown through this discovery process, I can empathize with my students because I am growing and becoming right along with them. I no longer have to be an authority figure looking graciously down from my pedestal at their pitiful attempts to express themselves on subjects I have had to choose because they are not "capable" or in forms I must tell them to use because I "know" they can't write without them. No, I am right in the middle of the fray, discovering along with them.
> And it feels good.

Though they'd once been committed to teaching structure more directly, Ruth and Kathy now believed that for students to apply the skills they already had, we had to get their minds off structure while they produced rough drafts. Early process advocates like Murray and Macrorie were right, they concluded: The first step in teaching grammar was to get students' minds off it so they and their tutors could discover their "hidden skills." Until ESL students stopped overmonitoring, it was a waste of time to teach them formats and rules, for it was only after they began to write freely that tutors could distinguish developmental errors from overmonitoring and outright mistakes or make valid decisions about what students needed to learn.

Once convinced that process-based teaching could work, Ruth, Kathy, and the other Team 1 TAs continued teaching all students alike: reducing anxiety, helping students find topics they liked, uncovering tacit knowledge students didn't know they had, and building students' confidence and commitment to writing well. Soon tutors would begin to teach revising and editing, helping students find order and focus in freely written ideas, modeling strategies for finding and correcting mistakes, and brainstorming ways to apply all these skills to academic assignments. It was what we learned during those first two weeks, however, when students were first unlearning "rigid rules and inflexible plans" (Rose, 1980), that convinced skeptical tutors to give whole-to-part teaching a try.

Based on changes in student writing they'd spotted within two weeks, Ruth and Kathy had shifted from a deficiency model in which their teaching and grading focused on surface errors to a growth model in which the focus was first on strengths and then shifted attention to factors—whether written, affective, or behavioral—that affected writing development. No longer did they believe ESL and basic writers should be treated differently, and for the next four and one half years of the study tutors continued to treat the two groups the same. From this point I will also stop distinguishing, and unless I state otherwise, the term *basic writers* will refer to both groups.

In September, Ruth and Kathy had been what researchers call "outliers," for they were far above the TA mean for resistance to the new teaching paradigm. By midterm, however, they'd shifted to the opposite pole and had become Team 1's most vocal advocates of change. "The bigger they are, the harder they fall," the old adage goes; and these tutors, who'd had the biggest stake in traditional methods, were now the strongest "converts" to a holistic approach in which writers produced whole pieces of writing before learning how to fix the errors occurring in certain parts. The very traits that had made them resist my untested approach—high professional standards and strong commitment to ESL students—apparently stayed with them once the two-week test was complete and kept ego involvement in their former part-to-whole approach from affecting their open-mindedness. Nor have these tutors abandoned process-based teaching, though both have now been teaching full-sized classes for several years. One day (while revising this chapter, in fact) I received a note from Ruth, who was then teaching English at a university in Seoul. Her comments on the risks Team 1 took during those early, adventurous days still influence the way I work with in-service teachers, making me more understanding of the resistance many feel: "As you write about us, please be kind. We were hanging on for dear life to what was known (grammar, five-paragraph themes, etc.) because the sea of the uncharted was so vast and deep. It just takes some of us a little longer than others to take the plunge."

As a result of Team 1's investigations, subsequent teams continued to teach native and ESL writers alike, addressing writing problems incidentally as they occurred and looking closely at what was going on in the small workshop groups. Insights from Team 1's work also led to program refinements and to adaptations of the research methodology. The following year, for example, new TAs kept more detailed records. Responding less often in "learning logs" to published research and theory, they began keeping participant-observation logs—systematic thinkwritten accounts of what went on in their groups. We shifted to observational logs because Team 1 found them more helpful than reading the work of others (Nelson, 1988). More clearly than research and theory in composition, tutors' logs helped us see how a variety of factors— attitudes, behavior, and written products—were related to the various methods tutors used. And, to the surprise of this quantitatively trained researcher, documenting group and individual *processes* helped tutors and me understand *how* and *why* specific outcomes occurred.

Playing the Predicting Game

In the coaching role I adopted with TAs, I read and responded to dozens of semester-long logs each year, a process that made me uniquely aware of emerging patterns that held (or did not hold) true across tutors and students. Five years of studying some 90-odd of these documents informed my intuitions about what goes on in groups by building up inductively in my mind a conceptual framework for understanding how basic and ESL writers develop, a framework with which I became increasingly able to predict what students (and tutors) were likely to do next. While reading them I therefore began to play a predicting game, looking for events that supported or conflicted with my hunches about what was going on so as to make tacit knowledge explicit and refine the framework further. So valuable were tutors' freely written logs, that increasingly over the years I found (as did tutors) that reading unedited logs informed my work more effectively than reading writing research and theory did.

Keeping and studying logs offered another benefit: Comprising the largest share of our data except for students' folders, these research logs actually made enjoyable reading. Almost always rapidly written, in largely unmonitored prose, logs were with few exceptions straightforward and unpretentious, and I found I could trust the strong, clear voices in which tutors wrote. I grew to "know" their characters, to "make friends" with WTC students, to empathize with basic writers through their tutors' eyes. Like good fiction writers, tutors told interesting tales—tales with suspenseful endings, well-rounded characters, interesting plots. The chapters that follow are strongly grounded in these data, which informed and reinforced our emergent analyses.

3

Interdependence in the Writing Group—"We Get By with a Little Help from Our Friends"

Frankly speaking, for that essay, even though it was written by me, I had a lot of help from my friends. The students around me were the ones who taught me how to write a good essay. . . .

So you see, in the Center we have the understanding that we are all in the process of learning, that there's nothing wrong to criticize each other, there's nothing wrong to give suggestions, and there's nothing wrong making revisions. That way both of us can improve. There's a kind of "You help me, I can help you, and both of us can benefit"—so we work together.

—Kamal

Now I know why Marie kept telling me she could teach me to lead a group. She could teach anybody; the potential is in the group itself.

—Ashley Williams, Team 4

Stage 1: Dependence—The Legacy of Negative Evaluation

Dependence was the entering condition of Center writers. Identified as unlikely to succeed without extra help and required to attend the WTC until certified, scores of basic and ESL writers acted like detainees, passively waiting for tutors to tell them what to do. Clinging to familiar formats and rules, censoring and monitoring heavily, these students expected tutors to mark all their mistakes and tell them exactly which corrections to make. Dependent on the threat of grades to force themselves to write, they docilely followed instructions even while resisting responsibility for their work. They complained when tutors suggested they find topics that interested them or replied that the number of words they needed to write would depend on what they were writing and who they were writing to. They blanched when tutors suggested they ask groupmates' advice about what revising and editing their work needed. Apparently, they were less concerned about how their work affected readers than about minimum standards for escaping from the WTC.

49

Afraid to take risks and unwilling to take responsibility, dependent students cowered in the shadow of evaluation. Writing for other than a grade, it seems, was an unfamiliar and unwelcome idea.

Using "topic of discussion" as a principle of division, Team 4 tutor Yitna Firdyiwek studied patterns of interaction in many groups. Early in his first semester of tutoring, after we'd talked in the seminar about how to encourage students to interact more, Yitna audiotaped a session in one of his groups, transcribed it, broke the transcription into nine topic-related segments, and examined the segments for patterns of interaction. The diagrams that resulted illustrate vividly how entering students clung dependently to tutors. Despite the fact that Yitna tried to get students to interact with each other, most of their questions and comments that hour had been directed to him (see Figure 3–1). Apparently, these dependent students were convinced that their tutor's ideas were more important than those of their peers.

Our charge was to guide these dependent learners into independence—and to do it quickly, in a semester, at most two. We therefore looked closely at high-achieving groups to identify factors that led to their success. This chapter outlines much of what we learned in the process while later chapters show the

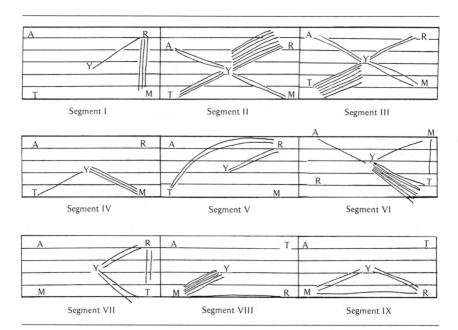

Figure 3–1 The "Switchboard Operator" Effect in Stage I (Dependent) Groups, as Diagrammed by Yitna Firdyiwek on Nine Topic-Related Segments of "Writer Talk"

problems we had. For ten semesters, five teams of tutors used theoretical sampling (Schatzman & Strauss, 1973), analytic induction (Goetz & LeCompte, 1984), typological analysis (Goetz & LeCompte, 1981), and a constant comparisons approach (Goetz & LeCompte, 1984) to monitor group and individual progress, study pro and con evidence on scores of hypotheses, and weed out naive assumptions or premature conclusions about what conditions best helped students learn. Later teams built upon what earlier teams had discovered, improving successful approaches, discarding weaker ones (Nelson, 1987, 1988). In the process, we discovered that when students worked together, helping each other improve their work and sharing what they knew, dependent attitudes and behaviors gave way to interdependence, which in turn hastened the onset of independent work.

Stage 2: Interdependence— A Missing Link in Writers' Development

A breakthrough in our thinking took place in the spring of Year 4 when we spotted this link between dependence and independence. At that point we abandoned an early bipolar analysis that had been accurate, in the beginning, for Team 1 in favor of a new three-phase theory of group development that was far more descriptive of the groups taught by Team 4. After the breakthrough, a new progression became clear: Gradually dependence gives way to collaboration, and independence germinates in that soil.

DEPENDENCE → INTERDEPENDENCE → INDEPENDENCE

The central stage—in which students together took charge of group work, practicing with each other's help unfamiliar writing tasks—wasn't a phenomenon tutors had never noticed. When we went back to their thinkwrites and logs, to their midterms and research reports, we found that members of every team had reflected on it. For example, you may remember Ruth Fischer's Year 1 comment: "We get by with a little help from our friends." What we'd not known was that interdependence was a pivotal link.

The Analytic Breakthrough— How We Discovered the Missing Link

Let me digress for a moment from this discussion of interdependence to show how the significance of interdependence emerged. Analytic breakthroughs were points at which we made what we "knew" explicit, often long *after* our teaching had changed in response to TAs' observations. This breakthrough reveals the extent to which the teacher-research process was at once inductive and deductive, holistic and linear, intuitive and analytic. It also shows how the program evolved in advance of our ability to describe what we knew how to do. Much like the students, who discovered "hidden skills" they hadn't known they had, we took a while to make our research-informed intuitions explicit. In addition, much of what we were learning kept shifting on us. Some of what I report we therefore felt a bit foolish "discovering."

From the start our goal had been to free writers of their dependence. How we did that, however, was hard to put into words. Having noticed an inverse relationship between *withdrawing* (decreasing tutor control) and *independent behavior* (increased student control), Team 1 defined these variables as reverse continua along which both tutors and students moved. Later teams felt uncomfortable with the continuum theory, however. Not that Team 1's bipolar model of growth was *wrong*, but it described how students had acted during Year 1, when sketchy screening procedures had reduced our clientele and left tutors with tiny "groups" of one or two students each. Under those conditions, the relationship had been simpler—the more tutors transferred control, the more independence grew. As screening improved and enrollment neared capacity, however, the bipolar model grew increasingly less accurate. Team 1 themselves had noticed that group collaboration and rapid progress in writing went hand in hand. We never saw the pivotal role of interdependence, however, until several teams had succeeded at evoking it in groups.

I don't remember who coined the term *interdependent*—I think Miki Jackson used it first on that breakthrough day—but it triggered a preliminary three-stage progression that almost immediately rearranged itself to bring order to our four-year analysis. In other words, *interdependence* served as "a key linkage" (Schatzman & Strauss, 1973), by organizing the data on dozens of variables and making clear how they related to one another.

"It looks to me like these students act increasingly *interdependent*," said Miki, a doctoral student who taught at an area middle school and who'd joined Team 4 to get practice with qualitative research. At once Yitna Firdyiwek saw the progression her words implied.

"It's as if students go through a shift." Yitna mumbled around a bit, talking his way through a thought. Then: "Actually, they may shift *twice*—from dependence to independence to interdependence, I think."

"That's it, that's it!" cried Kathy Briggs. "I see those three stages, and they're symmetrical like that, too."

The elegance of this theory wasn't lost on me. Like Kathy, I was convinced at once that the three-stage format was right. But though Yitna's proposition came close, it didn't quite match my memories of Center groups I'd studied and classroom groups I'd taught. Nor did it fit the images from logs dancing in my head. By the end of Year 4, I'd examined logs on some eighty-odd groups and used small groups myself for four years in a range of writing classes. So as tutors chattered I doodled, slashing at a legal pad, doggedly trying to find some way to make the progression fit. But despite its elegance, its lean economy, the obvious correctness of the three-stage form and the way its components sang back and forth to each other, something seemed not quite right about Yitna's progression:

DEPENDENCE leads to INDEPENDENCE which leads to INTERDEPENDENCE. . . .

It was so close, it *looked* like a fit, it *almost* described our data. . . . Suddenly, as a magnet reorders filings on a child's slate, Yitna's terms realigned themselves before my eyes.

"I've got it! I've got it!" I shouted. We've had the pattern reversed. Interdependence isn't final—it's an *intermediate* stage that occurs in the middle and helps independence along. We've just *seen* it as final because it takes up most of our time.

"See, if we reverse the terms, we get something like this . . . ," and I sketched a reordered progression on my legal pad:

DEPENDENCE → INTERDEPENDENCE → INDEPENDENCE

"I think you're right, and I think I know why we had it backwards. This middle stage is what we struggle so hard to achieve," said Kathy. "But once it occurs, independence is almost an afterthought. We don't pay much attention to that when we work with groups, 'cause once they get interdependent, independence takes care of itself."

"You're right, Kathy," cried Kai Wheatley, a writer in the MFA program. "Interdependence requires big changes in motivation. But once students *want* to work hard, independence is merely a matter of time."

"There's another reason why interdependence feels final," Yitna added, teasing out another thread from the tangle to explain the confusion we'd lived with for so long. "And that is that in practice the two stages overlap. At least, from our perspective as tutors, the *behaviors* overlap. Because we teach students in groups, interdependence lasts all semester, even after most students can make it on their own. But since we hardly ever see them outside the groups, we usually see them working interactively. They *can't* act *too* independent given the structure of the WTC."

Yitna was right in noting that even during Stage 3 it was rarely independent behavior we observed. For though students took increasing control of their learning, we observed their behavior in an interactive context. Only a few, for example, requested early certification or abandoned groupmates to work entirely alone. Instead, most worked in groups until the end of the term, with those who "loved" groups returning after certification to attend again as "volunteers."

Another factor that made the data confusing was that we weren't observing a straight-line progression at all, but an upward spiral of increasing independence back down which students could also regress when faced with unfamiliar tasks. I will describe upward and downward spirals in another chapter, for a lot more raw data would gurgle under the bridge before we'd be able to integrate all we'd learned into our new theory.

Convinced we were on the right track, however, I returned at home that night to my legal pad, and alone in the quiet of my study a number of puzzle pieces fell into place. Now that the progression's stages were in order, within seconds the data in memory split into two sets—those dealing with attitudes and those dealing with behavior—then realigned themselves again along tutor/student lines. We'd been aware of these patterns before the breakthrough, of course, but for the first time I could see their interrelationships. For example, as student attitudes shifted from

DEPENDENCE to INTERDEPENDENCE to INDEPENDENCE,

their behavior went through parallel shifts from

REACTIVE to INTERACTIVE to PROACTIVE.

(See Figure 3–2 for a definition of terms.)

Also clear once we noticed the interdependent stage was an inverse, three-stage progression of shifts in tutor behavior

from PROACTIVE to INTERACTIVE to REACTIVE

in which actively reducing anxiety and modeling writer talk gave way first to sharing authority (by actively drawing out students) and later to relinquishing it (by learning to be quiet).

Breakthroughs serve as watersheds in qualitative studies by shifting researchers' roles from exploration to confirmation, from generating hypotheses to testing and refining them. This breakthrough experience was no exception. For the next year we tested the framework, revising it at points to account for discrepant data, fitting small bits of analysis into the larger picture, and tinkering with the language to make it natural but precise. But even a cursory review of the data in our heads told us that we had finally found a key, organizing linkage. For it explained the patterns we'd stored in the logs, the tapes, the videotapes, the process writings of students, and our memories. For example, without even reviewing the raw data again, we knew tutors started semesters using a large number of proactive behaviors like these:

Clearly Proactive Behaviors

- Establishing a safe atmosphere
- Modeling behaviors and attitudes successful writers adopt
- Unteaching misconceptions about how writing is done

- Stepping students through activities for finding ideas and drafting
- Pointing out any strengths they could find in students' work
- Limiting their responses to positive ones
- Offering real-world rewards for trying unfamiliar tasks
- Rewarding critical attitudes and behaviors as well as writing
- Making clear what students might expect of each other in groups
- Suggesting writing strategies students need to succeed

Once students began taking risks, tutors added other proactive behavior:

- Reinforcing desired changes in attitude, behavior, or writing
- Letting students know privately when they violated group trust
- Setting up opportunities for students to help each other
- Focusing student attention on groupmates' attitudes, behavior, and writing when it modeled directions students might benefit by moving in

Just as the new framework would lead one to predict, when students began to catch on to what writing entails, tutors backed away from overtly proactive behavior to interact more as fellow-learners in the groups.

The term **REACTIVE** describes behavior in which a tutor or student waits passively, without acting, until a member of the other category solicits a response by giving an instruction, a suggestion, a hint, a request, or (rare in WTC groups) an order.

INTERACTIVE refers to self-sponsored communication among students and to all communication across tutor and student categories except responses to instructions, orders, suggestions, requests, or hints. In other words, in addition to non-directive talk about writing, interactive behavior includes instructions, suggestions, requests, hints, or orders from student to student and other students' responses to such efforts at control. By contrast, **PROACTIVE** behavior refers to efforts by tutors or students to elicit, from a member of the other category, behavior aimed at achieving a specific learning goal. Proactive behavior by tutors takes two forms, both designed to bring about changes in student writing behavior. On the one hand, tutors give verbal directives to students; on the other, they model the kinds of attitudes, strategies, and writing with which they hope students will respond. Proactive behavior by students includes asking for advice or information, making suggestions (or complaining) about group use of time, pointing out areas in which help is needed, and doing (or asking permission to do) self-initiated work.

We settled on these terms because they reflect better than others we've found the reciprocal nature of shifts in tutor–student relationships.

Figure 3–2 **Definitions of Terms**

Clearly Interactive Behaviors

- Sharing their writing, interests, and concerns
- Asking for help when they themselves had a real writing problem
- Asking friendly (not teacherly) questions about students' work
- Giving supportive but constructive criticism
- Withdrawing slightly to let students take charge of group interactions
- Abandoning direct instruction for incidental teaching
- Giving students chances to take stock of their own progress
- Encouraging groupmates to help each other solve problems
- Engaging students in decisions about what to work on next
- Letting students experience natural negative consequences

Waiting for natural consequences to take effect was important. When tutors relied on natural, rather than artificial, rewards and penalties a number of things could happen. Less serious students might fail to be quoted in the *Excerpts*, might receive less help and less praise from peers, might not get their latest drafts thumbtacked to the "chair rail" I had nailed up at eye level for posting students work, might not be featured (with photo and drafts) on the "Writer-of-the-Week" bulletin board. Nor might they have a polished piece ready for publication in *The Drafted Writers*, the WTC book, or make as good grades on papers for courses as did hard-working students.

Finally, as each semester wound to a close, our data showed tutors luring basic writers toward independence by withdrawing almost entirely to observant postures reminiscent of those dependent students had at first used.

Clearly Reactive Behaviors

- Finding other things to do (so groups had to work on their own)
- Avoiding involvement when present (except when groups got stuck)
- Offering information only when called upon
- Letting students handle problems themselves, through group interaction

In other words, by shifting twice, tutors reversed, anticipated, and modeled the attitudes and behaviors students would need to become truly independent. And in response, basic writers reciprocated, adopting the attitudes and behaviors tutors had modeled for them.

Tutor Behaviors:
PROACTIVE → INTERACTIVE → REACTIVE

Student Behaviors:
PROACTIVE ← INTERACTIVE ← REACTIVE

In other words, as tutors gradually withdrew, students moved from

REACTIVE to INTERACTIVE to PROACTIVE

Our pre-breakthrough findings on how to promote independence in students had emerged gradually and reshaped the program slowly until, at breakthrough time, WTC tutors were applying them with some success. Confirmed by scores of incidents in tutors' logs, by interviews with students, and by student process thinkwrites, early changes in methods were rooted in tutors' experiments, in hunches of mine, and in problem-solving sessions in seminar.

Throughout this analysis, tutors and I interacted as colleagues with complementary expertise (Nelson, 1988). I had a broader view of the data and monitored analytic processes, but TAs were the experts on individual students and groups. They collected much of the data with which we worked, while I read and studied all logs, comparing and contrasting approaches. On the foundation of patterns prior teams of tutors had noted and patterns I myself saw in the logs, I also suggested alternate methods and interpretations, alerted tutors' attention to emerging patterns, and later (while writing this report), refined and elaborated the analysis.

The rest of this chapter illustrates the breakthrough analysis in concrete ways. The next sections show how these six factors hastened independence by contributing to a climate in which interdependence increased:

- Group size
- Group makeup
- Mutual trust

- Bonding
- Motivation
- Confidence

Focusing on the second shift, the final section uses excerpts taken from tutors' logs to illustrate behaviors and attitudes from Stages 2 and 3.

Factors That Make Interdependence Possible

The Importance of Group Size: Five Heads Are Better Than Two. As I've noted, we opened the Center with fewer students than planned. When only a handful showed up that first semester, tutors advertised the program in freshman classes. We still fell short of capacity, but I silently rejoiced. After all, I reasoned, smaller groups would give each student more help. While one-to-one instruction would *of course* have been ideal, we were lucky to have a light load while establishing routines and developing a corps of experienced tutors.

"Groups" of one or two would let tutors learn more about what students needed before they had to deal with three and four students in the spring.

I was wrong to assume that a one-to-one ratio would be ideal. Almost immediately, in fact, tutors began complaining that single students were harder to motivate than groups of two or three. Enthusiasm grew fastest in the few groups of four, they said. Writer Ruth Furr expressed this theme in her research report:

> I have three new students I am working with, but it is too soon to see their patterns. I think they would all benefit from being in a larger group. I felt my best tutoring was done in my group of four. The students stimulated and encouraged one another. They got over the fear of reading their papers to others and they learned how to respond and help each other. *There was just more interaction and it helped them.* [italics mine]
>
> I think it's harder to work singly with students. It's almost like it's too overpowering for them. It's a more real-world situation for them to work among their peers. Hopefully I can get some larger groups going at the start of spring semester.

As screening improvements brought in more students, evidence began to build. All six tutors agreed that groups of four were easy to teach and that students worked harder and made more progress when groups were full. They also complained (and rightly) that meeting five groups twice a week was a strenuous load. They needed some time for planning in their ten weekly contract hours.

The next year I adjusted the schedule accordingly. We'd test groups of five for a term, I said, to see how they worked out. Tutors would teach four groups of five instead of five groups of four, reserving two hours a week for planning, conferences, and record keeping. Results were entirely positive. In the larger, more diverse groups, students took more initiative, talked more about their writing, and shared a larger knowledge pool. They also grew more confident and said they enjoyed writing more. That year Team 2 also confirmed Team 1's prior conclusion that ESL students held their own with native writers and were valued highly as resources by peers.

About this time, we began to suspect (on admittedly sketchy evidence) that all other things being equal, groups of six decreased in effectiveness. We watched closely for evidence conflicting with this hunch, but over the next few years it was repeatedly confirmed. In 1985, for example, the Center got a new secretary who (trying to help students get their ideal schedules) signed up some six-student groups before I could ask her not to. The semester was far from over when the results became clear. Excerpts from Kathy Briggs's logs illustrate this trend:

> September 25:   All present. This group was really crowded today. Sandy, Dean, Vo, Jon, and Hun were all here as usual. We were joined by Stewart

(making up an absence) and a new member was added—Hosea Williams. It was too many students.

September 27: All present. Somehow six people seems like a big group. Maybe it's because Hosea emits such an air of tension. . . .

November 29: All present. Really large group today. Song from my 7:30 group was doing a makeup—I don't normally take any makeups during this hour because the group (six) is large anyway, but Song had a special problem. . . .

Other data supported our finding that students learned more in groups that were neither too large nor too small to work in our system. During Year 4, in early fall, several tutors copied an approach I was using in their graduate class of nine—dividing the class into even smaller writing groups. Unaware of earlier teams' findings on group size, new tutors began, from the first of school, to break four- and five-member groups into mini-groups of two or three because they themselves had found four- and five-member subgroups beneficial. Pleased to see Team 4 rely on experience as a guide, I nonetheless suspected from our earlier observations that two- and three-member mini-groups might prove rather small.

Almost at once I was reading in logs that students in mini-groups had regressed and were acting less serious, less committed than before. Participation dwindled, and within a few days tutors abandoned mini-groups until nearer midterm, when students had grown interdependent enough to work with less supervision. Kathy Briggs was one of several to comment in logs:

Today I put them in mini-groups: Sandy & Hun; Vo, Jon and Dean. They were to read their most recent two pieces and get feedback. The mini-groups did not flow well in here. Sandy and Hun had gotten along pretty well together in the large groups. Together in a small group of their own, Sandy looked pretty uncomfortable. She usually gives excellent responses to group members. She read today, but she didn't look happy.

Everyone in Vo's mini-group read. They acted as if the purpose of the mini-groups was to race through reading. They gave very little support or feedback. Maybe it's my fault—maybe I put them in groups too soon. Or maybe I should have given more prior instruction.

Once the breakthrough emerged, the wisdom of Kathy's supposition grew clear: Dependent (reactive) students needed (proactive) training in order for interdependence (interaction) to help mini-groups succeed. For entering students not yet used to taking charge of their learning, mini-groups proved to be too much responsibility. Ashley Williams noted similar results:

Sung Tae worked with Terry. They and the group of Parvis and You Chi "finished" quickly. Sort of like they each found one thing to correct and thought they'd completed the assignment. . . .

I'm disappointed that more didn't go on in the mini-groups.

That smaller groups progressed less quickly was confirmed in the spring of Year 4 when an unexpected drop in enrollment led again to smaller groups.

Evidence about group size also came from students. While I was drafting this chapter, for example, Kim White, a Team 5 tutor, alerted me to some evidence from a "returning" student (one taking more than a semester to be certified). Noting the benefits of interacting with others, Diep said he wanted a chance to learn in a larger, more diverse group. In Kim's log I read: "Diep's freewrite mentioned how much he hoped the group would be five students and one tutor—last Spring his group had been too small and too quiet, he said." I asked Kim to copy Diep's piece, errors and all, for my file: "In this class, I'm hoping to have 5 students this semester. In last semester, WTC class had only three students, that is including me. so, when we have to make comments and suggestions only 2 students can response."

It's not that five was a magic number. Four and six worked about as well. But with four, when someone was absent, the groups shrank to three or two; and with six, if all were present, someone's work didn't get discussed. Team 4 tutor Yitna Firdyiwek concluded:

> It's in taking into account the inevitability of variation that five becomes the ideal number, for absences and makeups are factors we *know* occur in our setting. Four and six, then, are boundary numbers, the numbers five-member groups will have with makeups and absentees. But when we *schedule* groups with either four or six, they often become too small or large to work effectively.

Though I won't review those data here, these interactive processes were confirmed by my own and by former tutors' experiments using small groups in full-sized writing classes.

As Diep noted, smaller groups grew less interdependent, in part because they shared a smaller knowledge pool. This finding had important implications for learning, for dependence was both catching and self-perpetuating: The longer a student acted dependent, the less her groupmates learned. Dependent students lacked confidence, had low expectations for themselves, failed to take charge of their learning, contributed less information, and less often experienced the surge in feelings of competence that more forthcoming students felt after helping others succeed. Dependent on tutor approval, such students took fewer risks, and learning less, *remained* dependent and lacking in confidence. In other words, when basic writers failed to take charge of their learning, a downward spiral of decreasing expectations resulted: Instead of *proactively* making sure they learned what they needed in groups, dependent students *reacted* to what they thought tutors wanted from them. And, as peer influence affects adolescent behavior, passivity in one or more groupmates made others more passive as well.

In short, in our examination of hundreds of students and groups, we observed a persistent tendency: Students attending five-member groups were most likely to grow independent, for five-member groups produced the most student–student interaction and distributed it most evenly among groupmates without reducing too far the time groups could spend on each person's work. In addition, five-member groups acted more trustingly. Having somewhat larger groups promoted greater honesty, for when students felt uncomfortable, they didn't have to comment—there was always someone else to contribute a point of view. Five-member groups took more responsibility and maximized the critical distance students got on their work. Team 4 tutor Yitna Firdyiwek summarized these effects in a thinkwrite:

> In five-member groups writers can be subjective and objective at once. They can get involved but maintain distance on what's happening. Apparently five is also small enough to foster individual responsibility without being so small that students feel on the spot. Groups of five are small enough that students cannot hide—can't avoid making subjective responses—but not so small that they get anxious or feel the spotlight is always on them.

A Malaysian student, Kamal, put it more succinctly: "After we freewrote, we read our papers. There were only five of us, so I read too."

In short, five proved the optimal number for groups in the Center context—given our specific array of scheduling constraints, the length of pieces our students wrote, our fifty-minute sessions, the students we enrolled, the graduate students who tutored, and our process-based teaching approach. Five also proved the size most likely to lead to interdependence, make all students feel comfortable, force them to take charge of their learning by leaving them no place to hide, provide enough points of view to help them get distance on their work, and ensure an adequate knowledge pool from which to learn. Two heads are better than one, the old folk adage goes, but in these small-group writing tutorials, five heads were better than two. My point, of course, is not that this size would be elsewhere ideal (though a body of research seems to support that conclusion), but that, *compared to other-sized groups in our particular setting*, five-member groups contributed most to an interdependent stage without which few of our basic writers grew confident.

Diversity Is the Spice of Life—and of Writing Groups, Too. Size was not the only factor affecting group success. Diversity also increased the interdependence that helped students handle academic writing later on. Every team of tutors noticed that diverse groups learned faster. And in the sanctuary atmosphere— where thoughtless or unkind treatment of others or of their writing was rare— many kinds of differences enhanced development: cultural background, ability, gender, language, age, religion, and political leanings. Even having feelings of dependence in different areas contributed to the growth of interdependence in groups. American students tended to be passive learners, for example, though they rarely acted passive with teachers or with each other. By contrast, some nonnative students, while more passive in behavior, were models of strong motivation and determination to learn.

Here the log of Linda Topper, a beginning tutor, shows a more experienced tutor maximizing diversity:

> *9:30 A.M.*   Kathy [Briggs] suggested we wait until everyone scheduled at this hour filled out the forms before we decided who was in which tutor's group so we could form folks into well-blended groups instead of grouping them by the order they signed up in. I'm sure glad she did! I think this new mix will work better. I now have:
>
>> one American (a male native speaker)
>> one Korean-American, a returnee, here 12 years (since he was 6)
>> two Koreans
>>> —Mary, another returnee, here two years—she's 19
>>> —another Korean student, 10 years in the U.S.
>> one student from Ecuador, 11 years in the U.S.
>> one Malaysian volunteer [Kamal], 4 years in the U.S.
>
> Their ages range from 17 to 25.

Students from different cultures offered different points of view and served as expert witnesses on interest-provoking topics—such as the influence of Islamic sects on terrorism, routines of daily life in the People's Republic of China, what it's like to spend months in an Iranian political prison, firsthand experiences with racism here and abroad, how Olympic training differs in France and the United States, the impact of Confucian thought on Korean women's lives, and how French and German universities differ from CAU.

Japanese and Korean students who'd studied grammar for years could often recite grammar rules even tutors didn't know, though they frequently failed to apply those rules in speech and writing. Asians were often slow to speak up, remaining outwardly passive, though they modeled self-discipline and motivation for others. But by watching Hispanic students (whose typical patterns of strengths and weaknesses were the reverse) Asians learned the value of free-writing and free talk, relaxing the monitor and censor to draft and speak less inhibitedly. Later, near the end of the term, with papers being readied for *The Drafted Writers*, Asian students returned the favor by modeling editing strategies and teaching other students the rules they knew so well. Kamal, the Malaysian volunteer from Linda Topper's group, speaks of a breakthrough he had when he copied how a "Spanish lady" talked on the first day of his first required WTC group.

> My first day in WTC we just talked. There was a lady . . . she has a Spanish accent—and I think she is a Spanish lady. We had a talk. I had difficulty expressing myself, because first I talked soft. I didn't have confidence to talk. You see when I want to say something, I worry that I might mention the wrong word. But that Spanish lady—I think her name is Elena—she did talk, and she said the wrong words and everything. And I

said to myself, she could not speak English much better than I am, so why should I be shy?

There was instance where she went somewhere south—I think Florida—and she was very excited to tell about being on the beach. So, she start to say it, and I watch her and see how she talk. She just ramble on the words, and all I could get is the story. I understand what she's talking about, but she speak with broken English.

And I say to myself, "Hey, she speak like that. Why don't I just speak like that? Then I don't have problems." . . . So I start to imitate her. I just talk, and when I start talking my tutor understand what I'm talking about and I say, "Wow! I'm not that *bad.*"

So then I talk, I talk!

Still other differences made interdependence more likely. When Vietnamese read poignant narratives vivid with imagery, other students liked what they heard and copied the technique. Recently arrived Vietnamese were often reserved, however, sometimes requiring two semesters to speak out in groups. But once these students found topics they cared strongly about, they set a standard of commitment and improvement that inspired many others to work hard. Black English narratives tended to be honest, vivid, and melodic, powered by the rhetoric of a rich oral tradition. Once drafted, however, some papers needed organizing and editing, and ESL and standard speakers could often help with this. Thus did group diversity encourage interdependence: Recognizing each other's strengths built trust and confidence, and after some hesitation students grew interdependent, depending for help on each other rather than on tutors.

Though we adamantly resisted stereotyping, believing it to be one source of many of our students' problems, the bulk and richness of our data suggested that certain traits were "typical" of students in certain categories. Because they led us to make groups more diverse, these findings also led to greater individualization, for students had different levels of skill and progressed at different rates—even though all seemed to improve under similar conditions:

1. Autonomy in making decisions about their work
2. A reasonable expectation of real-world rewards and penalties (as opposed to grades)
3. Balanced evaluation based on individual levels of development and on the stage of completion a particular piece was in
4. Assurance that their self-esteem would not come under attack—that they need not feel defensive about writing, beliefs, ethnic background, or grammar mistakes

In an effort to distinguish between seemingly conflicting patterns, Team 4 reexamined my assumption of similarity—which Team 1 had made a "principle"—in light of emerging insights about diversity:

THE PRINCIPLE OF SIMILARITY: Given the kinds of process-based teaching going on in the Center, the range of change in writing attitudes, behaviors, and products was similar across categories of students, including native and ESL students.

What Team 4 found was not that the similarity principle was wrong but that it could not adequately stand alone, for it masked the great diversity among writers and writing processes that nudged us increasingly to individualize. Writers attending the Center varied in many ways—in culture, language, strengths and weaknesses, personality, writing experience, confidence, level of anxiety, and learning style. Despite underlying similarities and the similar conditions that fostered growth, diversity in groupmates' backgrounds led to faster progress. Finally, a complementary principle, long familiar to researchers, emerged from the data to account for this paradox:

THE PRINCIPLE OF DIVERSITY: Differences within categories of students tend to be greater than between-category differences because traits of all sorts are unevenly dispersed across categories.

In short, though each of our "categories" exhibited "typical" traits—so much so that we developed names for the more common patterns—members varied widely on any given trait, with each category exhibiting a range of behaviors and attitudes, not to mention diversity in the writing itself.

The cross-cultural example I've given illustrates this theme, too. Conventions for classroom behavior vary from culture to culture. By comparison with American or Europeans, recently arrived Vietnamese seem reticent in class because they tend to interact less with teachers and peers. Unaccustomed to open-ended teaching and class discussion, most show teachers a deference that rarely includes volunteering, questioning, disagreeing, or challenging in class. Some of our students didn't conform to these norms, however; the cases of Terry (from northern Virginia) and Tai (from Vietnam) show how unevenly reserve and participation were dispersed *within* ethnic categories. Though Tai was outgoing in class, even by American standards, Terry was more guarded and withdrawn than most Vietnamese.

From the first day of group, Ashley Williams noticed Terry's atypically reactive pattern:

Aug. 29:   I'm sure [Terry's] piece was totally sincere, but it was full of pat phrases ("There is no other country like America and so our country should never be taken for granted" . . .) . . . very straight, formal writing.

Sept. 5:   I'll start with the one native speaker. Terry. His entry essay was one of those formal types w/ repeated phrases. He is sort of a formal young man, too. . . .

Sept. 10:   Terry was, as before, visibly nervous when he spoke. . . . He is correct, formal, and inhibited about his writing, too.

Sept. 17:   Terry is still stuck in the rigid mode.

A month into the semester, Terry's behavior hadn't changed much:

Sept. 26:   Terry is a worry for me. . . . He's correct, formal, nervous, inhibited, jumpy. He wrote 6 sentences in his tiny, neat handwriting about the roads in W. VA. He used "these roads" five times in those sentences.

Finally, though Terry remained reserved, his writing loosened up:

Oct. 6:   If some night you are driving threw the coal mining sections of West Virginia you may see what looks like a whole mountain on fire. The mountain glows with red and blue colored flames which make it seem as though a volcano has erupted.

By passively failing to interact with peers for a full six weeks, Terry denied his group a model for native speech. Notice that Ashley intuitively drew Terry out well before we knew of the pivotal role of the interdependent stage:

Oct. 15:   I've been trying to draw Terry more into the group since he's the only native speaker.

Though Ashley proactively sought to draw oral and written language from Terry, Dianna Poodiack and I used an opposite strategy with our mutual student Tai. After two years in this country and one semester in the Center, Tai joked with American students, played the comic in group and in class, arrived early to chat with Dianna or me, drafted cartoons and satires to make groupmates and classmates laugh, sought out groupmates on campus, called English classmates on the phone, used a number of attention-getting strategies, and almost daily volunteered to read his writing first. So great were Tai's proactive efforts to practice English that, though unaware of each other's efforts at the time, Dianna (his tutor) and I (his freshman writing teacher) proactively sought to limit Tai's activity so other students would have time to interact more. Where group interaction was concerned, Tai's oral and written behaviors were above the mean not only for Vietnamese but for students of all nationalities.

Diversity was not limited to categories of students. Individual behavior also varied over time. For example, Terry was "rigid" and "inhibited" at first, but he began to relax as his group's trust level rose.

Oct. 22:   Terry seems so much more confident, both in his writing and in his group. He crosses his ankle over his knee, leans back in his chair, and volunteers an answer to a question somebody else asks. He comes first to class each day, and we chat about his major (law enforcement), his courses, or our (Baptist) churches. He is still restrained and correct, but he speaks less tentatively.

Terry now wrote less redundantly and with more concrete detail:

> The swamps are full of many strange creatures such as the alligator, who with his scaly green skin, lurks around every corner of the swamp searching for some unfortunate creature to pray upon. The alligator is very quick as he snaps his huge jaws closed upon his dinner.

On November 14 Ashley quoted a draft for another piece, showing how she taught incidentally, at Terry's point of need, while balancing attention to weaknesses with attention to strengths:

> Terry read his piece about the approach of winter, about snow flakes "like puffy white feathers floating to the ground" and "black smoke rising from chimbleys (sic)." He finished the piece with "old man winter is just around the corner."
> "Brr . . . " said Sung Tae, and the group laughed. . . . "It's good description," said You Chi, feeling her way. "Yeah," she said, confirming her [own] statement. "I liked the 'blanket of white snow'." . . . Nobody had mentioned his problems with *chimney*, so I asked him about the spelling of the word and reminded the group about going backwards through a piece to catch [spelling] errors.

Within a semester, Terry's behavior had moved closer to Tai's. Taking an active part in group activity, he became a regular source of humor and even developed attention-getting strategies of his own:

> Nov. 19:   "I might write about falling in the mud." . . . [said Terry]
> "What?" asked Mouna.
> Terry explained, "As soon as I stepped on the grass—Shuuuuu—." The group broke up! . . .
> Things gradually quieted down except for Terry tapping his pen hard on the table in front of him. It was loud and deliberate—the first time Terry has ever done anything to draw attention to himself. Mouna and You Chi smiled at him, and he started writing with a grin and a shrug.

These two tendencies—for members of the same category to vary widely and for individuals to vary widely over time—confirmed our hunch that how we taught affected writing development more surely than did cultural background, gender, age, or personality. They also shed light on a question a number of tutors had raised about whether or not ability grouping would help students improve. By reducing the range of group knowledge and experience, homogeneous groups kept students dependent on tutor input, robbed weaker students of strong peer models, denied stronger writers the confidence peer respect and praise bring, and reduced all students' chances of reaching the interdependent stage during which they practiced writing in groups, with the help of their peers, until they felt ready to strike out on their own. In short, when our teaching built on strengths, addressing problems as they arose, homogeneous grouping hobbled development whereas mixed groups strengthened conditions from which independence emerged.

For several years tutors checked and double-checked these findings, with twenty-eight tutors recording how several groups each evolved. Now, after we've observed more than 300 groups and kept participant-observation logs on 90 or more, the data confirm that *for our context* five is an ideal size and that, all else being equal, diverse groups more often succeed.

Bonding and Group Trust: Blessed Be the Tie That Binds. Bonding was another factor that increased interdependence, which, like group size, interacted with diversity. In fact, it was while we were wondering how to help less diverse groups that the power of the bonding variable emerged. One factor that increased bonding—openness or self-disclosure—showed up more often in the presence of diversity. In fact, in adolescent groups with all students from the same culture, peer pressure could maintain bravado and façades that reduced honest interactions and made risk taking unsafe. As diversity in groups increased, however, some of the "coolest" students revealed an engaging honesty that earned groupmates' respect and empathy while setting them at ease. By the end of the term, students' highest praise—"That really took guts"—was reserved for uncommonly honest and open writing. When diversity decreased, by contrast, self-disclosure grew rare, with fewer students taking part in the pivotal interdependent stage.

Let me illustrate the role of diversity with an example. During Year 3 the "All-American" student emerged—at least it was then that we attached a name to that category. All-Americans were students most tutors had trouble with, the problem being, to quote several, that these students were "so bland." All-Americans were eighteen-year-old whites from nearby suburbs, graduates of the area's affluent west-side schools. When they wrote, however, All-Americans played it safe, avoiding controversy in content and form. They chose typical "teacher" topics they had little interest in and built stiff, wordy, repetitive, formulaic essays from platitudes. Even more significant from an instructional point of view was that tutors had trouble motivating All-Americans. Most saw Center attendance only as busy work, as a hoop through which they were forced to jump for a term or two. Terry, the native speaker who at first had been so reserved, was in many other respects, fairly typical of this group.

All-American groups were frequently dependent, conforming, lacking in motivation, and uncommonly slow to improve. Tutors complained that these reactive students tried only to "please the teacher" because they were more interested in grades than in learning itself. New tutors had particular trouble motivating them. We soon learned, however, that adding a minority, a nonnative, or a mature student or two frequently turned floundering All-American groups around.

Despite their "blandness," middle-class suburban writers had much to offer. As they spoke standard English and could correct mistakes by ear, they became valued resources for ESL and dialect speakers. For international students, they modeled American styles of male-female interaction and acceptable ways of dealing with teachers and administrators. Unfortunately, their writing, which was often full of simplistic thinking and naive argument, tended to bore the others in their groups. When confronted by diverse points of view, All-Americans were forced to examine their biases, write more thoughtfully, and apply better critical skills to the writing they did.

Though many All-Americans rarely ventured beyond the river that separated the affluent west-side suburbs from the city, once they began to relax in the WTC's diverse groups, their open, interactive styles broadened and informed group thought. Like the ESL students who served as "expert witnesses," All-American students shared life experience, but the effects of these two groups' sharing were complementary. Despite ESL students' personal involvement in world events, their topics were often perceived as external experience, for they dealt with subjects Americans studied or learned about on the news: unfamiliar customs, religious and political conflict, coups, wars, famine, escapes from tyranny. The seemingly "public" nature of these students' experience can be seen in an excerpt from the logs of Geri Madigan, a graduate teaching intern who did teacher-research in the WTC. Assigned to observe master tutor Bonnie Martin to learn the Center approach, Geri documented what happened when Bonnie's student Loi drafted a powerful essay in which he detailed the political conditions leading to his narrow escape from Vietnam:

> Loi read his story of life in Vietnam in '75 when the Communists took over. What a powerful story! The ending was fantastic! Really good concrete details:
>
> summer over
> first day of school
> classroom was not filled with happy, joyful people
> instead guile, and "we looked at each other with fear in our eyes"
> teacher asked us to join a Political Group called "Young Communist Party"
> "use every minute we have to do something useful for them so we don't have any actions or ideas against them."
>
> The ending was fantastic!
>
> Day after day, these things made us feel like we lived with two persons inside us. One for them that always do and say good things about the communist government. The other is for our real life that never stop wishing there will be some changes which make our lives look better in a brighter future. That is what I am having now.
>
> We all exclaimed how good it was.

By contrast, All-Americans informed and unified groups by sharing what others perceived as "internal" experience. Here Ethiopian-born tutor Yitna Firdyiwek—who brought to the analysis his multilingual, multicultural perspective as well as his strong analytic bent—comments on the bonding that resulted from self-disclosure:

> ESL students have a picture, an abstraction, of how people live in this country, but when an American girl reveals that she has bulimia and is seeing a psychiatrist, she's not revealing an objective history but subjective experience. When American students reveal personally traumatic experiences—anorexia, parental divorce, abortions, drug problems, child abuse—it expands ESL students' awareness of the hardships of American life and generates sympathy, empathy and even *love* in the groups.

Ashley Williams described such a piece written on the first day of group:

> August 29: Perry lives in High Falls [a pricey neighborhood along the river] and graduated from Overlook H.S. He was obviously disturbed and irritated over being assigned to the WTC. . . .
> I reread his work, about his parents' separation. It had been given 2's [on a four-point scale] by [another tutor] and by me. It was one of many essays I read that might be categorized as the "Affluent Suburban Model"—not a great number of mechanical problems (no evidence of verb problems, objective case used incorrectly, etc.) but structure that was less than desirable.
> The paper was written about a subject that was obviously painful for him—his parents' separation—and that certainly took honesty. However, he just didn't quite manage to cut through the fog and write naturally.

Yitna also spoke of the impact of such writing on groups:

> Though some teachers are afraid to let such topics come up in group, they almost always create strong bonds between students when they do. And students don't fear each other because of these self-disclosures. I think they end up *loving* each other, feeling deeper feelings. You'll find students staying after group to talk about what a writer revealed.
> When American students do this, there's a different depth of experience, a kind of intimacy. *The WTC group experience is one of intimacy.* [italics mine]

Observational logs are replete with examples of intimacy. The following incident showed up in the field notes of Taejung Welsh, a Korean-born doctoral student in Bilingual Education, who spent two years studying the learning and teaching that went on in Center groups (see Welsh, 1988):

> 10:30. Victoria read a story on her boyfriend who died of leukemia: Knowing he would die soon, she had visited with him as long as she could. She had watched him suffer from the physical pain through his entire treatment on his spinal cord. This young man was so sure that he would be

much happier in his life after death that Victoria did not grieve upon his illness. Instead, they had developed a touching and profound friendship which had enriched and influenced her, even in choosing her major, medical technology, at CAU.

Far from all such exchanges were initiated by Americans. After seeing the strong and interesting writing such topics produced and realizing that they were truly free to write what they pleased, others began writing about topics important to them. Our policy, of course, was one of voluntary disclosure, of *never* asking students to write "personally." In fact, we distinguished carefully between writing *about feelings*, which often produced mediocre writing, and writing *with conviction*, which led to stronger work. In their writing, however, as in group discussions, it was students themselves who opted for personal contact, though some took longer than others to feel safe choosing personal topics. Students rarely had trouble writing when *they* chose the topics, however, and when they did, the writing was often strong, a tendency that meant many personal pieces got lots of praise. Ashley quoted a comment by You Chi that reveals the motivating power personal topics can have:

> In my mind, there are a lot of things that I want to write. Those topics that stay in my mind must have very simple but (it was) very strong. . . . The other topic I have interested in is described a relationship with my best friend. That is very special and different, I believe, from others.

As writing and discussion grew intimate, sensitivity and trust increased, as did commitment to improving their own and others' writing. The following excerpt* from Ashley's log shows her group shifting at once from lighthearted banter to attentive support when an Iranian student alludes to a "personal" piece, just after Terry's banter about a fall in the mud:

> Things gradually quieted down except for Terry tapping his pen hard on the table in front of him. It was loud and deliberate—the first time Terry has ever done anything to call attention to himself. Mouna and You Chi smiled at him, and he started writing with a grin and a shrug.
> After 20 or so minutes, I asked "Who wants to read?"
> "Terry does," answered Parvis immediately.

*In choosing quotes, excerpts, and examples for this book, I've tried to strike a balance between (1) supportable generalization (a goal that requires including lots of examples) and (2) providing rich descriptions so readers can know and remember individual tutors, contexts, students, and groups (a goal that requires a limited cast of characters). On the one hand, to show that the patterns we found recur across groups and tutors at various levels of skill and experience, I've included more than the one or two groups that would have been needed to illustrate all of our findings. On the other hand, to show that evidence for any finding can be found in virtually any group, I've limited the number of groups from which our data are drawn. Because we have so limited the data pool in this way, I've taken the liberty of repeating an occasional excerpt that illustrates more than a single theme.

"When you start volunteering others, that's a sure sign you want to read yourself," Terry retorted, humorously.

"But it's personal," protested Parvis.

"We're family," Mouna assured him.

Parvis read:

> I have this problem that I don't know what to do with it. As you know [he had written about it earlier], my girlfriend was killed in a car accident, and I promised not to get another girlfriend. I have kept my promise for almost 3 years, but I don't think I can keep it any more.

After summarizing the body of Parvis's piece, Ashley quoted Parvis's conclusion, closing with a transcript of his group's supportive response:

> There's a girl in his biology class he wants to take out, but he's concerned over his promise, and he admits, he's "embaraas!"
>
> I need somebody to share my mind with . . . is like that something is killing you but not suddenly, very slowly. It is like a executer who comes and takes a small piece of your body inch at time and lets you feel the pain!

Despite his initial protest that this piece was "personal," Parvis's choice of the second person ("as you know") suggests that in writing it he was in fact seeking "someone to share my mind with." Regardless of the audience Parvis intended, however, reading let him experience real-world writing rewards not always available to writers of academic prose: the release of bottled-up feelings, sympathetic support from friends, reduced isolation, personal talk with peers, and a developing sense of intimacy. The group responded as Yitna's analysis (see p. 69) suggested they might—with empathy, sympathy, and warm, supportive advice:

> Mouna spoke up as soon as Parvis finished. "Ask her out."
>
> "But I feel guilty," said Parvis.
>
> "We are fated," said Mouna (and I thought of Chaucer and Troilus!) "If you hadn't been driving, someone else would have been. You can't blame yourself. You are too young to do that."
>
> "I agree," said Kamarudin.
>
> Terry hadn't voiced an opinion, and I looked at him. "Well, let's see," he said considering Parvis's plight. "I think you should do it."
>
> "You can't hide your true feelings," added You Chi in her usual quiet, sincere voice—"Anyway, you like her."
>
> "It's not a good idea to keep remembering," Kamarudin told Parvis.
>
> "I think you should talk with someone," said Mouna. "When my father died, I kept it all inside for a long time. Finally, I let it out; I let myself grieve and talk about it."
>
> Din nodded at Mouna's remark. "My friend got a letter two days ago. His father had died. He just accepted it. He's very strong."

Given the degree to which diversity increased bonding, it's interesting to note at least three sources of it in this group. In the first place, these five students represented five countries: the United States, Malaysia, Korea, Jordan, and Iran. The group also included Mouna, a woman in her thirties, who according to Ashley immediately adopted a supportive and motherly tone with this otherwise youthful male/female group. Notice, by the way, how Ashley's interdependent students took full responsibility for responding to Parvis's work.

Self-disclosure and support were but two aspects of bonding that strengthened independence, hastening the speed at which student writing improved. Shared laughter was another behavior that more than repaid in improvement any group time it took up. Because students who chose what they wrote took writing seriously, aimless joking designed to waste time was rare, as was laughter that was mocking or unkind. When these occurred, however, tutors explained that they were inappropriate because they threatened the atmosphere others needed to learn. Once trust developed, sensitivity quickly followed, and the tone of a group could shift rapidly, with laughter providing comic relief after intense discussions, or disappearing immediately—as when Parvis read—when a risky or personal topic arose.

So closely did laughter draw and hold writing groups together that Yitna, who studied interactions in many groups, began to call it "the glue that bonds" and "the tie that binds." Using the system he'd developed for diagramming interactions, he illustrated in graphic form laughter's contribution to bonding. Figure 3–3 contains diagrams based on the segment from Bonnie Martin's logs in which Loi first wrote about his escape from Vietnam. Notice how different these diagrams on an interdependent group are from the earlier pattern of switchboard-operator dependence (p. 50). In addition to showing students interacting together, they show a single shared laugh generating more cohesion through person-to-person ties than any other category of interaction except total unanimity, something that occurred rarely in the Center's diverse (and honest) groups.

In his analysis, Yitna altered none of Bonnie's sentences. He did, however, isolate from Bonnie's much richer narrative those sentences containing direct or indirect quotations. I have reduced the number of sentences a bit further, for my purpose is not to get frequency counts on the patterns that follow but to show levels of cohesion in interdependent groups. Notice that except for affirmations of unanimity, laughter produces far more cohesive ties among groupmates than any other interaction observed. Notice also the degree to which these teenage men, instead of competing or posturing with each other, offer the support others need to continue taking greater and greater risks, drawing out a shy young man from Vietnam in consistently affectionate ways and closing ranks, when his confidence fails, to give the support he needs.

Without being aware of Yitna'a diagrams, Team 5 tutor Linda Topper also

Interaction as Recorded in Log	Cohesive Ties Produced

"Jack read first."

"I asked Bob what part of a spaceship the 'bridge' is."

"Bob, Dimitri, and Jack spoke all at once (It's the control room)."

"Jack told Bob he didn't like comparison of the captain as a 'King watching his empire fall.' He said when he thought of 'King' he got a mental picture of a fat old man in a rich purple robe, sitting idly with a crown on his head, wrapped in jewels."

Figure 3–3   **Interactions Typical of Interdependent Groups**

"Everyone laughed."

"I asked who wanted to read next."

"Dimitri pointed to Loi, saying, 'Let's hear from <u>the</u> <u>man</u> there.' "

"Loi smiled, and pulled the piece he's worked on for the last two sessions from his folder." [<u>He</u> <u>read</u>.]

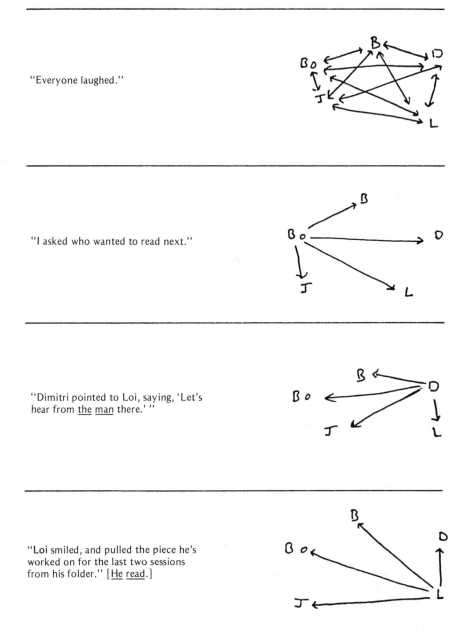

Figure 3–3   **Continued**

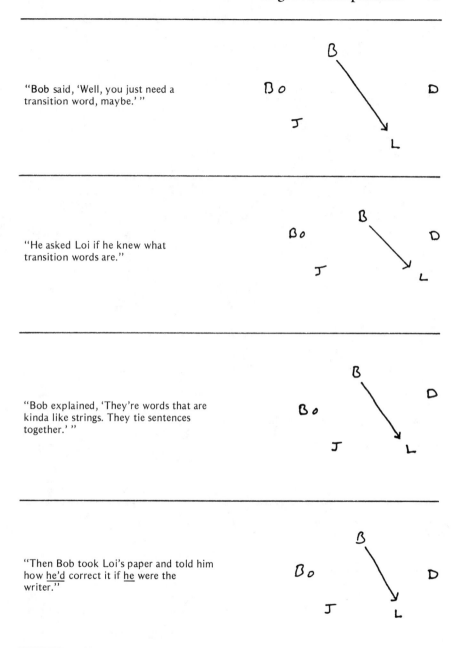

"Bob said, 'Well, you just need a transition word, maybe.' "

"He asked Loi if he knew what transition words are."

"Bob explained, 'They're words that are kinda like strings. They tie sentences together.' "

"Then Bob took Loi's paper and told him how he'd correct it if he were the writer."

Figure 3–3 **Continued**

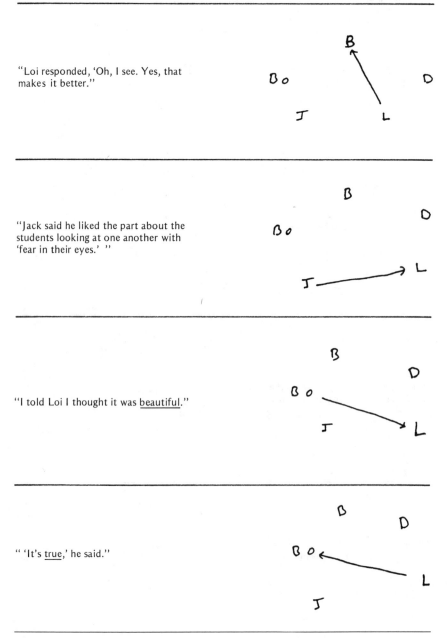

"Loi responded, 'Oh, I see. Yes, that makes it better.' "

"Jack said he liked the part about the students looking at one another with 'fear in their eyes.' "

"I told Loi I thought it was <u>beautiful</u>."

" 'It's <u>true</u>,' he said."

Figure 3–3 **Continued**

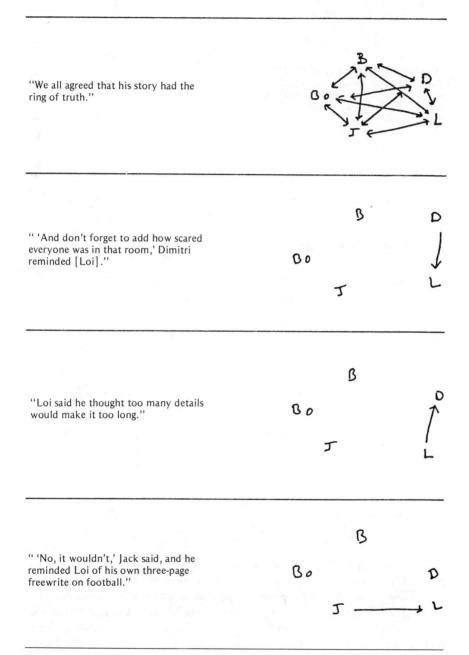

"We all agreed that his story had the
ring of truth."

" 'And don't forget to add how scared
everyone was in that room,' Dimitri
reminded [Loi]."

"Loi said he thought too many details
would make it too long."

" 'No, it wouldn't,' Jack said, and he
reminded Loi of his own three-page
freewrite on football."

Figure 3-3 **Continued**

"Dimitri told Loi that he had a 'few grammar errors,' but then said that Loi seemed to write with less errors than he did and he'd been in this country for eight years!"

"'My papers are full of errors,' Dimitri exclaimed."

"Bob laughed, saying that he was <u>born</u> in this country and he <u>still</u> made many errors."

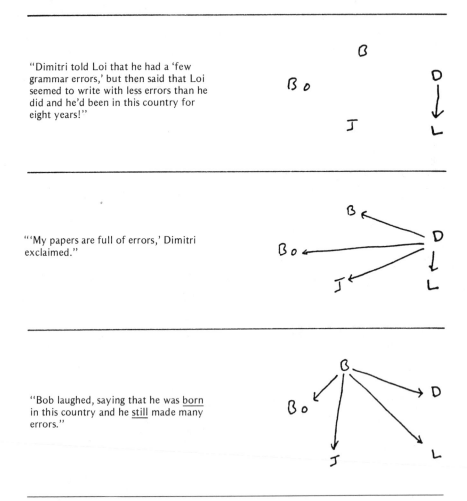

Figure 3-3   **Continued**

studied laughter's role. Her data confirm that in groups who laughed together, closeness and commitment increased, as did responsibility and pleasure in the task at hand. Others pointed out that laughter was both cause and effect of bonding and that students referred to people they laughed with often as "friends." Laughter also provided comic relief from the intense feelings that often came up when students wrote very personally. The same day Parvis read his piece on his girlfriend's death, for example, Ashley Williams reflected in her log on the relationship between "friendship" and laughter in Parvis's group:

November 19:   Just at that point the door burst open and Sung Tae came rushing in. "You won't believe what happened to me. I've really got an excuse this time," he exclaimed, and he handed me his piece [due that day for the WTC book] on the perils of the parking lot. "No criticism or anything, Parvis, but some Arab guy crashed into my car!" he told us.

After ascertaining that Sung Tae wasn't injured, I thanked him for bringing his paper in and he dashed off to tend to [his car].

Everybody in the group cracked up. One way or another, Sung Tae manages to provide some entertainment each time. After this session ended, Parvis and Terry took their time gathering up things to leave. Terry showed us his muddy jeans (from an encounter with the muddy walkway) and Parvis howled, pointing and laughing.

I thought several times today about laughter and what it indicated. The familiarity of this laughter assumed friendship—or at least a companionable sort of acquaintanceship/camaraderie—that had developed this semester.

Ashley's hunch that friendships were developing was supported by oral and written comments from tutors and students. Affectionate good humor strengthened tutor–student bonds too, as can be seen in this excerpt from one of Bonnie's Year 2 logs:

Loi and Jack stayed 15 minutes over. There wasn't another group in the room, and they just kept on writing. Dimitri and I went out into the other room to discuss his piece on his father. Mostly I praised him, though we did talk about moving one paragraph up as the second paragraph for better organization. Dimitri marked both places to remind himself to do that.

When I came back into the room after talking to Dimitri and calling Bob . . . , Dimitri was pretending to jump out the windows because it was a beautiful day and he hated being locked in. He teased Loi ["Loi is very shy."] about crawling under the table to read when we videotape. What a pleasure that kid is!

Students also took pleasure in the bonding that went on in groups. Kamal described at some length his delight at making "friends." Accidentally discovering Kamal's depth of group experience—he'd attended two full semesters to earn certification, then returned for three more as a "volunteer"—I invited him to speak to a new group of tutors currently attending the preschool seminar so somewhat nervous tutors could get a student's perspective on how well our as-yet unfamiliar approaches worked. The next day, while describing his view of the program to Team 4, Kamal shared insights about how developing friendships motivated groupmates to work harder and interact more:

KAMAL: And this is the interesting thing I like so much—when I go around in the University and meet my friends from the Center, they say, "Hey, have you finish your paper? I really like your paper, have you finish it?" This kills my prokanis . . . , prosctin . . . , proscatination—what is it?

KAI WHEATLEY
[in low voice]: Procrastination.*

KAMAL: This kills my procrastination. When my friend said, "Hey, have you finish your paper?" I went home to work on it. And the next day I am anxious to show that I already work on it. So I say, "Hey, I put your suggestion in my paper."

It's fun! It's fun being in the group. It's kinda interesting because every time I go in that session, I'm anxious to read my papers. It's a great thing that happened to me.

In fact, before I was very shy. I didn't want to share my paper. I was very afraid. But with my group I say, "Oh, I'm glad—I'm going to read my paper." That feeling drive me to write more and more.

I would never have met Kamal had I not chanced to borrow the WTC front-office typewriter one day while working at school during the summer break. It was then I learned that this student, who planned to teach college English on his return to Malaysia, had attended the Center for five semesters—two to get certification, three more to study the Center approach. Because of the improvement he and his friends experienced, and because our methods were "more compatible with Malay people," Kamal had been studying tutors and groups, without our knowing it, in hopes of importing our model to Malaysia on his return. Kamal's purpose and experience in five groups made him more analytical about our methods than were other students. His *affective* responses, however, were typical:

After I go again, I see that they have plan. At first I don't recognize a plan, but after I go back again I see the tutors have a method. They all teach same way, same order.

The order go like this. first they introduce us to group and tell us, "Just write, don't worry about grammar, spelling—stuff like that. You can fix them later." The next, part two, is this—we write. We write a lot, and we talk about our writing. And then three we do the revisioning—we help each other revise. And four we do editing to make ready for WTC book.

After a while I am getting better, and it fun, it *fun*! I *love* it!

This is something new for me and it worked for me. And if it worked for me, there's a probability it might work for others too. I discovered it because I attend the WTC many semesters. The first semester I was introduced to something new. That time I was like everyone else—learning eveything new, and I do not like to do it at first. The second semester, I am

---

*Notice that the by now independent Kamal proactively reveals his point of need, prompting Kai, who has not yet begun to teach, to respond reactively to his cue for direct instruction in vocabulary.

force to return because I do not get certify by the WTC. But the third semester, I study the WTC. I came to watch what is *the process* in WTC.

And then, the next semester, I watched *the students and what it does to the student*. I studied how the student act, and how the student learn. In fact, [leans forward and speaks in a lowered voice] there is a period of time when I also studied *the instructors* too—I study how I see them. Don't tell anybody, okay?

Then the last time I come, *I try to stretch myself, to test my ability to produce a maximum on my own—the WTC way—by writing my poetry.* And I found out it works! I got a considerable amount of confidence after five semesters, and so I decide to take a poetry [writing] course. I take it with the poet Judith Harris, and I made a 'A.' [italics mine]

When by accident I discovered Kamal and learned of the informal participant-observation research he was doing, I realized that, among Center students, he was surely uniquely informed. Just before school started every fall I had developed the habit of asking a former WTC student or two to talk to the new TA group so they could get a student perspective on how the new paradigm worked. I therefore asked Kamal if Team 4 might interview him about his findings, and that is where most of these quotes by Kamal come from. We used his independent analyses—and I quote them here—to provide another perspective against which to check our findings; but his thinking was consistent with ours in every way. It was Kamal's feelings as much as his formal "findings," however, that confirmed our hunch that the bonding students called "friendship" played an important role in interdependent groups.

Kamal was keenly aware of the impact of friendship on learning because it had affected his attitudes toward the WTC:

The thing that interests me most—and this is outside of what I was researching—is that after I've gone through one semester of WTC, I gained four friends. And after another semester, I gained another three friends. And the same thing for three more semesters. And when we pass around in the University, we greet each other and ask how we are.

It been four years now, and I still have those friends I made in the WTC. Some of them I just recognize, but others I meet to talk.

So when the group is establishing we don't see it as the WTC anymore. We don't see it as writing class, but we see it as friends. And we write about our life, and we share our problems.

Because of this I become to *love* the WTC, and I see that I learn a lot there. That why I go back again and again after I get certified. I go back five times, five semesters, to learn.

Noting that interdependence with friends motivated groupmates, Kamal stated that "individual attention from one person to another" added to basic writers' enjoyment of their work. Working together also built confidence, he said, because students "feel equal" to writers whose work they have helped make strong. This linkage among variables—friendship, equality, confidence, motivation, and pleasure—foreshadowed what other students have said of the interdependent stage. Here is Kamal on the topic:

> When the teacher make us read published essays, there is always a realization that, "Oh, this guy is a professional writer, and I'm just somebody, so *no way* I can write as good as he is. . . ." And because of that idea in my mind, I couldn't learn how to write. That realization and impact—it makes myself feel so *small*. It makes me lose my confidence. After all, I'm just *studying* to learn to write. . . .
>
> But my group is different, because when I read my friend's writing, I can find errors in his writing, okay? And at the same time, I can find errors in my *own* writing, so I'm *equal* with him, or with her.
>
> Let's say I have a ten pages paper, and I rewrite the whole thing, and the next time I come to my group I rewrite the same thing again. But even when my paper get long, people are willing to listen. And they give good suggestions.
>
> Of course, there are students who came because they didn't score high in the TSWE and they have a passive attitude—I was like that at first—but as time goes by, they *enjoy* it because it's kind of a *group*, you know. There is individual attention from one person to another.
>
> So you see, in the Center we have the understanding that we are all in the process of learning, that there's nothing wrong to criticize each other, there's nothing wrong to give suggestions, and there's nothing wrong making revisions. That way both of us can improve. There's a kind of "You help me, I can help you, and both of us can benefit." So we work together.

Ashley's log shows students actually working together in the ways Kamal so articulately describes. Though mini-groups had failed with these students earlier in the semester, as midterm approached and students grew more interdependent, Ashley began preparing them to work independently by breaking them again into mini-groups of three and withdrawing entirely except to respond to a question or two. Here one mini-group polishes a paper, giving each other the kinds of direct advice teachers often give:

> Sung Tae was working on his piece about getting to school late and the difficulty of finding a place to park. He was sitting in the parking lot, he said, when, finally, "I couldn't wait no longer," he read.
>
> "You can't do that," I heard Parvis tell him.
>
> "Why not?" asked Sung Tae. "Because it's a double negative," Parvis and Mouna chorused.
>
> "Huh?" asked Sung Tae.
>
> "A double negative," Mouna repeated, and she went on to explain that using a double negative "makes the sentence illogical. It means you *could* wait." Sung Tae changed the sentence. I haven't seen his paper yet, so I'm

not sure how he changed it, but I saw him line through a word following Mouna's explanation.

Sung Tae continued reading. "She had reached the maximum of my temper," he said.

"*She* had reached or *you* had reached?" Mouna asked him. Sung Tae looked puzzled. He stopped and apparently read the sentence once silently. "*I* had reached it," he said a little sheepishly.

Upward Spirals and Regressions in Confidence

Once it emerged, the three-stage progression looked deceptively simple— that's why we felt foolish taking so long to recognize it. But fine-grained examination of dozens of groups confirmed that writing development rarely followed a straight line, whether for groups or individual students. Instead, students and groups followed an upward spiral that included regression when new challenges occurred (see Figure 3–4).

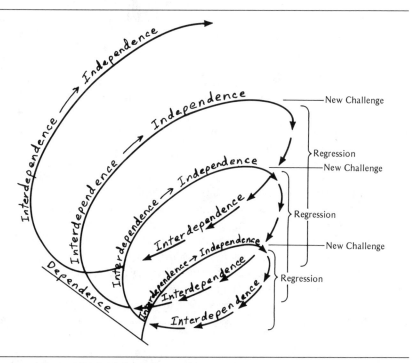

Figure 3–4 **A Tilted Spiral Showing the Regressions Made by Both Groups and Individuals in the Process of Development**

Even after groups reached the independent stage, confidence could regress whenever students took risks by experimenting with new content, strategies, or forms. Groups also grew more dependent on tutor advice and support whenever tutors introduced a new instructional focus—when they shifted from freewriting to revising, for example, or from revising to systematic editing. Students who'd grown confident writing what they chose grew frantic about papers for philosophy and history courses or felt paralyzed on finding that their composition instructor taught writing more traditionally than their tutor did.

The most common predictor of regression, however, was required but premature summative evaluation. When this occurred before students arrived at Stage 3 (independence), negatively biased (i.e., subtractive) grading, which helped CAU maintain standards by eliminating the weak, almost always produced setbacks in observable growth curves. Tutors were repeatedly surprised and disappointed to see regressions in writers who'd worked hard and made progress their first semester but needed to return to the Center for a second term.

In short, the dependence/interdependence/independence progression is a summary of the general direction in which groups moved. Detailed inspection of individual progress, however, showed that it followed more tangled and circuitous routes. Because each writer's path and rate of progress were unique, patterns in the data we collected were complex. But tacit knowledge of tangled and overlapping variables raced ahead of our more explicit, formal analyses. In other words, when tutors observed student writers closely, listened to their problems, and offered help at the point of need, their students experienced a great deal of success. Apparently these tutors intuitively discovered order in the piles of tangled analytic threads that the formal analysis would take years to tease apart.

Ashley typifies the tutor-researchers of this study in that her teaching anticipated the formal analysis. Abandoning Team 1's bipolar model of withdrawal in order to follow observation-informed intuitions, she acknowledged, *by her behavior*, that she recognized interdependence as a pivotal stage. Long after their groupmates were well on their way to independence, Ashley noted that Kamarudin (Din) and Terry lagged behind, and she consciously drew them further and further toward interdependence. In fact, instead of withdrawing, as the bipolar model prescribed, Ashley helped Terry by interacting *more*.

By mid-October Ashley had had some success: "I've been trying to draw Terry more into the group since he's the only native speaker. He seems more willing to respond to the others now." Later, Ashley realized that Din lagged even further behind than Terry:

> Right now, I feel that most of the students have really gotten on their feet w/ their writing, but Din is an exception. When I asked today if he had a topic yet, he shook his head "no"—again.

> I have had less interaction with Din, less conversation that was "personal" (i.e., directed to him about his life—the kind of casual conversation I have before class w/ students). . . . Am I right to want to draw them out conversationally as a prelude to writing? My hunch is that it does help (or am I rationalizing because this is the only way I can imagine?)

Though she saw the importance of proactively "drawing students out," Ashley never acknowledged interdependence as a stage. But because she watched closely and empathized with students, she began to resist Team 1's bipolar theory, which described tutor withdrawal as a straight-line continuum. In doing so, she helped bring that model's inadequacy to light. Her logs show where our thinking stood the semester before the breakthrough, when the tension between tutors' informed intuitions and the language of Team 1's bipolar proposition was at its height.

The Pivotal Interdependent Stage—
What Makes Secondhand Learning Special?

Once they reached the interdependent stage, students like Ashley's no longer reacted passively to authority. Tacitly agreeing to help each other improve, they built collective repertoires of strategies on which all groupmates could draw for writing they were doing—stories, essays, poems, letters, research papers, diaries, job applications, résumés, lab reports, and the like. And in the process of giving and getting advice, both basic and ESL writers learned to recognize what help they needed, got practice asking for it, and grew confident when the advice they gave peers was well received. Despite the loss of drive some suffered at first without grades, motivation surged when they experienced writing's rewards: pride of publication (in the *Excerpts* and *The Drafted Writers*), feelings of accomplishment, influence on others, better grades in other courses, competence, empathy and praise from friends, and (as with Parvis) emotional release.

Kamal confirmed the motivating power of those rewards:

> In WTC I found that even though my writing is not very good, it's very important to me, and I like to read it over.
> Also, when I read it aloud, my friends said, "Wow, that's good!" So when they do, my tutors said, "Let's publish that in *Excerpts*," and I felt, "God, I am a writer!"
> That feeling makes me come to WTC all the time. I attend five semesters, twice a week. And each time I attend WTC, I learned. That's why I love it.

The pivotal interdependent stage was a time of vicarious learning in which students experienced each other's struggles much as their own. Practice judging others' results with a distanced eye was practice that helped them gain distance on their own attempts. Midway through the shift in locus of control—halfway between students' dependence on outside evaluation and confidence in their own judgments about their work—this vicarious learning took a number of forms: changes in attitude, strategies, rules, technique, and style. When Jean-Claude heard the vivid details in Shelley's childhood memory, he imitated her style, and his stuffy comparison and contrast between Olympic training in the United States and France become more concrete and engaging than earlier drafts had been. Ji Ae probably knew the rules Kai Wheatley explained to Charles, but by watching as he took his pieces through draft after draft, she learned something far more basic than any rule. She learned she could wait to apply a rule until *after* she had a draft. Later, helping Charles learn to punctuate a tricky sentence, Ji Ae would gain confidence in her editing abilities.

Kamal had such an experience learning to edit in group. He'd studied English grammar and mechanics for years, he said, but understanding of the rules he'd studied developed only after he saw others separating and sequencing writing tasks:

> The process of editing—I thought it was difficult, but it's easy. Before WTC I use to think that you edit all at once, but I was wrong. You have to do it step by step.
>
> First I look at the tenses—present and past. I don't worry about the spelling—not yet. And then, after I look for tenses, I look at the spelling and sentence construction. But not at the same time, though.
>
> Step by step. Now I don't have to do it all at once.

Literary Epidemics

Interdependent students experimented with form and technique, and resistance to certain genres waned vicariously as students observed others' varied attempts. Poetry epidemics frequently swept through groups, for example, often with three to five members becoming involved. When this happened, students who had once said they "disliked" poetry listened with quiet attention as their groupmates read, setting aside resistance out of respect for their friends. Many basic writers stopped being afraid of poetry after hearing and enjoying poems written by friends and noticing the status these budding poets received. Several times a semester I would read in tutors' logs of tough young men who "hated poetry" in January writing tentative poems about love or injustice in March. So contagious were these "literary epidemics" that they sometimes infected neighboring groups that shared the Center's small rooms. Such attitude changes provided a base on which tutors could build, raising the level of group awareness and appreciation by sharing more complex poems they themselves had written or loved.

Working together to improve pieces on which they had critical distance but whose writers they felt a friendly commitment to, students practiced together a wider range of topics and genres than they otherwise could have in a semester's time. The vicarious interest that developed in pieces they had helped improve increased their commitment to one another's work, blurring the already hazy lines between group and personal ownership, breaking down fear and prejudice toward genres and topics and ideas, and motivating these budding writers to retain what they'd learned. Kamal said:

> Frankly speaking, for that essay, even though it was written by me, I had a lot of help from my friends. The students around me were the ones who taught me to write a good essay.

Students saw value in what they learned from each other and found vicarious, secondhand learning easy to retain. As Kamal put it:

> You see, I can remember more from my friends than when the instructor told me. It is easier to learn if my friends told me that "You should write this way because certain ideas are confusing, certain sentences are not constructed properly." First of all, I *enjoy* getting feedback from them, but another reason their response is good is that it's very effective.
>
> For example, if I rely on the instructor for help and the instructor says, "You should criticize this sentence," I'll always assume that the instructor knows everything and that I have to wait and ask *her* the right answer. But when my colleague tells me, "Your sentence is wrong," then I will say myself, "That guy—he's a fellow student of mine and he knows about this. It must be a common thing that I should try to learn."

Thus did practice blending critical distance with commitment foster secondhand learning, critical thinking, and confidence. For as Yitna had concluded earlier:

> In [WTC] groups writers can be subjective and objective at once. They can get involved but maintain distance on what's happening. Apparently five [members per group] is also small enough to foster individual responsibility without being so small that students feel on the spot. Groups of five are small enough that students cannot hide—can't avoid making subjective responses—but not so small that they get anxious or feel that the spotlight is always on them.

This simultaneous taking of subjective and objective views gave students practice using critical thinking skills. It also gave substance to the second shift in the progression, the shift from interdependence to independence. For example, Sung Tae's first semicolon appeared (correctly used) a few days after Ashley's group helped Terry with run-on sentences. Sung Tai himself chose to practice what he'd learned while observing Terry. According to Ashley's log Sung Tai's next draft began like this:

> At eight forty five in the morning, the alarm rings; I look at the clock and hate to get up. Another tipical morning.

> I'm astonished by the semicolon; he obviously listened the day we talked about run-on sentences and ways to punctuate them.

Thus did we learn that independence was helped rather than hindered by the secondhand learning done in interdependent groups. Gradually, then, many of us who taught in other contexts discarded past ambivalence about collaborative work. Instead of prohibiting helping each other as "cheating"—something I had once done—we tried our small-group approach in full-sized writing classes with students at many different ages and levels. Relying on Center experience and follow-the-kid research, we tested writing groups in beginning and advanced composition classes, in public schools, with doctoral students struggling to write dissertations, in adult education classes, with disturbed children, in language institutes, and in courses for writing majors at CAU. And, of course, teacher-research provided the tool with which we adapted our methods to meet the varied demands of these many conditions.

Stage 3: The Emergence of Independence

The Withering Away of the Tutor Role

Once all students were integrated into interdependent groups, Team 1's concept of withdrawal once again fit what went on in groups. Now tutors withdrew completely, except when called upon. And when they did so, students reciprocated by speaking up more, asking more questions, actively shaping group interactions to meet their needs, and letting groupmates know what rules they were ready to learn. Kamal described that process:

> When I read my paper aloud, I can hear a mistake so I say, "There's something wrong with this. I think I'll put it this way—That correct?" And I wrote it down what they tell me.

> Then it's time to finish reading my paper, and I read to my group some more, but I stop again. I say, "There's something wrong with this." And I ask, "What do you say this? Is this correct?" Then I made the revision.

Independence didn't increase on its own, however. In order for students to seize control, tutors had to relinquish it, and (like me) many found doing so a struggle. Here Ashley uses log keeping to monitor her progress: "I am going to work hard come Monday on talking less, 'teaching' less (at least in the didactic way), i.e., withdrawing more from group." Another excerpt shows Ashley nudging an interdependent group further by (proactively) offering students guided practice with identifying and asking for the help they needed. In other words, to move students to a more advanced stage, tutors may have acted *more* proactive at times, even though they were shifting responsibility to students:

> After [Sung Tae] read, I asked him "What do you think?"
> "I have a problem with tense," he said. And I attempted to discuss consistency with tense, explaining that I have a lot of problems with tense in my logs.

A Shifting Scale of Concerns

An Outside Researcher Confirms the Shifting Patterns in Tutors' Work. At the start of Year 2, Taejung Kim Welsh, a doctoral student in Bilingual Education, joined the tutor-training course as a participant observer as part of a three-course research sequence she took with me. Later, Taejung began formal observation of a Center group. Her dissertation (Welsh, 1988), which grew out of this project, documented two major themes permeating our work. First, her personal writing breakthrough in my teaching-of-writing course illustrated the broad applicability of writing workshop approaches. These proved as helpful for Taejung and native-speaking graduate students, many of whom were enrolled in MFA programs in writing, as they were for the basic writers of the WTC. Second, Taejung's analysis of one group's early weeks confirms the shifting focus that characterized tutors' work in the workshop groups.

Using microethnographic analysis of face-to-face interactions, Taejung analyzed the group sessions she observed during the first six weeks of a term. Focusing on how the tutor led students to interdependence—which, you'll remember, we "knew" about but had not yet named at that point—she documented the shift from tutor to group control and showed a tutor proactively setting up a safe environment before withdrawing so students could become interdependent in groups.

In the group Taejung observed, the salient feature of group interaction shifted from week to week. These were the shifts she observed (with our stages in parentheses):

Week 1. The Tutor Sets the Stage (tutor proactive)

Week 2. The Tutor Begins Modeling (tutor proactive)

Week 3. The Students Begin to Interact (interactive students)

Week 4. The Students Give Their First Constructive Criticism (interactive students)

Week 5. The Tutor Holds Individual Conferences (proactive tutor)

Week 6. The Students Speak More Than the Tutor (proactive students/reactive tutor)

Though specifics of behavior and timing differed from group to group as well as from tutor to tutor—for example, most tutors used conferencing more informally than this tutor—Taejung's description of the group shows the proactive/interactive/reactive progression that shaped student responses into a reciprocal dependent/interdependent/independent pattern.

Teacher-Research Logs
as Sources of Information about Learning

Shortly after Taejung completed her observations, six Team 4 members—Kathy Briggs, Kat Eckhardt, Yitna Firdyiwek, Miki Jackson (middle-school teacher and doctoral student), Kai Wheatley, and I—spent a full semester poring over dozens of logs and writing folders; comparing and contrasting tutors, students, and groups; looking for patterns in tutor and student behavior; testing for differences between pre- and post-test scores; examining pro and con evidence for our hypotheses; and struggling with the problem of how to focus this book. We also spent a lot of time interviewing Kamal to learn about his perceptions of how Center groups worked.

The interdependence breakthrough came too late that semester for us to draft chapters of this book as we had originally planned, for without it we had no organizing principle for the data. We therefore spent the term selecting and editing logs to use in the teaching-of-writing seminar and, we assumed at the time, for inclusion in this book. From those on hand we chose several that were complete, representative, self-aware, well written, and detailed. Most of that semester's work (which continued throughout the summer on these tutors' own time) was done with logs by Kathy Briggs (2), Lorry Lawrence (1), Geri Madigan (1), Bonnie Martin (3), Dianna Poodiack (3), Ashley Williams (2), and Louise Wynn (1). The following year, three research assistants (Yitna Firdyiwek, Kai Wheatley, and Karen Berger, then an adult education ESL teacher with the county schools) also worked extensively with these and other logs.

As logs were composed of freely written, unrevised, and unedited field notes, editing included working with punctuation, spelling, and paragraphing; cutting out extensive digressions and repetition; reordering jumbled passages; and explaining in-group allusions. We gave students new names, changed revealing details, added illustrative excerpts from students' writing, and checked back with tutors to be sure we hadn't distorted their intent. Analytic work included activities like these:

- Identifying categories in the data
- Coding data into these categories
- Looking for relationships among categories

- Generating and grouping the hypotheses/hunches/propositions that emerged
- Diagramming these relationships graphically
- Comparing and contrasting findings under different conditions
- Comparing and contrasting various kinds of data
- Comparing the perspectives of various informants
- Checking confirmatory and discrepant evidence
- Choosing vivid excerpts to illustrate patterns we found
- Doing fine-grained analyses of the excerpts chosen
- Searching for a unifying focus in what we'd learned
- Checking other scholars' theories against our own

Our hundreds of hours spent poring over logs were tedious but productive. Sloshing through the cypress swamps of our data time and again, we began to recognize patterns we'd missed before, and it was by this process that the breakthrough insight emerged. Reexamining the raw data through that lens—

DEPENDENCE → INTERDEPENDENCE → INDEPENDENCE

—we began to test how it fit what went on in groups. Four months later, Team 5 would again test Team 4's theory, using it to predict what would happen in Team 5's groups. Preexisting data, by contrast, offered a complementary test. Collected "blind" by tutors before the framework emerged, prior logs were entirely uncontaminated by conscious or unconscious pressures to make what went on in groups conform to this new progression.

In teacher-research it can sometimes be hard to distinguish between data collection, analysis, theory testing, and instruction, for in follow-the-kid approaches, the distinctions between teacher-research and teaching methodology blur. Like all logs, Ashley's reveal this link between teaching and research methods. Near semester's end they show her nudging a group toward independence by refraining from interacting except when students asked for help. Note that she observed her group *passively*, responding only to a question Mouna proactively asked. Notice also that, as Yitna's "overlap" theory suggests, independent student behaviors had to be observed against the backdrop of largely interactive groups:

> Parvis read his piece about his girlfriend's death. He had written a second draft which ended: "One thing really peest me off. that truck driver didn't even stop. I swear to God I ever see him again I will kill him."
>
> "I like the first one better," said Mouna and Sung Tae said, "Me too. You tell more about your feelings. It was flowing." Parvis read the first one again, and when he got to the part where he wrote about going off on the shoulder, Sung Tae asked, "Shoulders?"

"Yeah, the side of the road," replied Parvis. It was interesting to think that Parvis, who hasn't been here two years yet, was teaching Sung Tae, who's been here since grade school, a new word. . . .

A minute or two later, I heard Parvis ask, "*My* car?" I think it should be "*the* car." . . .

Mouna looked at Sung Tae and then answered, "But *you* were driving."

Parvis described the wrecked car. Mouna looked once at me and asked, "*Totaled?* Shouldn't it be *totally destroyed?*"

"I think *totaled*," said Sung Tae, and I agreed, explaining that it was probably slang but was widely used informally.

After the session, You Chi, the least independent groupmate—who'd spent the session in the mini-group with Terry and Din—proactively asked permission to take her writing home, revealing a budding tendency to work independently (no homework was ever assigned in the WTC):

"Can I take it home and work on it some more?" You Chi asked. I wondered how confident she was about the help her mini-group had given, so I asked if she'd gotten some useful responses. She smiled and nodded enthusiastically; I think she wanted to go over the changes—maybe assimilate some of them.

Even those Stage 3 students who withdrew to work on their own kept a watchful eye on what went on in their groups. Midway through fall semester, Linda Topper observed that Barqadle, an Ethiopian student who'd withdrawn to write, monitored group interactions even as he wrote. While proactively following a schedule dictated by his work's demands, Barqadle remained open to interactive learning as well:

Oct. 31:   I told Kamal that the story he'd written (about watching a group of superstitious men in a graveyard) reminded me of a story about how my grandfather met a ghost on a bridge. Barqadle listened, looked up occasionally, but wrote away. . . . Barqadle wrote a lot today; I was pleased at how he continued writing while we chatted about ghost stories.

Gradually, then, after practice taking charge of each other's learning, basic writers proactively took control of their own. Kamal described it like this:

So next, after revisioning, then comes editing. At first my friend say, "There's something wrong with that word. Doesn't sound right . . . , doesn't sound good. I think you can try to work on it."

Later I begin to learn that from reading my essay I discover my *own* mistake.

They stopped reactively hiding weaknesses to ask for help—as did Kamal:

So then I begin to *ask* for feedback, for response. It's very helpful.

They began calling down tutors who, a bit bored with their newly passive roles, sometimes let their attention wander from group work:

> I had gone back to my chair during this discussion (from listening to a question the other mini-group had), and Mouna asked me about my necklace. I started to answer her question, but Sung Tae said, "Hey, what about my paper?" His group got right back to work.

Something special was happening in groups like this, I believe. When skillful tutors like Ashley "withdrew," "sat on [their] hands," or became "anonymous" and "invisible" (to use terms tutors used in research reports and logs), they transferred to interdependent students not only freedom of choice but responsibility for learning to write well. And, in response, group members began reacting in ways, that, for dependent students, and especially Asian ones, would have been unthinkable earlier in the term.

Other Data Sources Shed Light on the Independent Stage

Logs weren't the only data we had on the three-stage progression. Tutors also interviewed students and read their process writing. Most independent behavior took place outside school, however, so it was often through chat that we learned how students applied, to papers for other courses, attitudes and strategies they'd picked up interacting in groups. Here is Kamal on the topic:

> Revisioning is very helpful for me to learn because there are times when I am not with a tutor, when I'm just by myself and have to fix my writing by myself. At that time, I read my writing aloud to pick up all the mistakes.
> But first, when I revise, I don't worry about grammar. No grammar, no spelling yet. Because that's not revisioning, that is editing. I do revisioning first, to get the ideas right, get the ideas right on the paper. Then comes editing.

The independence of Stage 3 students, who took full charge of their learning, also showed up in their proactive efforts to influence how tutors taught. Treating tutors, the WTC secretary, and me (the Center director, whom they rarely knew personally) increasingly like equals as independence increased, students proactively offered advice about how to do better jobs. In the Kamal interviews, which Kai Wheatley and Kathy Eckhardt transcribed, Kamal made scores of suggestions on a range of topics. I'll illustrate with those suggestions that cluster around a sample topic—vocabulary instruction—to show how deeply Stage 3 students thought about their learning and the proactive steps they took to gain control of it.

Supporting his suggestions with examples from his groups, Kamal explained patiently to the tutors and me that (for him at least) knowledge of vocabulary developed more easily when words and word meanings were studied in context, at the point of need:

> I think you do not need to "teach" vocabulary in the WTC because when other teachers discuss vocabulary, most of the words from vocabulary list I don't use so I can't remember. It's because there's no *purpose* for me in learning those words. I'm not interested in learning words which maybe I might use them someday and maybe I might not.
>
> But say if I want to write a paper, a critical paper, about how I think about a literature story . . . , *then* I would be *interested* to know words which can describe how I think about the book. And then I would *remember* them too.

According to Kamal and scores of other proactive students, learning done purposefully, at the point of need or choice, was easier to retain and use than was memorization and drill:

> In the WTC, when I *want* a particular word, I *ask* for it. And once I got it, I think I can *remember* it for quite some time. It happen a lot.
>
> Just now, when we had a conversation with [some teachers], I used the word *gorgeous*, okay? I learned that word from the WTC. One of my friends came to WTC and say, "Oh, today is gorgeous!" And I don't know how to respond. And I look at another of my friends, and he responds, "Yeah, is gorgeous. Is nice day. The weather is fine." So, when I had a conversation with the teachers just now, I used the same thing. . . .

> MIKI: You mean the vocabulary you learn in the center, you learn by, . . . listening? and by talking?
>
> KAMAL: Yeah . . . from interruption and discussion. I can get the vocabulary much easier from discussions than studying a list. And, at the same time, [voice rising] I learn its *meaning*. And through the conversation with my friends I know the correct usage of that word. . . . That why you do not need to "teach" vocabulary in the WTC.

Proactive behavior offered students unexpected rewards, like reducing how much they had to learn to become independent. Proactive students had both motivation and confidence, and they weren't afraid to ask for help they needed. Once students could spot their problems, Kamal and others advised, and cared enough to ask for help when they needed it, tutors didn't need to cover every rule in the book. Students would take responsibility for what they did not know. Nor did tutors need to assign dictionary or thesaurus practice to writers who cared enough to search for the perfect word, knew how far to trust references, and felt comfortable asking for help.

Proactive basic writers also noted another reward—the ease with which they remembered and could apply in other contexts features and skills they'd studied because they'd *wanted* to. (In this way they differed from dependent entering students who, as we saw in Chapter 2, could not tap their own "hidden skills"—which included rules they'd studied in school—and so had often been assumed to have very few.)

Though to my knowledge no tutors taught "vocabulary" in lists, it was regularly addressed at the point of choice or need:

> KAI: Well, how many vocabulary words would you say you learned in the center?
>
> KAMAL: Oh, there's a lot. I can't think of them right now because I don't have any list, but when I start writing, I just throw them out onto my papers. Whenever I start writing, they just come out. . . . Now, I will have mistakes—with the spelling—because I didn't study the spelling yet. But I know what the word is I am after, so I refer to the dictionary.
>
> I learn a lot of words in the WTC, and when I talk to American people, I can remember those words.

In short, proactive students said, what they learned at the point of need was easy to retain and use compared to what they learned from direct instruction.

Of course, we didn't incorporate all the advice we got. Stage 1 students' efforts to negotiate changes were almost always dependent attempts to avoid responsibility or to "psych out" the tutor who would evaluate them. Stage 3 advice, however, dealt with learning efficiently because proactive students wanted to learn as much as they could. This proactive advice, almost always offered gratuitously, nudged tutors' teaching in nontraditional directions. Rooted in student analyses of their own and their groupmates' learning, it drew tutors further and further away from familiar traditional teaching and increased their confidence in our research-based approach.

To learn efficiently and retain what they learned, motivated and independent students emphasized, writers need to *experience* written language in context—the attitudes, strategies, and rewards that accompany it as well as its formal content. After all, that's how writers learn language in the out-of-school world. Over the years, we therefore expanded our definition of "content" to include attitudes, strategies, and rewards that attend good writing in addition to conventions of grammar and mechanics, of rhetoric and style. Ironically, these four kinds of content—behaviors, conventions, rewards, and attitudes—are kinds of knowledge students had been taught directly in the past but had been unable to absorb, retain, and use until they experienced them holistically in the WTC groups.

Gradually, then, two shifts took place in tutors' understandings about when and how writing content is best learned. In the first stage they pulled away, often reluctantly, from preventive/corrective instruction and moved increasingly toward teaching at the point of need. Only later, however, as evidence accumulated, did many begin to feel confident with this inductive teaching approach. The chapters that follow will show how they set up writing experiences that allowed a range of opportunities for students to acquire knowledge—of structure and process, of attitudes and rewards—incidentally, at the point of need.

Hindsight/Insight/Foresight: The Rewards of Teacher-Research

The analytic framework wasn't complete in a day. It took a number of weeks to get the terminology right, and we struggled, frustrated, with the term *proactive* for some time, opting at last in frustration for precision over grace. Our ability to explain what we'd learned from our work was expanding, however, and the framework has since withstood many tests. Nor is it a theory divorced from application. It has had a tremendous impact on my teaching, for example. By making clear which behaviors to associate with progress, it has helped me evaluate the impact of classroom choices, provided guidelines for judging my own and students' growth, helped me decide what experiences students are ready for next, and reduced my uncertainty about how to evaluate them. Thus did recognizing the interdependent stage and the resulting framework we'd groped toward for so long increase the sense of control many of us had over our teaching and build confidence, autonomy, and self-esteem.

It also convinced those of us who tested it of how clearly teacher-research informs teaching intuitions. Long before the breakthrough revealed the role of "interdependence," tutors had sensed the exciting potential of the groups and, like Ashley, took steps to lead students to interact more. The day *before* she actually started tutoring, for example, Ashley (who was still nervous about the WTC approach) recognized, while observing two of her teammates' first tutoring efforts, the unique potential offered by group work:

> I watched Kathy B. and Yitna with their groups today. I had a good feeling about it, watching the groups jell. I went to watch the tutors but ended up watching the students, of course. Now I know why Marie kept telling me she could teach me to lead a group. She could teach anybody; *the potential is in the group itself.* Even if Kathy and Yitna had been less skilled, the group would have held possibilities. [italics mine]

From Ruth Furr's Year 1 observation that three or four students made faster progress than "groups" of one or two, to this quote from Ashley, written the first day of classes, Year 4, tutors implicitly acknowledged the power of interdependence and foreshadowed most of the other findings in this book as well. And, contrary to what I, at least, had expected, the most successful tutoring we documented resulted when tutors learned to trust a kind of knowledge that was less linear and explicit than intuitive. In other words, two types of analyses—one tacit and intuitive, the other explicitly rational—informed the teaching decisions tutors made. For guiding day-to-day teaching and "following the kid," they relied heavily on observation-informed intuitions. For evaluating their methods and testing their assumptions, however, they used the more systematic procedures of qualitative research.

Self-correcting predictions based on pattern recognition were a product of teacher-research that was both prior to and independent of formal analyses. Whether from collaborative oral discussion, personal log keeping, or reading each other's logs, preliminary findings shaped our evolving program. In fact, many of the insights in this book were made explicit after I'd stopped directing the Center. A Year 1 transcription of a research-session tape, made before "keeping records" expanded into "keeping logs," shows the confidence I expressed in the value of tutors' data early on:

> I did talk a lot about [your] publishing [your research]. You had such incredible evidence. I mean, I was learning more from reading your notes than from reading published research.

Tutors agreed about the potential in their data. From Team 1's Linda Blair (who found "keeping the records" so much more helpful than "doing the readings you assigned" that she quit reading assignments to keep "records" instead, despite the fact that she was unsure how that would affect her grade) to Team 5's Jody Bolčik (who refused to reduce the number of logs she kept even though keeping logs on all four groups was no longer required), tutors found reflective teaching critical to their success. "Hindsight/Insight/Foresight" Jody scrawled at the top of a log, capturing the process by which teacher-research informs:

HINDSIGHT/INSIGHT/FORESIGHT

> That's what I get from my logs, and it's why they're so useful. As I write about what's happened each day in my groups, I begin to figure out what my students need from me next. You see, by looking back over my day, I begin to understand whether we're heading in the right direction or not.

Later that year, Jody put her money where her mouth was. Where the value of logs was concerned, her behavior bore out her words. When family pressures complicated a stressful midterm week (long after I'd suggested tutors focus data collection by keeping logs on two groups instead of four), she refused to relinquish access to the hindsight/insight/foresight keeping logs on all four of her groups provided.

"Even though I'm feeling all this pressure," Jody responded, "I just can't stop keeping logs on all four groups. I find they're just too important to me as a teacher." When I asked *how* the logs were helpful, Jody explained:

> While writing, I look back over what we did each day, and that's where I figure out what's going on with students. Without the insights I get from studying what we've done, I'd have no way to figure out what my students need next. So even though keeping two logs would take less time than four and I could focus data collection on my research topic, I'm not willing to stop keeping logs on all my groups because it's from the logs that I'm learning how to teach.

4

Changes in the Drafted Writers: Reinterpreting Student Behavior in Light of Underlying Attitudes

"To W.T.C.," read the inscription above the watercolor sketch Thanh presented Linda Blair in the middle of spring semester. And below, in double capitals: "MY GRATITUDE."

Only a week or so later, to Kathy Trump's surprise, another Year 1 student, after sketching a long-stemmed rose, presented it to Kathy with a thank you note. Coming near the middle of the Center's first semester, these incidents marked a turning point in our early analysis. By giving expression to an outbreak of good feelings, they alerted us to unexpected levels of attitude change. The surprise Team 1 experienced taught us a valuable lesson: It told us we'd underestimated how important attitudes are, how much good ones fertilize writing, how much bad ones poison it.

For five years, teams confirmed the importance of attitude, noting that although we could teach writing behaviors—such as freewriting, brainstorming, organizing, asking for peer responses, outlining, rewriting, and proofreading—unless students took writing seriously, they could turn the best of our lessons into busywork, going through the motions without absorbing much at all. Daniela Hoefer, a bilingual tutor from Team 5, recognized the power of negative attitudes on students who came for tutoring to the Writing Corner, an appointment-based tutorial center for anyone at CAU. Studying a group of "demoralized and frustrated" students who "didn't think very highly of their own writing because their teacher didn't," Daniela noted that these students were not successful at improving their writing until negative attitudes had changed: "We can't approach writing until they get their minds cleared of their frustrations and negative feelings. . . . Once they have talked through their troubles we can focus on the paper."

It wasn't that we had not been aware that attitudes were important. From the start we'd assumed basic writing would improve when neutral or negative feelings changed. But we'd had no idea how quickly improvement would occur or how surely behavior changes would follow changed attitudes. Nor had we realized that attitudes and their attendant behaviors were almost always to blame when writing failed to improve. As far as we have determined from our data, attitudes *always* affected writing behavior, which in turn affected writing for better or for worse. We diagrammed this simple but powerful principle this way:

ATTITUDE → BEHAVIOR → WRITING

Because most basic writers arrived with attitudes that actively interfered with their writing progress, we searched for the sources of negativity and in the process discovered a more basic factor—awareness level—that motivated students to work harder and take more risks. Several kinds of awareness functioned in this way, reducing student naiveté in a number of areas:

1. *Awareness that they could improve* changed the attitudes of students who'd accepted the premise that writers are born, not made, and who assumed, since they couldn't yet write well, that they never would.

2. *Awareness that they should improve* changed the attitudes of self-satisfied students whose standards for writing were low.

3. *Awareness that they had to improve to be certified* influenced students who were trying to beat the system.

4. *Awareness that they could, in fact, take charge of their learning* eased the frustration of those whose nonacademic writing had never before been recognized or valued in school. It also reduced the resistance of those who had problems with authority.

5. *Awareness of their writing strengths* changed the attitudes of students who were unaware of potential in what they wrote.

6. *Awareness of strategies for revising and editing* changed the attitudes of those who felt inadequate because they did not know that writers do more than one draft.

7. *Awareness of writing's intrinsic rewards* motivated others who had been unable to motivate themselves with grades.

8. *Awareness that the freedom of choice tutors offered was real* motivated students who'd been afraid to take risks.

Regardless of the type (or types) of awareness students lacked, some sort of naiveté—about writing, about learning, about what was expected of them—affected student progress more than lack of ability did. Carmen, one of Dianna Poodiack's students, credits the role of awareness on a midterm self-evaluation:

> I'm more aware now when to make parpagraphs. I think, that I've learned it on my own, but without the WTC, I would never have stopped to think about it. . . . I felt negative about [WTC] at first because I thought that I didn't needed. But now I think that even the most skillful writer needs advice from time to time.

Awareness, then, was prerequisite to growth:

AWARENESS → ATTITUDE → BEHAVIOR → WRITING

"Breakthrough students" we called resisters who became aware, for once awareness triggered a shift away from the negative, the awareness/attitude/behavior/writing progression folded back on itself. The result was upward spirals of motivation and confidence. These, once established, often sustained themselves because of the rewards students earned when their writing improved. These rewards must also be included in the framework, for without them, upward spirals of growth could not exist:

AWARENESS → ATTITUDE → BEHAVIOR → WRITING → REWARDS

These last two variables—awareness and rewards—functioned differently from the other ones because they initiated and reinforced change as well as participating in it. Increased awareness initiated change, while rewards reactivated the spiral by reinforcing changes students had already made. Awareness marked a turning point in the progress of negative students, interrupting downward spirals of frustration and failure and initiating upward spirals of increasing success. Increases in awareness prompted willingness to take the risks that preceded positive changes in writing behavior (freewriting, experimenting with content, trying new genres). When these changes accumulated to the point that they triggered noticeable improvement in the writing itself, students feasted at a smorgasbord of writing rewards (recognition, publication, competence, confidence, praise, better grades), which in turn heightened their awareness of why writers love to write, reinforced attitude and behavior changes they had already made, convinced risk-taking students they were on the right track, and reactivated the spiral by prompting additional changes in behavior and attitude (see Figure 4–1).

In the spring of 1984, Yitna Firdyiwek summarized several Team 4 conclusions, noting the holistic nature of the spirals that resulted from increased awareness—or, as he put it, from "breaking away from old habits of perception":

> Breaking away from old habits of perception can take place in [several] areas one at a time or simultaneously and in any sequence or order. But even though students progress in different areas at different paces, the "direction" of the changes is consistently in [this pattern]: from changes in attitude to changes in behavior to changes in writing. In addition to this we have also noticed that there is a "spiraling" effect to the changes once they have caught on.

Two years before, a student of Team 2 tutor Jane Lofts Thomas described the upward spiral she experienced in the WTC: "The more I write the more I

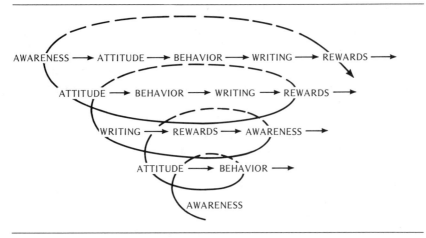

Figure 4–1   **The Upward Spiral of Increasing Motivation and Success**

improve, and the more I work on my writing, the easier it gets the next time around. . . . (1988, pp. 164-165)"

In addition to WTC data, Team 5 tutor Daniela Hoefer and I independently documented a "cyclic" effect in the students we worked with outside the WTC. I spotted the phenomenon in the spring of Year 1 while teaching my first creative writing course at CAU. By contrast with the (mostly) writing majors in that course, and with basic writers in the WTC, Writing Corner tutors like Daniela tutored any students, graduate or undergraduate, who wanted advice with a writing project, whether a paper for Freshman Comp or a dissertation proposal. We did have occasional graduate students in the WTC, but they came as volunteers, on a space-available basis. Most students, however, were required to come, at least at the start. Daniela noted what she called a "cyclic" effect while tutoring students in the Writing Corner's one-to-one sessions. In a research report titled "The Cycle of Motivation," Daniela described two types of Writing Corner "regulars." ("Regulars" were students who sought tutoring several times during the semester)—"demoralized and frustrated" students who "lacked motivation" and those "motivated" by "a real desire to learn about writing":

> Soon I noticed there were two types of regulars. One type came in because they wanted to improve their papers and ultimately their writing. The other type were people who didn't think very highly of their own writing because their teacher didn't. They also didn't enjoy their 101 class and some even failed to see the purpose of it.

To help "frustrated" students, who got little reward though they worked hard, Daniela returned to her logs to examine her successes, only to find that, for these two groups, patterns of success and failure predated her work with them. Those patterns were traceable to the teachers students had had.

> I was curious to know why some students felt motivated and why others didn't. I kept looking through my logs to find out if I'd been doing something different which might have motivated some, but realized that these students came to me already motivated. That meant I had to look behind the scenes. And there was my answer—teachers.

So Daniela studied what made some teachers more motivating than others: "Working in the Writing Corner, I have many opportunities to deal with students' concern over what will please their teacher [and] I have been able to learn about their teachers, how they run the class, and how the student feels about his/her teacher and class."

Students with motivating teachers went through upward spirals, she found, and her own praise and encouragement reinforced that trend:

> Every time they come in, their papers improve and there is less for us to work on. I usually point out their improvement and this praise seems to motivate them even further. It's like a never-ending circle. The more you write, the better you get, the more your grades improve, the more you want to write. They can't lose in this situation.

By contrast, attitudes were negative among unmotivated students who seemed unable to attract rewards for their hard work:

> On the other hand, there is the "unmotivated" camp. Leon, Abdul, and Craig are all frustrated with their class, their teacher, and their writing. When I see them, they are always complaining about something that has to do with English. Writing has become a chore—almost a punishment. . . . They come in with the attitude that even though they worked hard on a paper they will, as usual, receive a "re-write."

Illustrating her findings with three case studies from each category, Daniela supported her conclusions in detail and described the kinds of teaching both types of students received. In addition to the scarcity of rewards they suffered, unmotivated students had been allowed to make few decisions about their work. They also lacked assurance that they could succeed if they tried and focused most of their efforts on giving the teacher what she or he wanted. Daniela's research report continued:

> There is no enthusiasm when they come to me. . . . None of these can muster any enthusiasm for their topics and view their writing ability negatively. Their teacher gives them a list of topics from which they have to choose one; usually they pick one they think he will like. . . . Abdul practically starts off every session complaining about his teacher and his requirements, and so does Leon. They lack motivation because they feel their efforts are useless.

Students with motivating teachers had a different experience:

> As a reward for their efforts they get fairly good grades. All three of them have a B average. This gives them the motivation to improve even more. For example, My came in two weeks ago with a B– on her "fire" paper. She wanted to rewrite it and improve her grade even more. Betty wrote her rough draft for her research paper two weeks before it was due and Mark is always willing to rewrite his paper, even if he's already written six drafts as he did for his process paper.
>
> To add to this motivation, all three have a certain amount of confidence in their writing. When they first came in, they all believed they were poor writers. On a questionnaire, which all six students I studied filled out, [they indicated this]. When I asked toward the end of the semester why they came to the Writing Corner, [the motivated students] had more focused reasons. . . . This shows that they have been made aware of their strengths and that they no longer see themselves as poor writers overall but as writers who have a few weaknesses. This increased confidence also improves their writing because they get enocuragement from both their teacher and from me and feel they can improve.

The rest of this chapter illustrates, using data from the WTC, upward and downward spirals in risk taking, commitment, and confidence similar to those Daniela documented in her Writing Corner students. It also describes what we learned about positive and negative attitudes and confirms that for WTC students as well, past failures resulted from the past instruction they had had.

The Impact of Positive Attitudes on Writing Behavior

Though neutral and negative attitudes would also prove influential, Team 1 first noticed the attitude/behavior/writing sequence in those cases of positive attitude change. As student after student grew more serious about writing, they showed appreciation and affection for tutors and groups.

> I'm glad we're doing this. I mean it's fun writing about anything we want to write about, but I also need to know how to correct the mistakes I've been making all through school, and this kind of thing helps me do that.
> —Bev, quoted in WTC intern Geri Madigan's log, April 5, 1984

Grateful for the freedom to write whatever they pleased, some shared their relief at being allowed to do several drafts. Others expressed pleasure at feeling more competent:

> In school I was not exposed to the techniques of writing the proper way. I don't understand why teachers find it so difficult to teach students to write. Because of my lack of training, and not being exposed to writing I never

gained the much needed confidence that I needed to become proficient at the task of writing.

I came to the WTC unaware of how much I could learn or even if I wanted to at this point, but at last someone is giving me a chance.

—S. L., *WTC Excerpts*, March 19, 1984

I don't want to appear proud or anything, but I have confidence in my ability to write. . . . My joining the WTC course has helped me a lot. . . .

—S. P., *WTC Excerpts*, March 19, 1984

Attitudes also changed when students wrote something others liked, when they discovered writing could help them personally, or when they found out it could be fun:

I'm now beginning to learn to love writing. Just recently when I was very upset about something I sat down and wrote about it. As I was writing I began to feel encouraged. Now I write everyday, not to any one but to myself. I find that it helps me go through the day.

—R. G., *WTC Excerpts*, November 7, 1983

For some students, good feelings blossomed on discovering the sanctuary's potential for trust and intimacy. This freewriting, by a sixteen-year-old student from India, was written on her first day in an established group:

I think I am going to like coming in here. This is my first [day] and it seems like I know everybody in here very well. It's like they trust me. This has never happened to me before. I mean people talking so freely about their experiences to me and everybody else. I don't know why but I feel close to all the people around me here even though it is my first day here. Everybody seems so friendly.

Others were attracted to the diversity found in groups:

Well, to tell you the truth, I really didnt want to have to take this class. But now that Im here, it really isnt so bad. The people in my group seem very friendly and interesting. For example, everyone in my group originated or was born in a different area than the other. One from Vietnam, one from the Phillipines, one from New Jersey and myself from Madison, Wisconsin.

—T. E., *WTC Excerpts*, October 30, 1985

In his talk to the seminar the week before school began, Kamal told the Team 4 tutors how his feelings had changed:

I'd like to tell you my attitude before I came here. I thought WTC is a waste of time—"Here I am in *college* and have to attend *grammar* school again?"

When I came to WTC I gave a negative attitude—but if I *don't* come here, my registration will be on hold. Also, I was *embarassed* because my friends, they didn't come. They have high enough score on TSWE.

That why I *hated* WTC.
So when I came here, to this program, I was upset, and also I am afraid to write. But after class goes rolling, I *love* to come! Those are the barriers that I overcome.

Motivation and commitment also developed when students realized, often for the first time in their writing careers, that they were capable of writing well. This theme, recurring in transcripts, thinkwrites, and logs, was confirmed by Jenna, a creative writing student of mine, who had been far more successful, with school writing at least, than most entering WTC writers. Just as it did for basic and ESL writers in the Center, awareness that she *could* write well by using new strategies triggered an upward spiral of confidence and success:

I think I have finally struck gold! Actually I believe it to be more like bronze at this point. But at least I have acquired some riches. I am speaking about my writing. I think I have finally sparked the flame that will light the fire in future weeks. . . . I am letting myself, my personality, shine through. I am not going to worry about words such as "format" or about how to structure my sentences—I am going to write what comes to mind and what I feel comfortable with. Hopefully in this process I will be able to pen a paper which is enjoyable for the reader. Writing as of this week, seems to flow more like water than molasses. Maybe I am feeling more confident with my writing skills. Yes, that is it—I CAN DO IT!! Confusion still lingers at times, and my brain does not want to cooperate with my fingers, but at least I can see a light ahead. Hopefully I will be able to catch-up now. I shall have to see. . . .

—J. S., late February 1988

In short, a wide range of writing rewards that had nothing to do with grades reinforced changing attitudes and made hard work pay off. Of course, improved grades were not unappreciated, as is shown by a note from former tutor Kathy Trump, who had left the WTC and was then employed teaching English 100 and 101.

Marie,
    Rode up in the elevator with a student who, after discovering that I was a teacher in the English Department, volunteered the following: "The WTC is a wonderful program. I never would have gotten an 'A' in my English class without it."
    All of my Eng. 100 students who are working in the WTC are also *pleased* with their work there.
    Just thought you might like to know how successful you all are!

Kathy T.

These data illustrate a theme tutors discussed often—the role of motivation in writing development. Real-world rewards were what made the progression cycle back on itself, making upward spirals self-perpetuating. During week four of fall semester—while I was drafting this chapter, in fact—I entered a small WTC room where the Team 5 seminar met. There, for the second Thursday evening in a row, I found Jody Bolčik and her 3:30 group writing busily, all unaware that it was time for the graduate seminar.

"I'm really sorry we ran into your time," Jody said when her students had gathered their books and gone. Then she turned to the rest of Team 5 to explain about her group: "It's just that once we start writing, we all forget the time. On Tuesdays, when there's no class afterwards, I can't get them to stop. Last week they *all* stayed more than twenty-five minutes late. When I finally ran them out, it was ten till five."

Events like these convinced us something special was happening, for case after case showed changes in the formerly hostile feelings that had flourished in student naiveté about writing and learning. After several semesters studying student after student and group after group, the links between attitudes and behavior, behavior and writing grew clear. By far the most costly and unnecessary negative attitude was despair, rooted in the conviction that competent writers are born, not made. This perspective, frequently adopted by earlier teachers, had made dozens of students believe they could not learn to write. And the low self-esteem that resulted interfered with growth by lowering students' motivation, fanning frustration and anger. The result was they viewed our program as a wasteful drain on their time, as irrelevant busywork that could do them no good. Case study data showed that conclusion to be invalid, however, for in the Center environment learning to write well was something any basic writer who worked hard could do. The following case studies, written before this conclusion emerged, show several kinds of awareness breakthroughs affecting attitudes and behavior, which in turn affected written work.

Audry, Who Never Knew She Could

Team 1 tutor Kay Benton interviewed former students and included excerpts from transcripts in the eight case studies she wrote for a course in applied research. Here Kay, a professional writer, describes her successful effort to avoid a power struggle with a hostile, embarrassed student who was unaware that she was capable of improving:

> Audry was, I think, embarrassed about her writing problems, but at first she covered this embarrassment with her seemingly flippant "I don't care" attitude. She wanted me to look at her English papers, and when I informed her we would begin instead by freewriting, she was displeased and said freewriting was "a waste of time."

When she returned for her second session, Audry became angry with me. Her face flushed, she accused me of ignoring her English papers and said she didn't see how I could help her if I wouldn't even look at them. My outwardly calm voice belied the inner churnings against her accusation.

Staying cool paid off for Kay, and as Audry's attitude changed, so did her writing behavior and the writing she produced:

> Within a month, Audry was getting C's on her English papers and her self-image and outlook seemed to have changed for the better. She said she felt she might make it through English 102 this time. Though it was still difficult for her to write more than the absolute necessities on her papers, they soon increased in length from short one-half and one-page efforts to where she felt comfortable writing two and one-half pages.

Audry earned certification within the semester and, during a follow-up interview some months later, said the turning point had come because Kay, unlike other teachers, had treated her as if she actually could improve:

> KAY: You were taking English 102 for the second time when you came to the WTC?
>
> AUDRY: Yes, but I wasn't doing any better. I was a procrastinator first class and never got my papers in on time. The teacher told me I was going to flunk. She said I should go to the WTC for help with mechanics.
>
> KAY: What happened to you in the WTC? I recall very few problems with your mechanics.
>
> AUDRY: I got encouragement and that was all I needed. I found that my fear was all in my mind. I really thought I was horrible at writing.

Once aware of her own potential, Audry's fear subsided, and she was rewarded with a new sense of competence:

> KAY: After getting encouragement, what happened to your writing?
>
> AUDRY: My attitude changed. I was told "Yes, you can write, you can do it." The paranoid feeling left. I feel competent as a writer now. I know it is still hard, but the beginning step has been made.

Awareness that she could learn to write sustained Audry so much that she began getting A's on English papers—even without the support of the WTC:

> KAY: What about the English class you're taking this fall?
>
> AUDRY: I'm getting A's on my English 205 papers—and I am writing more. The last paper I wrote was five pages long. The old paranoid feeling sometimes returns when I first get an assignment, but then I remember *I can do it* and the feeling goes away. [italics mine]

Kay's case study of Audry illustrates how *awareness that they could improve* changed attitudes about writing, motivated students to try, and rather quickly affected their academic success. By contrast, Dianna Poodiack's case study on Farooq shows *awareness that he should improve* and *that he would have to do so to be certified* motivating a student whose standards for his work were low.

Farooq, Who Didn't Know He Needed To

Accepting the New Paradigm

For a spring semester course in writing research Dianna documented what went on in three writing groups. She taped almost every session, transcribed many tapes, and took detailed notes on those sessions she didn't completely transcribe. Unlike Kay, she did few formal interviews, assessing student perspectives by relying instead on transcripts of group discussions, on impromptu interviews, on volunteered information, on overheard conversations, and on the "process thinkwriting" we taught to help students take charge of their work.

Long before the awareness variable emerged, Dianna found that as Farooq's attitudes changed, so did his behavior, after which his writing rapidly improved. At midterm Dianna asked this group to evaluate their progress, and Farooq fondly titled his thinkwriting "Me and My WTC." He hadn't felt so positive two months before, however:

> ME AND MY WTC
>
> I was angry as I could be the momment W.T.C. Commission told me that I have to join the course. But I had to join the group. It was a feeling of being a hostage, like someone has rather forced me to do something. . . . At this point I didn't or I should say couldn't find any problem in my writing. I knew that it's not perfect but thought of it as something passable.

Farooq saw no need to improve until CAU's "literacy requirement" forced him to. But awareness that he had to improve to graduate affected only initial changes in attitude. It was group interaction that raised his critical standards and made him aware of other motives for working hard: "As the time rolled and I had spent a fair amount of time in W.T.C. group, I started to realize that just passable is not enough. . . ."

By the time he wrote this self-evaluation at midterm, Farooq himself could see the improvements in his writing:

> Honestly viewing and scrutinizing my choices I came to the conclusion that my writng and knowledge have gotten better, the uncontrollable thoughts called The stream of Consciousness has taken a new meaning. [The writing] is more precise, on the point, and disciplined, just like a self-correcting typewriter or a mustang of thought controlled by the guidance of W.T.C.

Taking a risk with a tutor he'd come to trust, Farooq very openly discussed his weaknesses and took responsibility for his own lack of growth:

> The W.T.C. program has been helpful in this sense which is a step ahed, but there is nothing that any body else can do about my laziness. If I don't have time to revise and edit my freewritings than I should concentrate on doing so or otherwise "tough-luck."

Comparing her logs with transcripts of audiotapes helped Dianna correlate attitude and behavior changes precisely. Though she'd once worried (in writing) that Farooq, a slow starter, might "never begin to revise," vicarious learning from observing a groupmate challenged his "laziness." After watching Tai revise a "dream piece" for half a semester, Farooq lamented his own lack of motivation. April 4: "I wish I had that much intention to do my work."

Once aware that "just passable is not enough," Farooq began to notice what others did to improve. Awareness that his work was weak fueled his desire, and just after he expressed this wish, it became reality, with committed revising behavior emerging immediately. Farooq spent the next month revising "The Convertible," a piece he'd drafted on April 2 and April 4. At the next (April 9) session, for example, he asked groupmates for advice as he read aloud this ironic piece on his heaterless car.

While his group made suggestions, Farooq took notes on the draft, relying almost entirely on other students' ideas to make the first revisions he'd done in the WTC. Near the end of Dianna's seven-page transcript of that session, this (barely) interactive group erupted in elation, revealing the pleasure they took in helping improve Farooq's piece. Note how Dianna (interactively) modeled the kinds of responses other groupmates would soon become confident giving. Note also that, though Farooq did not yet revise on his own, his growing enthusiasm (caught from Dianna?) provided a positive attitude model for his peers:

> Farooq asked, "So how can I say I cannot ignore it [the February cold in a convertible without a heater] any more?"
> I shouted, "You could say it just like that!" I laughed and so did Farooq.
> He said, "All right. Thank *God*!" [Reading aloud as he wrote on his draft, repeating the words after me,] "At this point you cannot ignore it anymore."
> I said, "That's perfect. That is *perfect*!"
> He continued, "You cannot tolerate this bitter cold." He stopped and muttered, "Oh, *terrific*!" and kissed his fingertips.
> Tai and Mike laughed along with Farooq and me. We were all excited about what had happened.

Transcript excerpts show the line-by-line revising Dianna and the other groupmates helped Farooq do. They also show his growing awareness of the need to improve:

Farooq read, "But boy it seems like a difficult task."
I asked, "Why wasn't it just 'difficult'? 'Seems' is a word that's shaky."
"Yeah," Mike said. "It sounds like you're not sure."
Farooq added, "You got it! It's like a weakness in my own statement."
He then wrote and read the sentence aloud two ways: " 'But boy it's difficult' . . . 'But boy it's a difficult task.' "

As interdependent behaviors increased, so did desirable attitudes like perseverance, excitement, and pride. During the tedious process of fine-tuning his diction, for example, Farooq used some of Dianna's suggestions in this piece. But, with groupmates' support, he ignored her advice when it failed to reflect his intent, revealing a growing tendency toward independent work.

I responded, "Yes, that's okay," then asked, "Would you use the word 'task' though or just 'Boy it's difficult'?"
Mike said, " 'Task' makes it sound laboring."
I asked, "So you think 'task' is *better*?"
Mike said, "Yes, it gives the impression it's more difficult."
Tai, Farooq and Mike were all talking at once. Farooq said, "That's why I used 'task'—it means 'achievement,' something like a conquest. I mean God! When you put the cigarette in your mouth and the cigarette's going 't-t-t-t-' [sound of shaking], it's *hard* to wait for warm weather."
Then Farooq exclaimed excitedly, "I *love* it! The paper's coming out terrific!" Farooq and Tai laughed, Tai adding, "I *know*!"

Farooq had experienced what TAs call a "breakthrough," a sudden increase in awareness that he needed to improve, which, by producing a shift in his attitudes, triggered an upward spiral of increasing success. This breakthrough came late—well after midterm, in fact. Farooq had remained resistant a lot longer than most: "Farooq had finally recognized the value of revising. Previously he had done only one or two drafts at the most. Now he was on a third draft and would bring in a typed fourth draft [done unassigned at home] at the next session."

Making Up for Lost Time

Fortunately, once breakthroughs occurred, late bloomers made up for lost time. One day Dianna arrived early at the center to find Farooq and Mike (proactively) discussing how to make better use of group time. The boys also (proactively) told Dianna that they needed more time to work on their own:

Mike and Farooq started talking about the very real need to come to the WTC three days a week instead of just two. [Farooq] said, "If only there were three periods a week! In group process, I understand everybody contributing thoughts—but individual gets mixed up [because the time is not enough].

Mike suggested, "With three days you could write two days, and revise one day talking as a group."

Farooq said, "I feel a great disappointment [when] I get here if I can't put [my] idea down on paper because somebody else needed help. The time [problem]. . . ."

Though we had yet to recognize the interdependent stage, Dianna's Year 3 logs illustrate how interdependent learning nourished independence. Like Farooq, who learned motivation from Tai's "intention to do his work," Mike was growing more involved by working with Farooq in group: "Both Farooq and Mike expressed a desire to come more often—a desire which may have grown out of the group process Mike referred to. At the same time, it was clear to me that what we had done to help Farooq, Mike sought also and had already benefited from in his own way."

In Farooq's case, new awareness of the need to improve initiated an upward spiral in a "holdout" student who had resisted working hard until well after midterm and who surprised Dianna and me by his sudden turnaround. Who would have guessed that Farooq the "hostage," once "angry as [he] could be," would soon complain of having too little time in group! Farooq's standards had risen again and with them his commitment to improve his writing on his own: "You've got to give individual a certain time period on his own—to put it down on paper, scrutinize it, instead of somebody else tell you it's fine. . . . And to put it on paper the way I felt it—nobody can help me with that."

Group interaction was no longer what these students needed most, though both gave group interdependence credit for their improvement. What they needed now was a shift, they informed Dianna, in the ratio of group to individual time. Having completed the first shift to interdependence and vicarious learning, Mike was now eager to practice working on his own.

> "What I've gotten out of this class is not the writing aspect," Mike commented. "It is more from helping people—from using sentence structure. Now I'm more *aware* of my own." [italics mine]

Similar awareness motivated Farooq:

> Farooq had also talked about the need for stronger advice, for more hard criticism from the members of the group, a clear change from his feelings at the start that his writing was "too good" for him to be here.

Although neither was totally independent yet, Mike and Farooq proactively practiced newly acquired skills: motivating themselves, finding problems in their writing, asking for help they needed, and sharing what they learned.

> Later we listened to Mike read "Colorado," and Mike explained some of his problems: "When I read it aloud it sounds rough. When I write and read silently I can remember everything I did." . . .

Farooq had some advice, something he had learned from his own revising experience. He began citing the advantages of typing when revising, saying, "Best shot you can take is to type it double space. It's a psychological effect. When I first wrote this paper [he motioned to his folded draft of "A Convertible," squeezed onto lined paper], it was congested, confused. When I type it, it gives a better idea of what's going on."

Continuing to discuss the advantages of typing a draft, Farooq said, "You find the mistakes perfect. It's so beautiful—you find the mistakes—articles, commas, etc. That [typing] is the only thing that helps."

I asked Mike, "What else do you need from us, Mike?"

He answered, "I'm having trouble making it flow."

Farooq said [glancing at me], "Wouldn't you agree with this? [To Mike] Do it again on another paper. Organize it. Write it over again."

I added, "Write it on every other line."

Farooq said, "That will give you an idea of what's going on."

In her report, Dianna summarized Farooq's progress, explaining why she had certified him even though he'd learned little during the first half of the term. More than his finished products, attitudinal changes and their impact on his behavior convinced Dianna that Farooq could now make it on his own: "The semester was nearly over, and I believed Farooq had become independent enough to carry these ideas with him after he left WTC. His changed attitude was apparent in the exciting way he had opened up to the revising process."

How the Attitude/Behavior/Writing Progression
Fits into the Analytic Framework

There's an obvious connection between the dependence/interdependence/ independence findings of Chapter 3 and the awareness/attitude/behavior/ writing/rewards progression outlined here. The latter analysis fits into the earlier framework under the paired shifts from dependence to interdependence to independence. As dependent students (passive, resistant, noncommittal, unmotivated) developed interdependent attitudes (trust, intimacy, desire to help others), dependent behaviors (waiting for instructions, writing to please teachers, competing, working only for grades) gave way to interdependent ones (accepting criticism, making helpful suggestions, writing to please oneself or one's peers). As the data on Mike and Farooq show, similar connections appear in the shift to independence. As the boys gained confidence, for example, they began to act more responsibly, use group time efficiently, arrive early, determine for themselves what to do in group each day, and request additional time in the group for working alone. Paired shifts can be seen in students' writing as well as in their behavior, as I will illustrate in Chapter 5.

The Bigger They Are, the Harder They Fall:
The Impact of Negative Attitudes

Tutors noted early on the results of positive change, but it took longer to notice the impact of negative attitudes, perhaps because negativism took us less by surprise. Unlike breakthroughs, resistance seemed so common, so predictable in basic writers, that at first we failed to challenge its inevitability. It may also have been that negative attitudes were more threatening, and that we therefore tended to avoid dealing with them. But cataloguing positive change, however comforting, was in the long run less beneficial to the teaching teams than examining negative (or even neutral) feelings and figuring out what to do to turn them around. A wide range of negative feelings affected students similarly: By blocking the development of motivation, such feelings reduced the purposeful practice students did. They also created the only behavior problems tutors had.

One of the first things tutor-research teams learned from their data was that to comprehend behavior, we had to understand the attitudes that led to it. For several years, resistance was our most persistent instructional problem, but as Linda Blair has noted, resistance was not always bad. It alerted tutors that students were about to learn something new and might need extra support in taking a risk. Resistance, we would find, was also an asset to those who experienced it, especially to active resisters who fought for their beliefs, for it showed they cared strongly, and those who cared had an edge on those who cared too little to resist. To illustrate this, I've selected case studies, written by three different tutors, which explore what Ashley Williams called ''the resistance factor'' because so many tutors misinterpreted it.

Three Kinds of Resistance; Three Shades of Gold. Viewed from a research perspective, resistance proved to be one of our most insight-producing variables, and several tutor-research teams found to their surprise that pain-in-the-neck resisters were more fruitful cases for study than students who neatly and gratefully conformed to theories or methods of ours. Resistance provided negative cases that challenged our assumptions, forced us to devise new approaches for resisters, and in the process improved the program that evolved. Whenever students or events shattered our expectations, we could be sure we'd taken a false assumption for granted or had overgeneralized and needed to specify more precisely the conditions under which a finding held true.

Tutors divided resisters into active and passive types. Ironically, many students with persistent writing problems were those who had resisted past instruction the least and now doggedly kept on writing as they'd been taught, following what Andy Cooper called ''a plethora of writing rules.'' Unlike active resisters, who fought for control of their work, these passive resisters avoided taking control, rarely questioning the logic (or illogic) of instruction. Lacking the confidence they would soon develop in groups, and seeing little connection between how they wrote and what they'd been taught, they had followed directions for years without seeing much improvement and without even getting good grades. Unmotivated, they saw our program as just another hurdle, just another crazy, meaningless hoop they had to jump through. After all, they had studied Composition for years without ever showing their writing to anyone but their teachers, without producing writing they or their friends enjoyed, without feeling any letup in writing anxiety, perhaps without even gaining mastery of grammar rules. Struggling to complete yet another writing requirement, many usually docile basic writers grew resentful and angry when they found out we had changed the rules. And, as they lacked the nerve to challenge tutors directly, some undermined the tutor's success in passive-aggressive ways.

Unlike dependent students, who blindly sought to please teachers, and unlike passive-aggressive students (resentful but compliant), active resisters were independent enough at entry to reject instruction that made no sense to them. Once aware that group work could help them improve, however, this desire to control their learning became an asset, for they did not need to learn independence from scratch. It was near the end of the program's fourth year when we realized that, properly handled, resistance indicated outstanding potential.

"The bigger they are, the harder they fall," Team 4 realized with relief after discovering that resistance, which showed how much students cared, functioned like a rainbow promise of gold to come if—but only if—tutors could stay in the advocacy role. We then began to welcome (and channel) this motivation, but awareness that we could do so took some time to emerge, and several teams of frustrated tutors groaned and tore their hair before we learned to cope with the hard feelings students showed. It would take even longer to come to understand that these students' negative attitudes, and their negative downward spirals of failure and frustration, resulted from their failure on the Center's entry exam.

Tutors got lots of experience with negative attitudes, for the Center's very existence enraged many WTC students, causing them to refuse to cooperate. The history of the program made this almost inevitable. The Center was formed after the CAU faculty senate instituted a "literacy requirement." This was an effort to raise university standards by eliminating students with weaknesses. All undergraduates were subject to the requirement, which they could fulfill in one of three ways: scoring above a cutoff point (35) on the TSWE (the Test of Standard Written English, a subtest of the Scholastic Aptitude Test—the SAT), writing a superior entry essay (as judged by a panel of raters), or earning certification by attending a tutorial group. To make matters worse, the original senate ruling applied to transfers and reentry students who had taken the SAT several years before and had in some cases completed writing requirements at other schools.

The embarrassment, frustration, and discouragement students felt at being tapped for this program often showed up publicly as anger or as passive resistance to the new methods tutors used. Most felt little incentive to work hard until they realized writing was possible, useful, necessary, and even fun. Once attitudes changed, these same students would criticize how they'd been taught in the past, but this happened only *after* tutors gained their trust, only *after* their eyes lit up with awareness of their potential, only *after* it became clear they could write whatever they pleased. Until that time, they aimed barbs at the WTC, at tutors, and at how tutors taught. Bonnie Martin documented this pattern in George.

George, the Fiction Writer

> George was one of those angry students. Because he viewed the WTC as a "remedial writing center," he was both hurt and insulted that he was requested to attend its sessions. On the first day he was quite defensive about his presence in the group.

Though most students grew cooperative when given control of their work, dozens entered angry, afraid, frustrated, or seemingly indifferent. Others—like George—failed to trust the freedom tutors offered. On entering the program, George showed little interest in learning. His only apparent goal was to escape as soon as he could:

> When [George] wrote his first piece, he turned it in asking, "Is this good enough to get me out?" Clearly his motive was to impress me enough that he could exempt early from the program.

One day the group wrote responses to pieces in the *WTC Excerpts* (see pp. 4–6). When George called one of these excerpts "too mushy," Bonnie noted, a female student defended it as being "open and honest." George concluded he'd finally discovered what Bonnie wanted, but she gave tutors' standard response to his mistaken assumption that if personal writing were allowed, it must also be required. Like other dependent students George had not yet learned that responsibility comes with freedom of choice. So instead of choosing a topic he cared about, he continued to try to figure out how to please the teacher:

> George looked quickly at me, and with a smirk on his face said, "So, what we have to do in this place is write about emotional stuff." In my teaching logs for that day I recorded his comment and then wrote:

I tried to clarify our goals. Good writing contains honest feelings, I told him. That feeling doesn't have to be a dramatic emotion, but it must be genuine. George nodded in agreement, although I'm still not sure that he understood my explanation.

Though George was still dependent on psyching Bonnie out, evidence that he cared about writing was available. When a groupmate responded that one of his pieces wasn't believable, George missed the next five sessions, suggesting that the groupmate's criticism may have hurt. Bonnie called and encouraged George to return, recording his angry (but honest) written response when he did. "He wrote an honest, blunt evaluation of the program. He said he resented it, that it was not helping him, and that he already knew 'enough about writing.'" Like Farooq, George apparently thought his writing was "passable."

Hostility was a problem tutors faced every semester, so solutions for dealing with it evolved gradually. Once we saw how often anger interfered with learning, I began to teach coping strategies in the seminar. Relying on anti-terrorist techniques devised by earlier teams and on standard conflict-management approaches, we tried not to take hostility personally, but to accept students' feelings as natural and to empathize with them. Oral responses during group wasted others' time, however, and exerted negative drag on improving group attitudes, so tutors learned to conduct these dialogues in writing, which channeled negative energy into purposeful practice and allowed tutors time to think before responding. In her case study, Bonnie reported a written dialogue with George, who had ended his angry piece on the following note:

> George concluded: "After writing this I may not be able to look you in the eye."
>
> Sure enough, George avoided me during the next session. I recorded in my teaching log:

> Today George avoided looking at me. He sat with his forehead resting in the palm of his hand and began *four* times on a piece. At the end of the session, he stuffed his notebook into his bookbag and walked slowly out of the room.

In the "sanctuary" Bonnie established, George expressed his anger and found that he could trust her not to get mad in return. Instead, she treated his written outburst as a good sign for his work. Bonnie sensed that the risk he'd taken signaled a "breakthrough," and—as she handled it well—it did prove a turning point:

> I deliberated as to how I should approach his anger. Because I saw his written expression as a breakthrough in honest writing—for the first time he wrote for himself, rather than to please me—I wrote on his piece that his expression of anger was "one of the first genuine things he had written." I

also encouraged him "not to feel any shame for being honest" in writing and to continue writing about it if that were necessary in helping him work through it. The written response was the only one I gave him.

Addressing George in writing let Bonnie plan her response:

> I recorded in my logs, "I've debated over and over about what to do or say to George, but my instinct warns me that it is best to leave him alone awhile and let him work through his anger." Significantly, however, I wrote responses to him, thereby letting him know that his confessions were not going unnoticed.

Bonnie had recently listed students she was worried about, and, to no one's great surprise, George's name "headed the list." After accepting his outburst, however, she saw signs of growing commitment: George asked about making up absences by sitting in on another group, and he did something else she'd never seen him do before—he sought control of the genre in which he would write:

> "Could I write something that isn't true? I mean, based on real things, but made up?"
> I said, "You mean *fiction*?"
> He nodded his head eagerly, "Yeah!"

Notice how incidental teaching, at the point of need, supplied the name of a concept George already knew. Here Bonnie supplied a term George must surely have "known," but had apparently not applied to his own work. Though he'd been comfortable expressing anger in speech, only when he ceased to censor his writing did George's negative attitudes change. And at the point that he learned he could write whatever he chose, George's motivation rose far above the norm.

George illustrates yet another kind of change-producing awareness—*awareness that the freedom of choice tutors offered was real*. Students unused to making decisions about their work sometimes took a while to trust the freedom tutors extended. After Bonnie accepted his risky decision to write about his anger at the Center, George tested this freedom by asking to choose the genre in which he wrote. When Bonnie confirmed that he could write whatever he chose, his writing-related behavior changed immediately: Suddenly he talked like a writer, acted enthusiastic, wrote to please himself, paid attention to how he wrote, dropped by to chat between sessions, and began picking Bonnie's brain about narrative technique:

> From that point on, it was George's story. He was now writing for himself, not for me, and not to earn approval under the guidelines of the required program. Suddenly he began to stop by the WTC on days he was not scheduled to meet, just to give an account of how his story was progressing. We talked extensively about point of view: it seemed so fas-

cinating to him that as a writer he could elect to tell the reader "what went on in one guy's mind" while only recording the external details and actions of a second character.

Like Andy, Bonnie was able to build on a student's hidden strengths, for independence and honesty on the one hand and interest in fiction writing and technique on the other led first to attitude changes and then to self-sponsored practice as soon as George was convinced that he could take charge of his work.

Bonnie confirmed these attitude changes in an impromptu interview:

> When George's story was in the final editing stages, I glanced through his folder to find the first draft for comparison. I noticed that the harsh piece he had written about the WTC was missing. When I asked him why he removed it, he said, "All that's over now. I just had to get over being mad."
>
> "What made you get over it?" I asked.
>
> "I just saw it wasn't getting me anywhere. Plus, once I wrote this story, I kind of started *liking* it in here."

George's case was one of many from which this chapter draws its central conclusion: Awareness (that he could control what and how he wrote) changed his attitude, which in turn triggered changes in writing behavior that brought payoffs he had never before received in school. George also illustrates another recurrent theme. "The bigger they are, the harder they fall," Team 4 tutors would exclaim when they realized that their angriest students often became the most dedicated writers the program produced. Like Farooq, held "hostage" by the "WTC Commission," some former resisters asked for extra hours in group. Like George, who'd been unable to look Bonnie in the eye, some dropped by between sessions to chat about technique. And like Kamal—whose Malay people's history as a colonized nation had made them second-class citizens in their own land and made Kamal hate the language of those responsible—breakthrough students changed from basic writers into confident students, into writers of fiction with a new interest in literature, into writing majors, into researchers studying how writers learn, and into graduate writing students seeking advanced degrees. These behavioral changes began, as we know now, when students learned to love writing in the WTC.

In my study of writers who teach in middle and secondary schools, I'd been alerted to the "harder-they-fall" pattern by an Atlanta writer who taught seventh and eighth graders and whose program had served as the model for the WTC. So, when Team 4 found this pattern in college writers, I went back to my tapes to confirm that Barbara had indeed noted it:

> It's interesting, Marie, but I've found that the students with the most potential often act most resistant. Writing's important to them because they have much to say, and I think they act resistant because they feel so vulnerable. It's like they defend themselves—you know—emotionally. So, if

we can make these students feel safe, they almost always become the best writers in the class.

Dozens of resistant students marched belligerently through tutors' logs acting either overtly or passively aggressive. Not only did resisters fail to work hard, however, they destroyed the sanctuary atmosphere other students needed in order to improve. Adding one hostile student to a group of four or five could reverse the upward spirals of motivation and success tutors had painstakingly established. Hostile students therefore posed a threat to tutors' success, and new tutors sometimes took their defiance personally, accepting the authoritarian roles projected on them and undermining our goal of putting students in control. Daniela remembered responding to authoritarian roles projected by Writing Corner students resisting how composition teachers taught: "These students treat me differently from students of the other group. . . . They see me as a knowledgeable figure who can impart her wisdom (or so they think). . . . Because I am treated as an authority figure, I tend to act like one."

Giving basic writers control of decisions about their work solved many motivation and behavior problems. On the other hand, it sometimes also left tutors hostage to dependent students who, avoiding responsibility, demanded that tutors tell them exactly how to proceed. Rather than abandon the goal of transferring control, however, most tutors chose to muddle through, despite occasional problems with overly dependent students, relying on the research team for help when resistance arose. And, as our accumulated know-how increased, WTC terrorists intimidated tutors less, for together we developed ways of handling these disgruntled students without reverting to traditional controls which undermine key aspects of the new teaching paradigm. For example, while studying the sources of their resistance, we learned that angry students were usually covering up insecurity, embarrassment, or fear.

We tested this hypothesis by acting as if it were true. When I read in the logs that tutors were unsure how to proceed, for example, I responded with administrative support and suggestions like these:

> Don't let his behavior upset you—he's probably just *scared*.

Or:

> Reassure her that you can and will help, and be as patient as possible. Let her write through her feelings and don't take them personally. They're probably directed at the literacy requirement—not at you.

Tutors were shocked at how simple our more successful strategies were, for most had viewed resisters as powerful enemies, which in fact they would have been had not I, as director, supported tutors completely. Being new at teaching and fearful of losing "control," they'd hardly suspected their most aggressive students were merely afraid. This excerpt from Ashley Williams's logs shows a Team 4 tutor applying what earlier teams had learned about dealing with resistance:

> September 12:   I just don't feel like things *went* today. . . . There are two members, Parvis and Sung Tae, in whom I sense some resistance.
>
> Parvis, an Iranian student living here with his brothers . . . likes science and probably views this [program] as a real drag. When we freewrote, [Parvis] was the first to stop. ("Time's up," he announced). He looked at his watch several times. . . . Lazy and lackadaisical are the words which come to mind when I think about his behavior in class ("My tutor says to write but nothing comes to mind. . . ."). I know he *isn't* lazy, though—he gets up at five A.M., studies chemistry, and works as a cook. How can I get through to him?
>
> Maybe I should get him to write about his feeling on WTC. If he does dislike it and writes honestly, maybe that would give me a chance to start a dialogue with him.

Ashley made other allusions to Parvis's resistance and lack of motivation. On October 1, in the ill-fated mini-groups, he had acted unwilling to help the less proficient You Chi: "You Chi worked with Parvis; he simply told her he'd give her an A on [her paper] . . . , and I'm really disappointed (and a little irked) because I feel Parvis made so little effort to help." Ashley's experience with Parvis shed light on the hypothesis that resistance, passivity, and fear often co-occur:

> When I wrote earlier that in class he appears lackadaisical, M. N. wrote "scared" [beside it in my log]. I notice more and more how true that is. On close inspection, I see that his lip quivers (And this is the "laid back" kid who likes fast cars and discos!)

Sometimes it took a while to realize that students had changed, but tutors learned (and taught others) to monitor attitudes closely rather than assuming their students would never change. Here Jody Bòlcik tells how a more experienced tutor helped her learn to look for breakthroughs in attitude:

> Linda Topper, Kathy Briggs and I had gone to lunch, and I was feeling frustrated. Kathy suggested I have the group do a "What does this group mean to you?" thinkwrite so I tried it in all my groups. Chet read first—Chet who was so hostile before: "I feel I can come to group with an open mind. WTC is giving me more confidence in writing."
>
> At 2:30 we again did the thinkwrite. I read mine first. Then Ailene. Ailene expressed the need for more talking, more participation from the group members. (It was so good to hear it from someone else.) Soyeon wrote about people being absent and said it was hard when everyone didn't come. It's true. It really affects the groups.
>
> Marie, these thinkwrites are priceless; a lot of the students were hostile in the beginning, but by the time we did this (Oct. 10), nearly everyone had

turned around. More importantly, a few people expressed a need directly to other group members—a need for more group response.

How relieved we were to discover that our worst behavior problems resulted from students wanting so badly to succeed. And how often student and tutor frustration shifted to excitement when we learned to channel that negative energy positively.

Staying in the Advocacy Role

Not without chagrin at having so misunderstood our students, we refined new paradigm approaches time and again, repeatedly taking comfort in Linda Blair's conclusion that resistance was healthy and showed our students were ready to take risks. Incorporating new data, we extended Linda's theory, abandoning the perception that open hostility was "bad" and experimenting with ways to preserve self-esteem so threatened students would feel safer taking risks.

Our most successful strategy was staying in an advocacy role, which meant that tutors would not act defensive when they or the program came under attack. As advocates they had other options, however. They could show that honest self-expression was safe by accepting hostile feelings, by divulging feelings themselves, by soliciting empathetic responses from the group, by matter-of-factly acknowledging the power of "bad" feelings, by writing personal responses (as Bonnie did with George), by suggesting that groupmates write responses to each other, and by treating resistance as a problem groups could help solve. In the process of responding to students' anger, tutors could also address students' underlying fears.

Staying in the advocacy role wasn't easy, however. Unlike the more traditional teaching most of us had known, it required making standards clear *while extending the right to ignore them* (though not with impunity). Except for removing disruptive students from groups, staying in the advocacy role meant allowing them to resist and relying on natural penalties to motivate them to work harder. Of course, we sometimes worried about irresponsible students who seemed completely dependent on teachers for motivation. At first it seemed naive to expect basic writers to take on this responsibility, and a couple of teams debated prodding "holdout" students by reinstating assignments and grades. But as student after student grew more *aware*—of their need and potential for learning, of writing's intrinsic rewards, of the consequences of not working hard—we saw so many rapid turnarounds that in the end we concluded students were helped, not harmed, when we waited patiently for them to take charge of their work.

Successive teams of tutors took comfort in past teams' conclusion that resistance was less related to our approach than to lack of awareness on the part of students. As Andy, Ruth, and other Team 1 tutors found, once students tasted real-world rewards and penalties—once they knew they could and would have to work hard and improve—basic writers began to work for writing's intrinsic rewards, to think of themselves as writers, and to take charge of their work. The bigger they are, the harder they fall, we reminded ourselves when those who held out the longest improved the most in the end. In short, we found that letting students resist taught them the main thing— self-motivation—that they had failed to learn in their past instruction. And once awareness turned their attitudes around, our resistant students confirmed the wisdom of our decision. Of those who required a second semester in the program, for example, many wrote in their process logs that they needed and/or wanted to return. In the long run, then, the research confirmed our decision not to motivate (i.e., control) students with assignments and grades, for there was little connection between performance on assigned writing and the ability to write correct and engaging prose.

Waiting for awareness and motivation to develop paid off, for the hardest nuts to crack were those who stood to benefit most. New tutors, we therefore concluded, need not accept guilt trips from dependent students unaware of what writing entailed and all too ready to blame lack of progress on someone else. Tutors' role, instead, was much as I'd first envisioned it:

- To explain CAU's literacy requirement clearly but succinctly
- To create conditions under which students become *aware* of the need to motivate themselves
- To create conditions under which students become aware of how much they do not know
- To base teaching choices on writing experience and teacher-research
- To use methods consistent with linguistic research and theory
- To model attitudes and behavior that help many writers improve
- To offer a range of writing rewards and consequences
- To create a supportive atmosphere in which students can take risks
- To train students to give support and constructive criticism
- To transfer to students increasing responsibility
- To use balanced evaluation techniques
- To maintain an advocacy role
- To remove disruptive students from groups if need be

Under these conditions, if students failed to work hard, tutors could rest assured that they themselves were not to blame and could wait, patient and confident, for natural consequences to motivate students. Students might see their progress outstripped by groupmates. In addition, their work might fail to appear in the *Excerpts*, fail to hang on the eye-level "chair rail," or fail to be featured on the Center's four bulletin boards. They might be the only ones in their group whose writing got little response or who had nothing ready in time to publish in *The Drafted Writers*. If they continued to resist taking charge of their own learning, students could also lose their early registration priority or require a second semester to be certified. By replacing reminders, complaints, and bad grades with natural consequences, tutors in the advocacy role won the trust of resisters, who then began to take group work more seriously—at which point they, like their less dependent groupmates, found that they were learning to judge their progress themselves. As Linda Topper's student Tung exclaimed near midterm: "*WOW*! Everybody have a finished piece. I better get *busy!*"

Natural consequences like these jolted students into awareness, but any negative impact they may have had was short-lived, for once dependent students resigned themselves to hard work, they received rewards for their changed behavior and attitudes:

> In the beginning I was confused and frustrated basically because it was my first semester at Central Atlantic. I had signed up for fifteen credit hours and thought I could handle it. But, out of nowhere comes a message in the mail telling me I have to take another class in order to receive clearance to register for next fall.
>
> I felt railroaded, jipped, slam-dunked. Deep down inside I knew that my writing could improve. I can't spell very well and any mechanical aspect of my writing stinks. But, I know I have good ideas and someday I would like to put them down on paper so that I might sell those ideas. So, the whole idea of taking a composition class that could not harm my gpa was alright with me.
>
> I'm glad now that I have this class, the rest of my school work is crumbling down around me. It's nice to have one class that I can count on not being so demanding but carries a big reward.
>
> —freewriting by Vinny

You Can't Push a Rope—Contradictions of Control

Staying in the advocacy role was hard for other reasons. Beginning tutors—like Andy Cooper in Chapter 2—might feel guilty when they couldn't cover everything their students needed in a semester. So when, despite their efforts, students failed to respond quickly, tutors felt even more tempted to hurry the pace of learning. But demanding that students function "at the college level" failed until students felt confident at all levels below. Like individuals, each group's progress had its own rhythm, moreover, and tutors were unsuccessful when they tried to hurry things. Students not yet fluent at generating ideas probably weren't ready to practice organization until they'd had more time to develop their thoughts. Nor did those who could not yet freewrite learn much from grammar study until they knew which of their problems were actually mistakes and which were merely regression errors caused by overmonitoring.

An example of how pushing students short-circuited progress showed up when a tutor I'll call Kate tried to get a dependent (reactive) group to act more independently (proactive) than they felt. Ignoring both awareness and attitude development, Kate focused her efforts on getting students to change their behavior, revealing her lack of confidence in the attitude/behavior/ writing progression that had shaped the WTC program for a full four years. "You can lead a horse to water, but . . ." the old adage goes, or, as a friend of mine used to say, "You can't push a rope."

In her rush to independence, Kate's good intentions backfired, for she failed to honor the premise on which independence depends: By refusing to transfer control of their work to her students, she destroyed the atmosphere in which attitude change might occur, thus precluding the upward spiral of which students were capable.

This, of course, is my *interpretation* of what happened. Let me provide the evidence on which my conclusion is based. Early that fall semester, Kate complained of being overworked, saying she stayed in the Center until after midnight each night, working with students who needed help and writing extensive logs. Though I assured Kate she need only work her contracted ten hours a week and suggested she narrow her research focus to make log keeping manageable, little change occurred in her behavior or her complaints. I was puzzled at why this tutor was having so much trouble until one night, working late in the Center, I overheard this exchange.

As her evening group broke up at 9:30 P.M., Kate invited the students to stay for extra help. When none responded, she turned to a 30-year-old Vietnamese, calling him by name and insisting she *didn't mind* staying at all.

"This time I do it myself," replied the softspoken student.

"Oh, I'm perfectly willing to help," Kate persisted, "I really don't mind."

Making a final effort to assert his independence, the student explained that he'd like to complete a draft before getting more help. Amid the eye-rolling of groupmates escaping hurriedly past my typewriter, Kate "offered" again to "help" this polite but reticent man, insisting she *really* didn't mind, that *of course* she would stay *if he wished*.

Probably tired after working all day at his full-time job in the city, Thieu stayed until after 11:00, getting extra "help" from a tutor unable or unwilling to transfer control. Apparently Kate was so concerned about how I would judge her teaching that she tried to force behavioral changes (like staying late for help) in order to have dramatic results to report in her logs. His impeccable manners prevented Thieu from challenging Kate's behavior, but her manipulations produced a quiet sigh from him and destroyed her credibility with others in his group.

Unfortunately, Kate had put the cart before the horse, for changed behavior has little effect unless it is rooted in awareness and attitude change. Though she could now report in her logs that Thieu stayed late for help, his staying against his will made me wonder how much he learned. After all, as our data on Farooq and George show, self-motivated practice, even fairly late in the term, led to faster improvement than tutor-assigned work. As Andy Cooper had concluded in December of Year 1: "I found that self-help is much more motivating than correction and leads to more dramatic results. . . . The secret to rapid improvement is to show them they can work on their own and can teach themselves most of the time."

Kate's controlling behavior was self-defeating in the context of whole-language teaching approaches, but it appears less bizarre in light of a composition tradition that defines assignments in structural or behavioral terms. In many composition classrooms and texts, writing assignments are defined in terms of the third and fourth variables in the awareness/attitude/behavior/writing/rewards sequence. Traditional assignments are couched in structural (writing) terms, and "process" assignments most often in behavioral terms. This is why, in describing the WTC program, we've used the term *process-based* rather than *process-oriented* to suggest that while students need to learn writing processes, they need to learn them in context, at the point of need.

By requiring unmotivated students to imitate behaviors motivated writers adopt voluntarily, Kate nipped her group's motivation in the bud, and they became less productive than most Center groups. By treating students as if they had control of their work when they didn't, Kate also created unnecessary resistance and kept students more dependent than they wanted to be.

Although this case was extreme, it differed more in degree than in kind from problems other tutors and I experienced. Teacher-research helped us all find similar ironies in our teaching, inconsistencies between how our students learned and the traditional assumptions and methods we often clung to. All of us fought impulses to "police" irresponsible students and to go light on "cooperative" ones who improved little. Given the fact that our own teaching success was at stake, it was also hard not to nag charming but dependent students about what might happen if they didn't work hard. In short, we had to battle a persistent tendency to codependent behavior not wholly unlike Kate's.

Separating Conflicting Roles

What we needed, we decided, was a way to avoid falling into familiar but controlling enforcement roles. We therefore separated advocacy from law enforcement entirely, appointing a single scapegoat (me!) on whom to blame any and all unpopular policies. Thus it was that as Center director I became increasingly involved in law enforcement and antiterrorist activity. Now when resistance lowered group trust or shattered the sanctuary, tutors could tell disruptive students they'd broken "the director's rule" and would have to leave the group until after they'd talked to me. I would then schedule a conference with both student and tutor, listen carefully to each side, ask questions of both, and agree to let students (who needed certification) return on probationary terms spelled out in a contract all signed. In five years we only resorted to contracts two or three times, but the right to invoke this consequence made tutors feel more secure, reduced the pressure they felt to nag, and convinced many resisters to change their attitudes.

One such contract specified that, to return to his group, an offending student would refrain from sighing loudly, arriving late, rolling his eyes in exaggerated disgust, arguing aloud (arguments made in writing were fine), and making snide comments about others' behavior or writing. This contract also, at the student's request, required that the tutor stop pointedly calling on him by name, thus showing respect for his right to respond voluntarily, when—and only when—he felt he had something worthwhile to say.

To succeed, this system required at least two things of tutors: accepting students' feelings and staying in the advocacy role. By contrast, I as director became the official "bad guy" on whom tutors could "blame" any policy students could find to resist. Blaming "the director" reduced power struggles in groups by casting tutors as allies with inside information. In this role they dispensed hot tips on how to get certified quickly—like writing a lot, helping each other, revising and editing carefully, completing at least a couple of pieces good enough for "the book," and generally demonstrating that students could make it on their own. In short, tutors explained "the director's requirements" with impunity once students viewed their advice as assistance, not as commands.

At last our definition of the tutor's role was consistent with our goal of putting students in charge of their work. By letting me play the bad-guy roles—of cop, prosecutor, and judge—most tutors avoided adversarial behavior and in the process gained hostile students' trust. Of course, beginning tutors sometimes failed to stay cool under fire, but by empathizing with students' feelings of hostility, we very nearly eliminated disruptive behavior in groups.

Thus did our "follow-the-kid" approach of collaborative teacher-research free us from preconceived notions about the meaning of "negative" acts. By studying the intent behind writing (and other) behavior, we reinterpreted many troublesome attitudes, responded to them as signs that students cared about their work, and helped a whole category of students we'd failed to reach before. In short, applying "follow-the-kid" research strategies

- Gave us a more consistent definition of the tutor's role
- Taught us the importance of interpreting behavior and motivation from a learning rather than a teaching perspective

- Convinced us to stop attacking problems at the behavioral level, addressing first the issues of awareness and attitude

The point, however, is not that others should adopt or adapt our methods, for they were developed in a particular setting and would have to be adapted for another context. The point is that teacher-research can help any teacher find what will work in her classroom just as it helped us learn what would succeed in the WTC.

5

Writing Works When the Writer Does: Changes in Student Writing That Follow Behavior Change

Given their histories of failure rooted in harsh evaluation, it was small wonder that basic writers had lost touch with their potential, with writing's rewards, with motivation, and with "hidden skills." Fortunately, awareness increased with experience and led to better attitudes and harder work, which in turn caused student writing to improve, in the process reinforcing the new behaviors and attitudes. Typically, the first effect was that students tried harder, their many drafts attesting to the new importance they attached to writing. But caring and feeling positive weren't always related, and even students who cared a lot rarely began working hard until events convinced them that their writing had improved.

As researchers, tutors were not unlike their students. Before being convinced that the Center approach would work, they waited to see results show up on the page. Awareness and attitude breakthroughs might be fine for a start, they said, but they weren't enough to merit certification. For that, students would have to produce writing faculty would approve.

The proof is in the pudding, in other words, so teams also studied whether, how, and how much student writing improved. And as we shifted the focus of our analysis from changes in basic writers to changes in their writing, we confirmed that behavioral changes led to better writing, which brought increased feelings of competence, completing the awareness/attitude/behavior/writing/reward progression. Chapter 4 described interactions among the first three factors in this progression. This chapter documents relationships among the last three.

The Muse Helps Those Who Help Themselves

Once convinced they could or should take charge of their work, even the weakest writers somehow began to improve. For example, students with little control of surface structures began writing vivid, powerful, logical, convincing, or touching pieces, surprising themselves (and us) with their verbal facility and convincing themselves that these pieces were worth taking through many drafts. Examining her students' growth through the lens of her own experi-

129

ence, fiction writer Kim White concluded, during Year 5, that if students
would put out the effort, they could all learn to write well. Consider the
following excerpts from a "thinkwriting" assignment I had Team 5 try near
midterm to help them focus their analyses in preparation for writing end-of-
term research reports:

> The most important thing I know from my data is that some students are
> doing well and others aren't. This can have many causes, but one pattern I
> see is that effort (and the output of pages and rewrites that follows) has a
> direct connection with success that is clearer than individual talent.
>
> Writers are experts in not writing. We know all the ways that writing
> *doesn't* happen—what rooms aren't right, what pen sits too heavy in the
> hand, and on through a litany of excuses. But the list does not account for
> the primary reason that writing works: Writing works when the writer does.

Kim, who was pursuing an MFA in fiction, understood all too well the
nature of writing blocks, but she'd also seen what can happen when people
write a lot:

> I spent the last four years identifying all the ways that I could not write,
> and in turn, keeping the analysis clear by not writing. When I returned to
> school this fall, however, and began to write logs for this class, I noticed my
> own and other tutors' writing developing and wrote, "the muse repays
> quantity."

Kim was not the first to note that practice led to improvement, that serious
attitudes produced the hard work improvement requires. Even the Center's
most talented students—and many proved gifted with words—developed little
unless—or until—they began to work hard. In fact, Kim found, the "elusive
muse" wasn't hard to attract. She would visit any writer willing to put in
some work:

> It seems, when I read over student work and consider the changing
> attitudes of students, that the muse also reads basic writing and that she may
> not be a respecter of persons. Those who work hard, and write write write,
> improve. Their pieces take on smoother language, sometimes surprising
> metaphors, and maturity. But for those.who don't really exert an effort—no
> matter how gifted or observant they are—the effect will not be as great. In
> fact, there may be no improvement whatsoever.

In this thinkwrite, which focused her research report, Kim challenged an
assumption we heard repeatedly from other teachers of basic and ESL writers.
Because "writers are born, not made," they often said, there's little a teacher
can do to help "students like these":

> My theory is that students who work with a sustained effort improve.
> This may seem an obvious point. It falls from puritanical wisdom: *God helps
> those who help themselves*. But, it seems to work against another common idea

that students succeed in composition classes because they are more talented
to begin with.

I think talent is no small thing; talented students who work ignite on the
pages. But, the nongifted (or *previously considered*, nongifted) student also
causes a small conflagration. [italics mine]

In less than three months, teacher-research had led a first-year teacher, herself
a skillful writer, to the conclusion from my earlier study reached by the writers
who teach—that given the right kind of training, anyone can learn to write
well (Nelson, 1982a, 1982b).

In noting the "small conflagrations" students caused on the page, Kim
confirmed the breakthrough pattern we'd seen so often in logs—the pattern
of shifts in awareness leading to sudden "improvement" (defined as "the
difference between later work and the entry essay"). She also noted that
though awareness might dawn slowly, once attitudes changed and students
began to take risks, they worked so hard on writing that they more than made
up for lost time:

> [Improvement] is more affected, I think, by their output in the last half of
> the semester, than by a constant small effort. It is not as simple as "God
> helps those who help themselves," but it does come close to that. . . .
> Perhaps there is a wall that must be broken through, or another sort of
> barrier. This [the improvement that follows these increases in motivation] is
> what I am examining.

In a thesis written while she was at Oxford and without access to Kim's Year
5 work, Jane Lofts Thomas (1988) quoted a Year 2 student who used the same
"wall" image to describe her breakthrough. Helen, "a girl who came into the
Center feeling a failure as a writer, found that when she freewrote her words
exploded all over the page." Jane's narrative continued:

> The story she wrote about leaving her native country, which first found life
> in a freewrite, marked a breakthrough. Previously, she had only produced a
> few hesitant sentences when asked to write, yet after [she wrote] the first
> draft of her story, the growth of her writing ability accelerated rapidly.

Jane quoted Helen's description of the process:

> Writing this piece constituted an emotional release but also liberated Helen
> from the constraints that had been imposed on her writing. . . .
>
> > I had written about this experience before, but I had never written
> > *honestly* about it. Before I didn't know how to start. I would just write by
> > saying first I did this, then this, and I would then come to the end. I
> > hadn't written down my emotions before, how I really felt about this
> > experience. When I wrote on that topic before I felt nothing. This time I
> > got very upset, but *it was like breaking through a wall.* I had never really
> > faced up to the experience before. [italics mine]

Making the Transfer from Self-Directed
to Assigned Writing

Most tutors began the semester helping students find topics they cared so much about that they would voluntarily go through several drafts. Of course, tutors also helped the students learn to organize new material and manipulate unfamiliar ideas. Academic and professional writing require these abilities, and the Center was founded because students weren't succeeding at such tasks. In the long run, however, we found that our students were more successful when they practiced drafting, revising, and editing on self-assigned pieces *before* applying these strategies to academic work.

The case studies that follow, first drafted by Linda Blair, show students applying Center strategies to academic papers assigned by English teachers; subsequent chapters show how students dealt with assignments from other fields. These studies also contrast changes in the writing of breakthrough students (who began the semester resistant and afraid) and cooperative students (who had a more typical pattern of slow but steady progress across the course of a term). Tracing the ebb and flow of regression and growth, Linda charts basic and ESL writers' reliance on "hidden skills" and shows how students in charge of decisions about their work increased their output, expanded their repertoire of strategies, and became more confident of their writing abilities.

Changes in Student Writing

After several weeks of tutoring in the WTC, Linda asked students to jot down perceptions about their work so she could get a feel for any problems they might have. Having collected these data, Linda grew troubled by what she learned. For example, Elena, an 18-year-old from Spain, had been in the United States about four years when she wrote these words:

> By now writing comes more easily and freely. I just write what I think, no matter what. But in a way it doesn't help me with my English class. Since English class writing deals with not only ideas in paper, but also in sentence construction, vocabulary, techniques, etc. this class in that sense don't help much.

Elena echoed the concern of many entering students exposed for the first time to a workshop approach. Though few doubted that such teaching could help with creative writing, they saw little relation between WTC thinkwrites and the formal academic prose they needed to learn. Nor could they imagine how to move from first-draft disorder, errors, and emergent thoughts to tighter, more logical, more carefully edited papers later in the term. To help students separate and sequence writing tasks, tutors would shift group emphasis several times in the semester (see Figure 5–1). Although the tutors explained this practice, some students remained confused and others worried lest fluency-oriented activities might shatter, rather than strengthen, the fragile control they had over editing skills. To complicate matters, tutors (who were new to workshop methods) had to have faith that I'd help them teach revising and editing, for they had yet to be stepped through those processes in my class.

During our two-week test of the method that first semester, Linda had been convinced by data like that in Chapter 2 that the workshop approach would benefit ESL writers. Elena's comment shook Linda's confidence, however, forcing her to examine her assumption that students could automatically transfer what Linda taught to academic writing. At this point we were all feeling our way, exploring writers-who-teach approaches with which we had little practice. Of that vulnerable period in her development, Linda wrote:

> There I was, with a lot of theories and a student who didn't see a connection between the tutorial center instruction and her English class. How could I, as her tutor, help her develop a connection? I decided to test Marie's belief that if oral ability is more readily "acquired" than "learned," the same must be true for writing.
>
> This is how I began. I told my students to jump right in, that they all knew about themselves and had plenty of material to work with. I said write whatever came to mind without worrying about the intial appearance or correctness because they could organize their ideas and clean up errors later. The task was to write down as many ideas as possible or to follow a single idea that interested them if any came to mind. If it got too personal, they wouldn't have to share [what they'd written] with me or their group.

Some students saw at once that separating and sequencing tasks—such as drafting and editing—were tools they could use with assignments for other classes. But conflicts (or rather *perceived* conflicts) between Linda's approach and that of a composition teacher caused Elena to cling to error-avoidance strategies and prevented her from writing fluently. Linda's report shows Elena overcoming this resistance. But first, by way of comparison, Linda traced the progress of those more typical students who accepted without resistance the strategies she taught.

Karin: A First-Year International Student

A pattern we found in nearly every tutor's logs was that writing improved when students chose their own topics and forms. When students knew their subjects well, they developed pieces more fully. When they cared about ideas, they *wanted* to make them clear. And when they weren't required to follow

1. Developing Sanctuary and Fluency

getting to know each other
learning to follow the rule
building trust in the class
working together to help each other improve
learning to give positively phrased criticism
writing a lot
experimenting with topics
figuring out which topics motivate you to write more
abandoning false starts in search of topics you like better
experimenting with different genres
learning to keep learning logs
getting comfortable with word processing
trading work with writing partners
meeting in permanent groups
listening thoughtfully
practicing positively phrased criticism
taking risks in your writing

2. Giving and Getting Advice

reading your writing in class
asking when you need help
giving honest but kindly advice
using process logs to direct your own growth
working productively in your group
helping solve any problems that may arise in group
writing more than you ever have before
caring about your writing
revising over and over again
learning to find and correct your worst errors
letting me know whenever you're having trouble so I can help

3. Revising and Editing

breaking the revision barrier
taking one or two pieces through several drafts each
learning to judge whether your revisions work or not
noticing how other writers get their effects
experimenting to find out what works for you
asking others for help when you run into writing problems
editing many times—looking for one kind of error each time
developing an essay about ideas you care about
letting groupmates know what kind of advice you need
keeping your tutor posted on your progress and that of the group

4. Getting Your Work to an Audience

choosing the pieces you want to publish
working with others to design the WTC book

Figure 5-1   **A Shifting Scale of Concerns for Evaluating Writing**

copyediting your work for publication
submitting favorite piece(s) for publication
organizing your portfolio to reveal the progress you've made
celebrating getting your words into print

Figure 5-1   **Continued**

formulaic structures, organizational patterns emerged more naturally. Some of these changes took awhile to appear, however, because conditioned concern for correctness could be so ego-involving that students took self-defeating steps to hide what they had been trained to see as deficiencies.

Karin's case illustrates this pattern. Viewed in the context of her later work, her entry essay revealed correctness anxiety, and though a team of tutors rated it competent, they retained her in the program because they suspected (and later confirmed) that she'd memorized the essay in advance. The following excerpt is typical:

> I have been here in the U.S.A. some months, and I came here because I wanted to learn to speak English. I had studied English ten years in Finland. But here I have noticed that I just don't know a word. When I started to study, here in Central Atlantic University, I didn't understand anything my professors were speaking. Now I understand some words from here and some words from there.

Karin wrote fairly well-structured sentences, controlled time sequence with ease, and knew when to use prepositions (if not always which ones). But this introductory paragraph did not address the assignment, and what followed (a biographical sketch) was also unrelated. To escape the humiliation of a re-quired basic writing program, Karin had memorized her lines—despite the fact that her stated purpose for attending CAU was to improve her English. Karin's breakthrough apparently came at entry, on becoming aware that in the sanctuary atmosphere, hiding writing deficiencies was unnecessary: To our knowledge, correctness anxiety never reared its head again. Taking at face value Linda's suggestion that she write freely, Karin began at once, and her writing quickly improved. As the contrast between the memorized essay and her later work shows, Karin's seeming "deficiencies" were merely apparent ones. Her first attempt at writing freely began like this:

> I have been very sad already two months. I have a serious problem. I have put about twenty pounds weight on within some months. This sounds funny but it is not. Every monday I decide to start some kind of diet. So I did today also. This morning I ate just one grapefruit, and I trank one cup of coffee. Now I am so hungry I would (could) eat a horse.

This freewriting is structurally weaker than the memorized entry essay. The rhythms don't sound like English, and though Karin knew her topic, the *would/could* confusion shows her still monitoring to some degree. Still, knowing she could later rewrite or discard the piece let Karin approach a risky topic with a strong, personal voice.

Linda said Karin adapted to freedom of choice with ease. Soon she was writing eagerly of her life, borrowing ideas from Center freewrites for use in composition class. That fall she'd passed English 100, for nonnative speakers, and she was enrolled in 101 (for practice) in the spring. The next freewritten excerpt shows Karin monitoring less, in the process tapping more of her tacit knowledge. The sentence patterns are English, with no foreign-sounding word-order intrusions.

> When I was just four years old I already knew that my future was going to deal with horses. maybe I just watched too many Westerns and old movies. I used to build up horses from our furniture, and then I rode like a storm wind around our house—You can guess how happy my mother was!
> When I was seven years old I rode a pony in Paris. After that I lost my heart to horses completely. I started to take riding lessons in Finland. I was twelve years old when I won my first competition. You may not believe it but it was a great feeling, even if the fences were not very high.

Karin had mentioned horseback riding in several earlier pieces, and luckily her professor let her choose her 101 topics: Because she knew and felt strongly about horses she wrote with authority of them. The storm wind metaphor and furniture horses are vivid. Conversational style, varied sentence patterns, and ease evoking feelings also typify this draft. Karin was finally ad-libbing instead of composing by way of the monitor, and the main thing this passage needed was proofreading for comma flaws.

Group interactions informed Karin's work in other ways. Hearing others' writing in group helped her find topics, and soon, Linda said, Karin seemed more comfortable getting groupmates' response. As reliance on tacit knowledge grew, her drafts grew more nearly correct, at least where global or acquired features (like idioms, articles, prepositions, and the like) were concerned. Drawing on the textbook knowledge of grammar and mechanics that the memorized essay had displayed, Karin began correcting errors while reading aloud to the group. Apparently she was learning to adjust the monitor, turning it down to find and develop ideas, then up again while focusing on various aspects of form.

Unlike Elena, Karin had little trouble applying the strategies Linda taught to papers assigned in 101. Once she became aware of the freewriting strategy, she experienced no further blocks and needed no further breakthrough to improve steadily the rest of the term.

Vinh: Seven Years a Refugee

Vinh was typical in that low test scores brought her to the WTC. Like many Vietnamese, she took to freewriting with ease, but for some time she hid from Linda her problems with English 100, a 101-alternative for nonnative speakers. Though she felt no resistance to Linda's workshop approach, Vinh became blocked repeatedly in her English class. The contrast between her writing for that class and her work in the WTC group can be seen in the two excerpts that follow, both written during the week of November 17. Vinh asked Linda's group for help with the first, a paragraph-writing exercise for her English 100 teacher. Though she'd followed instructions and had copied the topic sentence from the assignment, she didn't feel she'd been successful:

> Why does the president of the U.S. prefers the Senate and the House to belong to the same political party with him. It's just that the president would gain more favor from his party members without much confusions and disputations. Otherwise it will be a disaster of confusions in governing for the president with so much different ideas from other parties.

The second piece, written more freely about her mother's death, is representative of Vinh's style for self-assigned narratives. It illustrates how grammar and clarity improved when students who could write what they wished selected topics they knew well and forms they were comfortable with:

> I just could not sleep because of the old air and the weakening sunlight rays that sneaked into the room through the window's blind. I sat up in my bed and hugged my pillow. I suddenly felt so lonely and tears started to roll from my eyes to say "hello" to the morning.

The contrast between the two excerpts is vivid. The teacher-assigned passage was confusing, garbled, hard to follow. Global lapses muddled its intended meaning, and Vinh misused verb forms, prepositions, and some mass/count nouns. Even in the copied question, she forgot the question mark, and a verb agreement error mysteriously appeared.

On the self-assigned topic, by contrast, without prescribed constraints, Vinh's writing became straightforward, descriptive, and involved. Except for a distributional "error" common among native writers (using the -*s* possessive before an inanimate noun), syntactic and inflectional problems disappeared. Articles and prepositions were correctly chosen and placed—though these are difficult features for nonnative speakers. And although Vinh's diction (*just* and *so*) reflected an adolescent speaking style, sophisticated sensory and kinesthetic details were plentiful: Sunlight rays sneaking into a room and tears saying "Hello" to morning conjured up vivid pictures in her groupmates' minds. Linda's data contributed to Team 1's hypothesis that struggling with unfamiliar topics and forms assigned by teachers before they became confident writing their own ideas could prevent both basic and ESL writers from functioning at the grammatical levels they were capable of.

Like Karin, however, Vinh quickly turned her writing around. Succeeding at something many professional writers struggle to do—making a point by showing rather than by telling—she tasted her potential on this impromptu piece. Though Vinh only once referred directly to her feelings, sorrow at her mother's death permeated the piece, evoking groupmates' empathy with skillfully chosen details.

Linda watched Vinh's progress carefully that semester. Vinh took a while to become aware of her potential, in part because of the harsh written comments and poor grades she received in English. In her candid but accepting group, however, Vinh learned to separate and sequence writing tasks, turning down censor and monitor to find topics and develop ideas, then turning them back up to prepare her writing for public view. Writing on familiar topics built her confidence, and later, when other structured, academic assignments came along, she was able to attack them successfully. By that time Vinh was aware that she could write well, for her groupmates had frequently told her so, supporting their opinions with comments on what they liked in her writing and validating its potential with suggestions for improvement.

Of course Vinh needed to learn to write structurally tight paragraphs on politics and government in response to professors' demands. But before she could write fluently about her own ideas, formulaic paragraphs on government proved an unrealistic demand. Years of unmotivated practice with just such assignments had convinced Vinh and her teachers that her writing was deficient. But a few weeks of writing on topics and in genres of her choosing confirmed that if Vinh took risks and worked hard, her writing would quickly improve.

Chat: A Newcomer with Limited English Proficiency (LEP)

Unlike most Center students, Chat's speech was limited, his oral abilities falling far below the mean. In other ways, however, he followed a typical Center pattern: Like Karin and Vinh, he showed little resistance to Linda's approach, and once he entered the sanctuary, his writing quickly improved. Chat joined his group late, around the middle of fall semester, just two months after arriving with his diplomat family from Thailand. Because she could find no record of TSWE or SAT scores, and because his spoken English was extremely weak, Linda believed (but could not confirm) he'd been accepted by mistake. Referred by his English teacher, who called his situation "desperate," Chat spoke haltingly, checking his dictionary even in conversation, and Linda noted that from the first he was "a real challenge." Chat's first attempted freewrite, on a topic he knew well, lacked almost entirely the rhythms of English prose:

> Suddenly, the boy who was about my age rode a bicycle across the street without looking at the traffic before. I collide not hard with the boy first and then his bicycle, but exactly he had to hurt because "body cover metal collide with metal cover body."

Though Chat zeroed in immediately on a topic he knew well, unfamiliar word order, agreement errors, and an awkward quotation left this passage difficult to understand. Asked for clarification by a fellow student, Chat described the accident clearly, so Linda suggested he jot down his spoken ideas and make an effort to add more details. She also asked about the quote, a direct translation from Thai. Chat was ready to redraft; an excerpt shows how he did.

> A bicycle which was covered by the boy and a car which covered me collide with each other. The boy must hurt more than me because my car hited (hit) him directly. On the other hand, I wasn't hited because my car protected me. The boy did not hit me but hit the car.

Despite limited vocabulary, Chat improved his unusual narrative. The language was still stilted, the use of *covered* unidiomatic, but the word order was now that of English. His inclusion of both *hited* and *hit* showed awareness of irregular past forms, but revealed that this feature was at best under partial control and that Chat's drafting process was not yet completely "free." Combining sentences from the first two drafts, Chat grew a bit more fluent in the third draft. In it he added details, continued correct subordination, and got rid of some unneeded redundancy:

> Suddenly, the boy who was about my age rode a bicycle across the street without looking at the traffic before. the bicycle which was covered by the boy and a car which covered me collide with each other. The boy must be hurt more than me truely because my car hit him directly. On the other hand, I wasn't hit because my car protected me.

Retaining the corrected past form, Chat extended the correction to a second instance of the verb. And though he dropped one capital letter, their otherwise correct use showed this to be a regression error he could catch while editing.

Submitting this piece to his English teacher, Chat earned "No Credit" for the paper and later earned "No Credit" for the English 100 course. (The 100-level courses were unique in the university in that they were graded *A*, *B*, *C*, or No Credit rather than *A*, *B*, *C*, *D*, or *F*. Aware of the growth patterns of writing abilities, which require time and practice to develop, English Department faculty had felt it unfair to give *D*'s and *F*'s to students who had worked hard just because they'd not reached the level of competence needed to get credit for required English courses.) Retaking the course in the spring, however, Chat voluntarily attended another WTC group, so Linda was able to follow his progress for a second term. (Because he had no SAT and TSWE records, the computer failed once again to flag his registration file, so he was not officially required to attend WTC.) From a freewrite begun in his second group Chat developed a formal paper for his English class, writing drafts at home but bringing them in for group response. Unlike Elena, he experienced no resistance and from the beginning could adjust his monitor at will, even though he'd never before been taught that strategy.

Chat revised repeatedly, then edited his paper till flawless, and the next four excerpts illustrate that process. First he explored a topic he knew well:

> I don't know when chopsticks has been using in Thailand. Certainly They are used by many people for a long long time. Using chopsticks is not too difficult. You use only four fingers to grape the chopsticks. If you try to use only two or three times you will get use to it.

A second revision, done voluntarily at home, achieved a more formal tone by shifting to the third person and deleting repetition of the word *long*. Chat corrected passive and agreement errors and added a new idea he would later elaborate. Though short, this section was flawless:

> Chopsticks have been used in Thailand for a long time. Everyone who uses chopsticks has his own style. There is no right or wrong way to use them.

Once he had a focus, Chat developed his ideas, inserting a definition and historical detail to produce a formal introduction and gradually shifting his diction toward a more distanced tone:

> Chopsticks have been used in Thailand for many years. The technique of using chopsticks is passed down from generation to generation. According to Longman dictionary of contemporary English "Chopsticks is either a pair of narrow sticks held between the thumb and fingers and used in East Asian countries for lifting food to the mouth." The use of chopsticks in Thailand came from Chinese immigrants who came to Thailand a century ago.

Finally, because of the agreement error, Linda suggested rechecking the definition (despite Chat's insistence that he already had) and mentioned that book titles are usually underlined. Notice in the following excerpts from his final draft a second correct passive and precise vocabulary—terms for fingers which Chat learned during discussions in group:

EXCERPT I

From the Introductory Paragraph

Chopsticks have been used in Thailand for many years. The technique of using chopsticks is passed down from generation to generation. According to the *Longman Dictionary of Contemporary English*, chopsticks are "either of a pair of narrow sticks held between the thumb and fingers and used for lifting food to the mouth." The use of chopsticks in Thailand came from Chinese immigrants who came to Thailand a century ago.

Correcting the definition in the introduction, Chat sketched the history of chopsticks and materials for making them. In the excerpt from the midsection he used himself as an example to describe clearly, precisely, correctly, and with a confident voice the process of using chopsticks.

EXCERPT II

From the Midsection of the Essay

Let me tell you how I hold chopsticks. I use four fingers to hold them. I hold one chopstick with my index and middle fingers. The other one I rest on my ring finger. And I press my finger on this chopstick because I want it to be stationary at all times.

Without using a formula for a definition or process essay, without even being told he needed an introduction, Chat crafted into this essay these formal features and more. Choosing a subject he knew well, he fleshed it out, organized it, and edited it effectively—*after* considering a range of suggestions from his group. Despite limited vocabulary and syntactic repertoire, Chat produced an engaging and almost flawless formal essay, which he later handed in to his English teacher. Chat was bridging the gap between personal and academic writing: That semester he made *A*'s in English 100 class.

The bigger they are, the harder they fall Team 4 would call this pattern—in which the weakest students showed greatest improvement. And the pattern fit large numbers of students like Chat who, though they entered with seemingly "hopeless deficiencies," could within a semester or two compete successfully in classes with students who'd never needed the WTC. This finding was confirmed in an early interview with a colleague, an applied linguist who directed the TESL certificate program and coordinated the English 100 course, a 101 substitute (with four class hours instead of three).

MARIE: I'm trying to evaluate the WTC and its effects on students in writing classrooms so we can improve the program this coming year, and I remember something you said to me once. Would you talk about [its impact on English 100 (Composition for Foreign Students)] a little?

LINGUIST: The WTC has made quantitative quality differences in the writing proficiency of my students. It's just a wonderful resource

> because previously you would have a class of students, some of
> whom you were pretty sure were not going to pass the class. You
> could just sort of tell by their first couple of months' writing that
> it was impossible to take them where they needed to go in a
> semester's time. They were going to get "No Credit" [for a
> grade] and have to take it over again.
>
> Now, what I've noticed is—and I haven't documented this, it's
> an intuitive account—that if you put them in the WTC, that will
> do it. That will bring them up to a level that we [feel is adequate].
> I now try to get my worst students into the WTC and I find they
> do well in the course and get a passing grade. Sometimes they
> even turn out writing that is better than the students who didn't
> have large problems during the first couple of weeks, so the WTC
> clearly has a beneficial effect on their writing.
>
> I would like to have some way of getting the English 100 stu-
> dents into the WTC in a more systematic way. If my students
> who need the WTC can go to the WTC, it reduces my work
> enormously.
>
> —Research Interview, Fall 1982

My colleague offered no numbers to support his intuitions, so I checked
the registrar's database to determine just how well Center students were
doing. That term, of those Center students also enrolled in English 100, 4
percent got no credit and 4 percent withdrew. Sixteen percent made *A*'s, 52
percent got *B*'s, and 24 percent received *C*'s for the term. We were still
inexperienced and our program as yet unrefined, but the record set by Year 1
students wasn't bad, given the high rates of failure in the English 100 course.

Two years later, interviewed by Taejung Welsh (1988), whose doctoral
research was done in the WTC, the linguist had not changed his view:

> I send my lowest-level students to the WTC and they turn out to be among
> the better writers, not only passing the course but among the highest group
> in class.

Year 2 tutors would back away from working with English assignments
because they found students who worked for grades grew less independent.
Despite this fact, Linda's Year 1 data show students succeeding, both those
who adapted quickly and those who resisted at first. While the dependent
Elena resisted taking charge of her work, saying that wasn't what other
professors expected her to do, Karin, Vinh, and Chat grew fluent choosing
their own topics, genres, and organizational patterns. And that process made
their potential apparent to them, stirred latent motivations, convinced them
to work hard, and rewarded them with improvement they themselves could
see. At a workshop Linda and I gave for ESL teachers in Virginia, long before
either of us recognized the spiral progression, Linda noted the role of awareness breakthroughs in the development students were going through:

It's like learning to talk. Once a person recognizes her ability, there's no end to the process. I remember when my own daughter began to speak. She voiced her opinions on just about everything—whether they were sound or not—and we encouraged her to. At the same time, of course, we let her know where the gaps in her logic were.

Five years later, Daniela Hoefer used similar language to describe the effects of awareness breakthroughs on students who came for help with writing to the Writing Corner, Central Atlantic's other, appointment-based writing center: "Once a student has the attitude that she can learn to write and wants to learn, there is no limit to what she can do, and I'll be here every step of the way to help and encourage."

Resistance and Breakthrough Students

Writing improvement fell between one of two extremes. It varied from successions of small, incremental insights that led to the steady progress of a Karin, a Vinh, or a Chat to dramatic attitude reversals that led to the sudden activity and improvement of resistant students. "Breakthrough students" we called those writers, like George and Farooq, who improved in sudden and unexpected ways, causing "small conflagrations" by "igniting on the page." Many tutors noted that breakthroughs followed resistance, and in her research report Kim White described a "wall" that, until students "broke through" it, blocked development. Kim included a diagram of patterns in her data (see Figure 5–2) with the following revised hypothesis:

Perhaps there is a wall that must be broken through, or another sort of barrier, and students can achieve more by concentrated bursts of writing than with constant half pages. This is what, today, I am examining.

Kim's diagram confirms the tacit acknowledgment by five research teams (as seen in class discussion and in written work) that breakthroughs were discontinuous from other events on students' upward spirals. This difference is consistent with our emergent theory that awareness functions as the initiator of change, shifting the angle and/or direction of movement taking place. Immediately before "igniting on the page," students like Farooq and Mike "broke through" internal "walls" of resistance when they saw what group-mates (Tai and Farooq respectively) had done.

In other words, "breaking through" is the point on a learning curve at which a new writing insight, large or small, first fuels motivation and affects effort, thereby increasing success. Even the less dramatic breakthroughs of less-resistant students—and those of breakthrough students who'd had earlier "conflagrations"—can be explained if we view the awareness/attitude/behavior/writing/rewards progression as a spiral we can observe from any angle

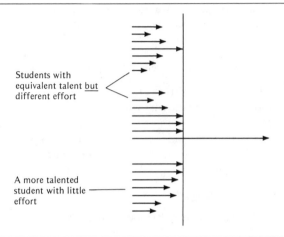

Students with
equivalent talent <u>but</u>
different effort

A more talented
student with little
effort

Figure 5-2   **Kim White's Diagram of Her Hypothesis about the Relationship of Effort to Breaking through the Wall**

(or point in time). The spiral also explains less dramatic changes common among cooperative students who entered the Center somewhat more aware.

Team 1 saw many breakthroughs and frequently used that term, but they made no connection between breakthroughs and resistance. Neither Linda Blair nor I knew it at the time, but the wall of resistance Elena erected to Linda's approach made her a very likely breakthrough candidate.

Blocking and the Influence
of Conflicts among Teaching Approaches

Like those of many Asian students, Chat's problems occurred despite his considerable knowledge of grammar and mechanics and his years of practice composing in English by way of the monitor. Elena's problems seemed to persist despite a different strength—the fluent (if not always quite correct) oral language she'd picked up. (Remember, for example, that Kamal refers to her as the "Spanish lady" from whom he learned not to monitor his speech when talking in English; see page 62.) In Krashen's (1978) terms, Chat's strengths were largely *learned* (that is, studied in school), while Elena's seemed to be for the most part *acquired* (picked up in use). Making a similar distinction, Vygotsky (1962) would probably have seen these as differences between *scientifically* and *spontaneously* developed concepts. Despite the limitations they must have suffered as a result of having most of their knowledge in one knowledge category or the other, both students' work was stunted less by this imbalance than by lack of balance in know-how (composing strategies).

At entry, for want of another approach, both relied on the monitor, and despite contrasting configurations of weakness and strength, the path to success was therefore similar for both. Elena and Chat had to learn to balance writing strategies, to separate and sequence subsets of complex writing tasks, and to use the monitor to apply rules they'd studied *after* tapping whatever oral English they'd acquired.

Karin, Vinh, and Chat illustrate a more common pattern—expressing little resistance and developing gradually. With obvious relief they gave up monitoring on first drafts, looked for topics they liked, and—relying on language intuitions—drafted whatever topics they liked in whatever genres they pleased. Elena, by contrast, stalled quickly, spinning into a downward spiral because she did not trust the workshop method Linda used. Her resistance, we found, resulted from the conflict—or rather, the *perceived* conflict—between Linda's workshop approach and that of Elena's 101 teacher. Fortunately, Linda did not act threatened by Elena's resistance. Instead, she encouraged Elena to talk and write about the problem. Once Linda understood, she adapted her teaching accordingly, at which point Elena "broke through the wall" and reverted to the norm—the upward spiral of increasing motivation and success.

In fact, this conflict in approach was largely in Elena's mind—though that didn't make its impact any less real. Elena's professor empathized with beginning writers and had a reputation for spotting potential in students' work. She has even been credited by a successful novelist (one twice nominated for the PEN/Faulkner award) with years ago providing the encouragement that convinced him to become a writer.

We cannot know what might have happened if Elena's resistance had threatened Linda more than it did (or if Linda had not had support for process-based teaching). But in the sanctuary, Elena's conflict surfaced, so Linda could help her work through her anxiety. Elena's attitude breakthrough was a long time in coming, however, and her situation got worse before it improved. Though she'd been feeling better about her writing in the Center, Elena felt "lousy" about her first paper for 101, an assigned response to William Stafford's essay on the process of writing. The professor gave her "no credit," wrote "rewrite" on the essay, and suggested Elena get help in the Center "as soon as possible." Because Elena was already attending the WTC, the note undermined her confidence in Linda and the group. Soon Elena was completely blocked, even in the group, for anxiety about what her English teacher expected kept her from applying the new writing strategies she'd learned. This excerpt from her three-page piece on the Stafford essay attempts to work through an issue the tutors and I were also grappling with:

> Are writers born or created? As the predisposition for writing is inborn with, a writer has to be created or educated through life. Writers are normal people withe the capacity of transforming words into writen language. Anyone can writte, but are few the ones that can express ideas clearly. the difference between people who write and writers, it's writing itself.

"Where should I start?" wondered Linda. "Spelling? Idiom? Syntax?" These seemed superficial compared to Elena's jumbled ideas. The first clause of the second sentence was barely comprehensible, and the second contradicted what little was clear from the first. Linda finally decided Elena needed to get back to basics—to get logic and organization right before focusing on surface-level problems, particularly in passages she might later rewrite or discard. Linda therefore began by saying, "Try freewriting about the assignment" to help Elena discover the deep structure of her ideas without worrying (in this draft) about surface-level mistakes. But though Elena had written gladly and fluently on her own topics, on this formal 101 essay she refused to try. She knew what her professor wanted, she said, and freewriting was not it!

The more this student struggled dependently to please her English teacher, the more anxious and blocked the perceived conflict between what she saw as two conflicting paradigms made her feel. This seeming catch-22 undermined her faith in both approaches: She didn't rewrite the 101 paper and she also stopped writing in group. It had been at this point, in fact—while feeling doubly vulnerable—that Elena had written the comment that bothered Linda so much:

> Since English class writing deals with not only ideas in paper, but also in sentence construction, vocabulary, techniques, etc. this tutorial class in that sense don't help much.

Elena did not realize how mistaken she was. Soon she was three papers behind for English 101 and could not freewrite at all, though her first WTC freewriting had been this nearly correct piece:

> Finally I am where I'm supposed to be. After twelve years of education I have to continue studying for a future, wherever it means. I don't even know what career I'm going to choose, but there is no other choice but being in a university.

Fortunately, Linda did not act defensive, for she trusted me to back her approach. She therefore sought support for Elena from members of the group and shared a similar problem she herself had had in a graduate course, where a professor had threatened her confidence by making harsh comments about her writing style. Linda told Elena's group about reading drafts to Team 1 at lunchtime to get ideas for improving her paper and to reduce anxiety.

Finally, events coincided to reduce the pressure Elena felt. At Linda's urging she talked to her 101 professor, an understanding woman who said Elena could pass if she turned in all assignments by the end of the term. Linda kept encouraging Elena to thinkwrite, reminding her she needn't show thinkwriting to the teacher and saying this process might give her ideas for revising the orginal draft. At last Elena tried again:

> I have mixed feelings in my response to Stafford. He is persuasive and is convincing me, but I also disagree with him. He expresses himself clearly

and some of his ideas are wise. But some of his opinions make me mad. He says how freely writing comes, and here I am having pain while writing this paper.

Through the process of freewriting Elena broke through the wall of resistance, and what resulted was honest and convincing. It was also "correct" and structurally sound. Intuitively attempting a slightly more formal style, Elena produced a classic thesis statement in the first sentence, established a framework for comparison and contrast in the next, and marshaled evidence for her thesis in the rest of the paragraph. These features revealed considerable tacit knowledge of logic and structure and confirmed Elena's ability to critique the Stafford piece. All she needed was to elaborate and support her ideas to produce a quality essay for English 101.

This was not the first time writing about a block had freed a stymied writer to draft in a clear, straightforward way. Apparently—as with Karin, Chat, and Vinh—Elena's problems with logic and structure resulted less from "deficiencies" than from misconceptions about how writers work. For when Elena stumbled, while drafting, onto a complex idea, she also came up with a framework for organizing her thoughts. Perhaps reading had informed her structural intuitions at the paragraph and text levels. Perhaps this form grew organically from the logic of her ideas. At any rate, her paragraph showed traces of complex thinking, and Elena experienced a breakthrough in her undeveloped critique of the essay her 101 teacher assigned.

A history of preventive/corrective teaching and first-draft evaluation apparently led Elena to depend on the monitor while drafting, then panic and depend on Linda when the monitor failed. To encourage more independence (a risk requiring extra support), Linda agreed to read 101 drafts after group meetings but insisted Elena draft and revise them at home, reserving her time in the Center for self-assigned writing tasks. In their brief postgroup sessions, Elena read drafts aloud, asking for comments and questions, just as she did in group.

Less resistant after writing about her anxiety, Elena tried another draft of the essay on Stafford. This one showed some signs of growing independence and an emerging awareness of the centrality of ideas:

> There is freedom when writing. Thoughts flows and can be materialized when they are put into written words. No one tells me what I write is wrong, because my ideas are my own and are my righth. When I present a paper its full with my thoughts and ideas, and is also clearly expressed in written language; there are people not channeled to my flow of insights.

This excerpt contained regression errors—like spelling and agreement problems—that Elena would detect later, during editing. She'd also misused a preposition, forgotten to check punctuation, and failed to make clear the relationship between the paragraph and its last sentence. In addition, she had used *its* for *it's*, a mistake she made often. In her struggle with Stafford's unfamiliar ideas, surface structure deteriorated (compared to Elena's self-sponsored writing of the same period). On the other hand, the content of this piece improved, for in arguing her point, she tapped her strong response to Stafford and with it the motivation to keep trying until her point was clear. Linda, a bit more confident now, pointed out these strengths, focusing on the potential Elena could develop in subsequent drafts.

Viewing attention lapses as a source of regression error demystified some discrepancies between oral and written language and explained how "hidden skills," somehow forgotten while drafting, could suddenly be available for revising and editing. In short, this ebb and flow pattern of regression and growth convinced us to upgrade our estimate of basic writers' potential. Instead of marking deficiencies, we were forced to conclude, these lapses signaled the growing edges of competence. And students apparently recognized this too, for they changed their ways of dealing with such errors, quickly developed confidence, and began to work hard.

Meanwhile, Elena tried another revision:

> My response when I readed Stafford essay on writing have a lot of mixed feeling. He is persuasive and is convincing me, but there are points where I also disagree with him. He expresses himself clearly and some of his points are wise. But some of his opinions make me mad. Stafford talks about how freely writing comes, and here I am having pain while writing this paper.

Once again showing a decrease in correctness, apparently because unfamiliar tasks distracted Elena's attention, this latest draft illustrates a different kinds of regression. In an earlier draft, surface structure had regressed when Elena turned down the monitor to freewrite on a school topic. In this passage, by contrast, her correct thesis statement ("I have mixed feelings in my response to Stafford") deteriorated when she turned the monitor back *up* to revise.

Elena was not the only student whose first attempts at revising made her writing worse instead of improving it. Unaware of their strengths and inexperienced at critiquing their work, many students systematically revised the best parts out, carefully cutting all passages on which they had taken some risk. This problem was most common early in the term, before the groups had much practice identifying strengths, before they'd built common repertoires of useful writing techniques, before they'd seen how taking risks stretches expertise, before critical distance had developed in the interdependent groups. Perhaps lack of exposure to good student writing also contributed to counterproductive revising, for entering students compared their work (much as past teachers had done?) to published, professional models with which few could at that point compete. At any rate, many cut or altered their best prose, and only after getting groupmates' responses to many drafts did they develop a feel for the kinds of revisions live readers approve.

Elena's early revising was not all bad, however, though her thesis statement had regressed, and Linda made a point of noting improvements in the piece.

Except for a missing comma, the end of the paragraph was fine, and this draft contained crossouts, insertions, and other marks suggesting she had tried several unfamiliar revising strategies. In a page and a half, Elena had (1) made eight diction substitutions, (2) inserted a missing article, (3) marked two sentences with "rewrite," and (4) corrected irregular past forms (changing *throw* to *threw* and *have* to *had*). Linda showed these markings proudly to the group, rewarding Elena's efforts (even unsuccessful ones) while soliciting supportive but honest comment on the changes.

Next Elena wrote a ninth and near-final draft—a not uncommon number for students who take charge of their learning. This draft showed further evidence of self-sponsored revising. In it Elena (5) used arrows to reorganize, (6) corrected two of the regression errors in her thesis statement, and (7) added more details. By using the third person ("one") she also (8) shifted to a more formal tone. Her new first paragraph looked like this:

> My response while I was reading Stafford essay on writing have a lot of mixed feelings. He is persuasive and convincing, but there are points where I also disagree with him. He expressed himself clearly, and some of his ideas are wise. But some of his opinions make me mad. Stafford talks about how freely writing comes, and here I am having pain while writing. What I can not understand is how an essay on writing, and how to accomplish it, could leave one in a situation like this.

This revision makes sense, flows fairly smoothly, and focuses on Elena's concern—the difference between her experience and that of a famous writer. Linda therefore judged the revisions successful and, to develop Elena's critical distance on the revising she did, arranged for her to continue getting responses to her drafts. As researchers, however, we evaluated our work not only in terms of our own teaching intuitions but by external criteria. For example, we tested our students' progress against the Center's mandate from the faculty senate—to prepare basic and ESL writers for academic assignments. Students' grades in other classes also helped Team 1 judge their success, and this essay, which earned a C– (though the final draft still had errors), confirmed that Linda hadn't threatened Elena's success by emphasizing practice and process in addition to rules.

In fact, we found that when students adopted a strong, personal voice, included firsthand examples, developed their own ideas, and let live audiences help them shape their essays, the grades they got often improved *before their editing did*. This passing grade, which Linda said was "gold to Elena," was also "all Elena needed to spur her writing on." In fact, by validating Linda's and the group's responses, the grade reinforced the risks Elena had taken while revising, securing a still-tentative upward spiral of increased motivation and success.

Meanwhile, as Elena revised the 101 essay at home, self-selected writing done in the Center grew fluid and vivid. A strong voice was emerging. So were concrete details. And, though verb sequence remained inconsistent, all *attempted* past tense endings were correct in the following excerpts from freely written drafts:

> Well, whenever I go to a small town I not only feel people watching me I also heard talking about me. . . .

> The thing I hated the most was at night after returning from being with friends, I had to give my nightly report. It is a complete invasion of my life. . . .

> I try to recall all the sensations I felt during the different times I went to the country, forest and mountains. My heart is pumping faster as I walk and the weight of the pack seems to disappear. My throat is dry as I feel the sweat from my forehead dripping in my face.

> I got interested in the idea of writing about superstition. I don't believe in any superstition except for the believe that mondays and fridays are hazard to my health. I don't have any amulets for good luck, I just try to use the same pen or pencil when taking test, so it gives me some confidence.

As Elena grew more confident with teacher-assigned topics, her behavior in group (and in English class) grew proactively independent. In addition to finding topics she wanted to write about, she began to catch misspellings, to add or delete omitted or redundant words on her own, and to ask for suggestions while reading aloud in group. Elena revised most papers six or seven times and began adding past tense endings even *while drafting new text*, a change that suggests this feature was gradually coming under automatic control. Under Linda's guidance, she made a checklist of problems for use when editing. She also kept a list of prepositions before her, read aloud to a sister for help with tenses, doublechecked *its* and *it's* to avoid a continuing mistake, and kept a dictionary handy as she wrote. And, as these strategies served her academic writing well, Elena not only *felt* confident, she also made better grades.

Mechanics remained imperfect in Elena's writing, and foreign-sounding rhythms sometimes interrupted English ones, but Elena's confidence grew steadily. She finished all back assignments by the end of the term and told Linda she no longer feared reading drafts aloud in English 101, though she'd once felt inadequate in this class of native speakers. Elena found she could meet other professors' expectations for writing, even on in-class assignments offering little time to revise. And in Elena's folder Linda found an outline (complete with thesis, three topic sentences, and jot lists of supporting details) for a five-paragraph essay written, successfully, on her own.

Though she'd once seen no connection between the two, Elena was now using writing strategies picked up in group with writing assigned across the curriculum. Better grades also confirmed her new-found independence. Not only did she earn a *C* in English 101 that fall, in the spring Elena returned to the Center as a volunteer and that semester earned a *B* in English 102. Her

commitment to writing was also growing: She enjoyed writing about literature in 102 so much, she told Linda, that she'd registered for extra literature
courses as electives for the following fall. In short, Elena typified breakthrough students by investing in writing far more than was required.

Confidence, independence, and increased commitment almost always accompanied writing improvement, and upward (and/or downward) spirals
were virtually universal. Despite these patterns, however, each student's progress had a unique rhythm, for anxiety, motivation, and timing were individual. Elena's initial writing block had been instruction induced, but once she
and Linda discovered its roots, it disappeared. At the point of awareness, it
seems, Elena broke through her resistance and reverted to the other, more
typical Center pattern in which increasingly positive attitudes motivated
writing behavior that in turn led steadily to improvement and other writing
rewards.

"The bigger they are, the harder they fall," Team 4 would conclude, and
Linda's Year 1 case study shows Elena fitting this pattern. Once Elena became
aware of potential in herself and in her tutor's approach, she abandoned all
resistance, quickly began to improve, and grew even more committed than
Karin, Chat, or Vinh—the three less-resistant writers whose progress Linda
traced. In short, Linda's Year 1 case studies confirm the upward spiral almost
all basic and ESL writers went through in the sanctuary of the small writing-
workshop groups.

Regression, Risk Taking, Sanctuary, and Vulnerability

Whenever students accepted new writing challenges, features of their writing that formerly were controlled might regress while attention focused on
unfamiliar aspects of the task. Patterns of regression shifted forward with
practice, however, as students first made the new familiar, then gradually
made the newly familiar entirely their own. We therefore began to view
regression as a good, not a bad thing, as a facilitator of, not an impediment to
growth. In fact, this two-steps-forward-one-step-back alternation of regression and growth was enough to convince us that, though students sometimes
made errors they had not made before, these were not caused, as we had at
first assumed, by lazy attitudes. More likely, these lapses occurred because
students' attention was distracted while they flexed unfamiliar muscles and
took what they saw as risks. In the long run, letting down their guard against
error while drafting paid off, for by practicing unfamiliar strategies, techniques, formats, and rules, students extended the boundaries of their writing
expertise. Gradually, by successive approximation, their writing began to read
like more accomplished prose.

This slow, bit by bit accretion of writing know-how and basic skills was but one compensation for regression errors. By defining where the borders of students' knowledge lay and identifying the features they had under partial control, regression errors taught students what they needed to work on next, thus helping them become independent of tutors in determining what they were ready to learn. In other words, regression patterns helped students (and tutors) focus instruction "at the point of need" (Britton et al., 1975), in "the zone of proximal development" (Vygotsky, 1978), at "the ideal instructional level" (Krashen, 1982).

With students' growing experience, their individual patterns of regression shifted. Regression patterns also varied from student to student, depending on which features and rules each had under partial control. Despite such variations in regression patterns themselves, however, the fear of regressing (of being seen as a "failure" or "fool") had conditioned almost all entering Center students to avoid the risk taking that learning to write demands.

Risks seemed always to be associated with growth, and sanctuary students accepted, even *relished*, risks, but the incidence of risk taking didn't decrease much with improvement. For though subskills could be mastered and written drafts improved, critical standards rose at least as fast as abilities, forcing students to face the potential for failure with each new challenge.

Instead, in the supportive atmosphere of the small workshop groups, the interpretation placed on risky behavior changed. Those who wrote with passion on topics they cared about, for example, seldom chose to abandon a piece until their ideas were clear, so they read it time and again to get suggestions for revision. They also noticed (and imitated) others' effects, borrowing from groupmates and professional writers alike. In other words, as upward spirals of increasing success swept through groups, students reached for levels of competence just beyond their grasp, maintaining in the process a fairly high level of risk.

Even though the level of risk remained high, however, the meanings students attached to "risky" writing behavior changed. For example, on seeing the role risk taking played in others' improvement, those who'd seen risks as self-defeating in other contexts began to act as though risks were a route to mastery—or at least a certain way to earn prestige. Risk taking now exuded an aura less of fear than of challenge, and repeated risk taking earned students a status not unlike that awarded athletes, politicians, artists, and entrepreneurs—people in other fields where disciplined risk taking is required.

By midterm the highest compliment writers in most groups could earn was a thoughtful moment of silence followed by "That took guts." It wasn't surprising, when we thought about it, for fearless behavior is highly valued in young adults. Just as people of college age want to make their own mistakes in life, bold experimentation became the norm in the WTC. It was this youthful willingness to learn by trial and error that interrupted the downward spirals evaluation fueled and initiated upward spirals in their place. And fortunately, as consciously protected risk taking rose, student writing approximated increasingly complex models. For growing feelings of competence and increased peer prestige, which included both friendship and respect, had boosted WTC writers' aspirations, causing them to compete with themselves by motivating the search for new and still more exciting ways to improve their work. These changes became possible once they understood that regression indicated potential for increased success.

Recognizing regression patterns not only helped students write better, it helped us teach better by showing us what was strong in our program and highlighting weaknesses. Spirals made clear, for example, the role of subtractive grading (counting off for first-draft mistakes, using the threat of failure to motivate hard work) in keeping basic writers "frustrated and demoralized," thus almost ensuring their achievement would be low. Conversely, once we made them explicit, we could see that upward spirals co-occurred with risk taking, which confirmed that a sanctuary atmosphere was critical. While downward spirals co-occurred with evaluation anxiety, risk taker's upward spirals validated the time tutors had invested in making risk taking safe. They had done this in a number of ways:

- Maintaining a sanctuary atmosphere by removing any student who attacked or made light of other students or of their work
- Shifting responses from an evaluatory to a problem-solving mode
- Letting students choose which writing problems to work on next by letting them choose both (a) What to write and (b) What kinds of response to seek
- Emphasizing potential rather than failure
- Pointing out strengths—in awareness, attitude, behavior, or writing—*before* calling attention to weaknesses
- Expressing evaluation as helpful suggestions, not criticism
- Showing students that similar problems occur in all kinds of writing and plague all writers, regardless of expertise
- Tempting students with a diverse array of writing rewards
- Offering only intrinsic rewards and penalties
- Giving attention or praise for moves in *potentially* productive directions, even if the immediate result was not improvement
- Eliminating penalties for risk taking that fails
- Letting natural penalties for not improving take effect

These patterns confirm the second part of the shift in tutors' teaching. Chapter 2 emphasized how tutors backed away from preventive/corrective instruction in structure (grammar, mechanics, paragraph, and essay formats) to teach rules and patterns in the context of students' rough drafts. This chapter shows tutors also avoiding prior instruction in "process writing" by teaching drafting, revising, and editing strategies sequentially, at the point of need. Growth-model assessment of tutors' teaching, which had the following components, made tutors' rapid development possible. Notice that what tutors needed to learn about effective teaching approaches parallels the conditions their students needed to learn to write:

1.   A laboratory setting in which to try out the methods they studied
2.   A sanctuary atmosphere in which they felt safe taking risks
3.   Specific, positive assessment of and feedback on strengths
4.   Suggestions for improvement by fellow learners at the point of need
5.   Consistent administrative support for trial-and-error teaching
6.   Summative evaluation withheld until the end of the term
7.   Incidental training, at the point of need, in a model of self-assessment (collaborative teacher-research) capable of informing tutors' decisions about their work

In less than a single term our collaborative research model convinced most tutors that students would be more successful with the workshop approach and made the tutors adept at providing settings in which students learned about the many aspects of writing simultaneously, through the whole-language approach of immersion in meaningful, writing *experience*.

Linda Blair's data were consistent with all of these patterns. Her case studies also foreshadowed a theory of writing breakthroughs that explained the sudden upward shifts in rate and degree of improvement that were the direct outgrowth of the risks Center students took. The case studies showed that breakthroughs need not be dramatic, one-shot events, that breakthrough patterns occurred in small increments as well as large, and that the mechanisms of learning were similar at all speeds. After all, total awareness of what good writing requires never arrives in a single insight, no matter how brilliant the flash. Breakthroughs large and small served instead as turning points after which students expanded new insights gradually. Smaller breakthroughs did not reverse spirals, they *refueled* them, intensifying the upward progressions students had begun by increasing the angles of their learning curves.

Conversely, however, the Elena data foreshadowed another pattern—that in contexts perceived as hostile or neutral to their success, students could regress back down spiral paths they had recently climbed. The sudden behavioral shifts of some returnees, for example, followed severe regressions in confidence and independence, backward slidings (caused by negative evaluation) down spiral paths these students had climbed with gusto the term before. In short, this chapter's data support two Chapter 2 conclusions—(1) that regression is not bad in and of itself and (2) that by using teacher-research to interpret regressions, beginning teachers can learn to increase support at the point of need. Chapter 6 develops our breakthrough theory more fully, showing how it emerged from and remains grounded in tutors' data and describing how we confirmed and refined it over time.

A Note on the Use of Teacher-Research and How It Empowered Tutors

Elegant grounded theories to account for anomalous cases do not emerge rapidly from qualitative data. This book, for example, took eight years of work by five teams of tutors and me, not to mention other teacher-researchers, interns, doctoral students, colleagues, and friends, who contributed in substantial ways. In other words, this kind of research is labor intensive. This project required many hundreds of hours from numbers of people.

It was the impact on our lives as professionals, I believe, that motivated and rewarded the work we contributed, and that impact goes far deeper than published findings. In fact, compared to the tacit knowledge we gleaned, this formal analysis (what we can put into words) is only the tip of the iceberg. By far the richer results of our study lie in the extent to which each of us developed complex understandings of students, of the settings in which they struggled, and of the complexities of writing and learning. Equally important to us as teachers, of course, were the confidence and independence we developed through the process of working together on this research. Just as students developed competence and independence even as they relied on each other during the interdependent stage, so were beginning tutors and I empowered professionally through the collective process of assessing our work. By shifting responsibility for evaluation from administrators to teachers themselves, teacher-research helped establish, for the tutors and for me, a supportive environment in which change was not threatening because we could change at our own pace, could evaluate our own results, and could help each other improve when results weren't entirely good.

Teacher-research taught us to hear and to trust our intuitions which it informed by close observation, reflection, and team problem solving. It taught us that our hunches were increasingly consistent with the best theory and research going on in our field. I saw teacher-research improve our work in many ways. It informed incidental responses to classroom events, and it increased our ability to plan the kinds of experiences from which writers grow. Close observation provided detailed and accurate information, making on-the-spot assessments more accurate and increasing our chances of responding appropriately. Though they were useful in day-to-day teaching, however, "hypotheses" that bubbled up during observation didn't become formal "findings" without extensive testing. The confirmatory stages (I use the plural, for there were many) included painstaking elaboration and repeated refinement brought about by constant comparisons with other students and groups. Through this cumulative and recursive process, our initial hunches—our framework's initially tentative "hypotheses"—were shaped into better and better predictors we could use when planning for and when responding to events.

Long before the analytic breakthrough, for example, intuitive recognition of cyclic patterns let new tutors predict end results of their work with great accuracy. As development and regression follow spiral patterns, close observation, for as little as a few weeks, helped even beginning tutors "predict" with some confidence how far students would likely progress *under current conditions* and determine what changes higher rates of success would require. Instead of making tutors' expectations more rigid or confining students to predetermined achievement levels, holistic prediction based on positive evaluation helped us intervene to help even weak students improve. Extrapolating from informed intuitions by projecting current patterns *hypothetically* onto the future, tutors assessed which students would need support of various kinds and intervened to give it, *before* it was too late.

Tutors' logs contain scores of these intuitive predictions—often parading as hunches, relief, speculation, or worry—about student writing development and how to facilitate it. During Year 1 I had been a bit awed by the rapidity of TAs' development as compared with that of the preservice teachers I'd worked with before. I suspected I must have received an outstanding group. In the years that followed, however, my involvement in TA screening, selection, and placement convinced me that though many assistantship applicants were strong, it was less special ability than open-mindedness informed by teacher-research that accounted for the effective teaching TAs did—and for their commitment and professional self-esteem. After all, most TAs had no prior background in education. What they learned in a single semester *demanded* an open mind.

For eight years now I've tracked TAs' developing intuitions—through their writing, conversation, and classroom behavior—and my own intuitions have been informed by studying theirs. I think this holistic process must be like a cloze procedure, with intuitions developing as a result of our human ability to recognize gestalts. After watching a student swing through a couple of turns, most WTC tutors could, without conscious calculation, recognize a spiral, spot its upward or downward direction, and estimate its angle (that is, its rate) of change. Factoring in other variables (like the level of expertise available in the group or other obligations—sports, jobs, family—competing for a student's time), tutors made intuitive but highly accurate estimates of how far, given unchanged conditions, students or groups could progress, assessed what they could change to increase the equation's final term, and intervened quickly, before time for improvement ran out.

Though comments in logs were typically informal and tentative, almost never being phrased (or intended) as formal predictions, tacit recognition of upward and downward patterns coupled with informal estimates of the angles of learning curves helped beginning tutors judge how much help Center students needed. The validity of their judgments was repeatedly confirmed by our rigorous and collaborative certification procedures. Working in pairs, tutors reviewed all drafts in portfolios, referring to logs to refresh their memories of student behavior and attitudes and, in borderline cases, conferring with me before deciding which students were or were not ready to be certified.

Having spent several years working with preservice teachers in the past, I was startled to discover the predictive power granted by thoughtful teacher-research to the TAs and to me. And though I do not refer to formal, statistical prediction, I would pit any Center team against the best tests available and expect the team to offer more accurate assessments of which students are able to learn, of how well they will do, and of what help they need. The degree to which early teams' hunches foreshadowed later analyses confirms the face validity of the conclusion that first-semester tutor-researchers (and I include teaching interns, who did *not* take the seminar) assessed with uncanny accuracy how their students were doing and what help they needed next.

In a single semester, teacher-research made it possible *and appropriate* for tutors to take responsibility often assumed at the college level but rarely allowed in schools—even though certified teachers have far more training in how to teach. Teacher-research empowered the Center's beginning tutors to adopt roles many schools relegate only to highly paid experts—testing agencies, curriculum planners, and textbook writers. In the WTC, tutors wrote curriculum, planned and sequenced instruction, did formative and summative evaluation, and assessed and monitored their own progress as well. They not only did these with a great deal of success, in the the process they developed a strong sense of competence, confidence, autonomy, and professional self-esteem. Given current efforts to reform public schools and restructure teacher education, I believe the small-group collaborative model of teacher-research offers great potential for change at other levels as well.

6

Putting the Magic Together:
The Breakthrough Phenomenon

As we have seen, risk taking proved central to development and led to progress for even the slowest writers. As students recognized this, their attitudes toward risk taking shifted from an inhibiting fear of failure, low grades, ridicule, and rejection to a tenacious desire to overcome obstacles and in the end to the exhilaration that facing challenges successfully brings. Kamal described the writer's high he experienced after his awareness breakthrough:

> I did not know that summer would make a difference in my life. Yet it did. It helped me to discover the hidden writing talent in me. The talent which I always thought does not exist. It makes me think differently. Its like magic. Before I knew it, things simply flips over and I couldn't help myself from being carried by rapids of spontaneous creativity flow like a raft being sailed down the river current.

Awareness arrived in different packaging and at different speeds, but even students' slightest misperceptions about writing marked potential points at which new insights could occur. Resistant students showed the most dramatic improvement, of course, so the "small conflagrations" they "ignited on the page" got a lot of press in tutors' logs and analyses. Nor did their breakthroughs go unnoticed by status-seeking peers. Afterward, motivation swept through listless groups like waves stirred up by a twister touching down on a placid sea. Group members picked up quickly on what breaking through entailed: courage, risk taking, and a valued payoff—writing good enough to make its creator feel happy and proud.

Helping Students Recognize
Their Own Breakthroughs When They Occurred

Though their groupmates rarely failed to notice breakthroughs, breakthrough writers themselves often failed to understand what they'd done, especially when they were the first in their groups to break through. Apparently these potentially motivating events were so unlike what students had come to expect in school that unless they'd observed other breakthroughs, many viewed their own as either neutral or negative. Misguided instruction about what good writing entails had taught students to avoid writing honestly, to assume that strong feelings during writing were a bad sign, to distrust the risk taking that makes success possible. In other words, being taught by people who were not writers themselves taught many students to distrust their linguistic intuitions. All it took to activate these intuitions, however, was the breakthrough awareness that it was not only safe but productive to rely on them.

In *Writing Down the Bones: Feeling the Writer Within*, poet Natalie Goldberg (1986) tells of seeing "peculiar phenomena" "time and time again" in writing groups:

> Someone will write something extraordinary and then have no idea about its quality. It doesn't matter how much I may rave about it or the other people in the group give positive feedback; the writer cannot connect with the fact that it is good writing. He doesn't deny it; he just sits there bewildered and later, through the grapevine, I hear that he never believed a word of what was said. It's been over years that I have observed this; it isn't just one downtrodden, insecure character in one writing group that has not been awake to his own good writing.

Goldberg's view is consistent with that of tutor-researchers. According to her:

> We have trouble connecting with our own confident writing voice that is inside all of us, and even when we do connect and write well, we don't claim it. I'm not saying that everyone is Shakespeare, but I am saying everyone has a genuine voice that can express his or her life with honest dignity and detail. There seems to be a gap between the greatness we are capable of and the way we see ourselves and, therefore, our work. (p. 154)

After watching basic writers squander potential breakthroughs because they were too naive about writing to recognize them, tutors learned that rewarding (with attention, exposure, and praise) both good writing and the behaviors that produce it helped basic writers recognize what they'd done. The following Year 3 data on Vietnamese student Loi (whose work was briefly noted in Chapter 3), show a breakthrough-in-progress (of which Loi seems unaware) guided skillfully to completion by a tutor's thoughtful response. These poignant excerpts describe Loi's breakthrough from two perspectives—that of Geri Madigan, graduate student in applied linguistics, just beginning an internship in the WTC, and that of Bonnie Martin, the tutor of Loi's group.

Recognizing potential by the power in Loi's writing, Geri, who spent her first few days in the Center observing and documenting student responses to Bonnie's teaching, noted Loi's strengths (length, power, detail, strong conclusion), then described behavioral changes preceding them. It was on this day that Loi's polite but persistent resistance gave way to the risky topic (that is, one he felt strongly about) that helped him break through to a new level of involvement:

> Feb. 23: [Bonnie read Loi's] story of life in Vietnam in '75 when the communists took over. What a powerful story! Really good concrete details:
> summer over
> first day of school
> classroom was not filled with happy, joyful people
> instead guile, and "we looked at each other with fear in our eyes"
> teacher asked us to join a Political group called "Young Communist Party"
> "use every minute we have to do something useful for them so we don't have any actions or ideas against them."
> The ending was fantastic!
> Day after day, these things made us feel like we lived with two persons inside us. One for them that always did and said good things about the Communist Government. The other was for our real life that never stopped wishing there would be some changes which made our lives look better in a brighter future. That is what I'm having now.
> We all exclaimed how good it was.

These powerful descriptive details alerted Loi's groupmates to a break-through Loi himself did not yet see the significance of. But attitude changes (increased pride and confidence) surfaced quickly once Loi's group alerted him to how much his piece had improved. Loi knew his freewritten revision flowed more freely; what he was unaware of was the *significance* of that fact. Learning from Bonnie's response that this improvement related to risk taking was just what Loi needed to refuel his upward spiral:

> BONNIE: I think you should feel good about your writing. Do you feel good about it? At how good it was!
> LOI: I feel better than before.
> BONNIE: Did you feel bad before?
> LOI: Before whenever I write, I think of story but can't put it out.
> BONNIE: Was it easier with this one?
> LOI: Yes, I can feel better [smiling, broad grin]. Now I can't *believe* myself. [Voice rising] I say myself, "How can I *do* it? I *wrote* so *muuuuuch*! I so *surprised*! I so *surprised*!
> BONNIE: I notice you were writing a lot.

Loi's face just lit up like a Christmas tree as he talked. He was actually glowing!

Bonnie again told Loi how proud she was of him. He didn't have his first draft there so she could compare, but she remarked about how many more details were in this draft and told both boys to be sure to leave their first drafts in the folders so they could trace their progress later.

Bonnie's report, which reveals a different perspective from Geri's, shows even more clearly the stages breakthrough students go through:

1. Becoming aware of the need (or potential) for improvement
2. Taking a risk with content, form, or new writing strategies
3. Submitting results to others for evaluation—necessary when students can't judge what's happened on their own (which is the norm, especially before they've seen others break through)
4. Becoming convinced of potential in their writing or in themselves
5. Embarking on an upward spiral of increasing success

The sanctuary atmosphere was essential for steps 2 and 3—trial-and-error learning and sharing writing with peers—and so without it breakthroughs rarely occurred. At step 2, Loi felt vulnerable, for freewriting this revision required him to flout many composition rules he'd been taught in the past—such as planning ahead, monitoring structure, censoring personal feelings, and maintaining a distanced, third-person voice. By definition breaking through to tap tacit knowledge and linguistic intuitions required students to give up conscious control. This made writers anxious about exposing their weaknesses. But without step 3—getting positive assessment—anxious students like Loi could not tell when their risk taking worked, so their sense of potential remained tentative. Once tutors and groupmates confirmed that they'd improved (step 4), our least-confident students experienced bursts of confidence that boosted their growth curves, kicking off upward spirals of increasing success (step 5).

The Relationship between Topic Selection and Breaking Through

Patterns in tutors' data first challenged, then reversed my thinking about how breakthroughs occur and how best to facilitate them. As a writer I did my best work on topics I cared about. As a teacher I knew peer responses prompted more revision than did my own. For a long time, however, respect for students' privacy and their lack of confidence with peers made me hesitate to suggest that they read risky pieces aloud, particularly when those pieces were highly personal. My hesitation disappeared bit by bit, however, for the relationship between breakthroughs and personal topics, coupled with a tendency for breakthroughs to be incomplete if not read and with writers' tendency to take great pride in such pieces, convinced me that my reluctance sprang from a false assumption, a patronizing belief that students could not protect themselves, could not decide on their own whether or not to read what they wrote. Taken together, these patterns convinced me we were in error not to facilitate breakthroughs by suggesting students read their best writing. This was the time to focus on strengths regardless of content when encouraging students to read to the group. When we did so, almost all students chose to read, surprising us over and over at the risks they would take. Interestingly, I discovered, once I began to encourage them all, I could not predict which students would feel shy about reading. When improvement in the writing—fluency, voice, imagery, coherence, honesty, or control—was the reason they were asked to read, most did so. However, when students felt uncomfortable, for whatever reason, they matter-of-factly declined. "Not today. Another time. This one's personal," was always a legitimate excuse for not reading in group.

Breakthroughs increased when tutors asked students to read whatever they'd written,. however, and I never saw evidence that students regretted doing so—except once or twice when novice tutors pushed them against their will. Once convinced they did not have to please tutors to get good grades, dozens of basic writers proactively declined to read until they felt safe enough in the group. And though many assured us they would not have read without "the rule"—making light of others and/or their writing was prohibited—they amazed us repeatedly by sharing painful, even shameful events that had shaped their lives. Apparently the chance to work through such experiences in writing gave them enough distance on the event that they *wanted* to share.

Of course, basic writers felt vulnerable when reading breakthrough pieces, all of which were risky in content, in process, or in technique. Some waited days before reading aloud, asked others to read for them, or hid their work until group trust and bonding increased. Surprisingly, however, it was less often privacy than worry about structure and style that made students hesitate. Some writers felt vulnerable about surface-level correctness (spelling, grammar, mechanics), while others focused on "organization," "transitions," "language," "style," or "technique." Because breaking through had involved giving up conscious control of structure to focus on meaning, feelings, or ideas, breakthrough students felt more vulnerable to structural issues than they apparently did to issues of privacy.

Despite their hesitation, it wasn't hard to see why writers chose to read (the writer who never read personal drafts was a rare bird in our sanctuary). Those who did invariably earned a coveted reward—the admiration of peers, as in "That really took guts to write!" To support all students' writing development, in other words, what needed avoiding wasn't personal writing itself but our tendency to make too much of the personal factor and (in order to leave control firmly in students' hands) any hint that personal writing was required. If we treated personal topics matter of factly, and offered support and empathy when appropriate, the inner explorations writing such pieces required proved to offer great rewards to students in Center groups.

Some writers broke through when a heartfelt topic engaged their attention so strongly they forgot to monitor or censor as they wrote. Other breakthroughs resulted from conscious decisions to try a new writing topic, strategy, or technique. Loi's breakthrough seems to illustrate both patterns. Though the piece is written in a strong personal voice reflecting painful struggles and private hopes and dreams, Loi's reticence about reading sprang from another source, for he had read a draft with *nearly identical content* the week before. Unsure whether his freewritten revision had worked, however, the nervous Loi asked Bonnie to read Draft 2 for him. Here's how a skillful writer and dedicated teacher (unlike most tutors, Bonnie had taught high school for three years) recorded Loi's breakthrough incident in her log:

> Loi's reading was what simply made my day. . . . Loi asked *me* to read it, and I did. The revision was very good—the transitions in the opening came from *him*, the tenses and tense sequence were much improved, and his description of the "Young Communists Party" was much more detailed. The ending was also smoother:
>
>> Day after day, these things made us feel like we lived with two persons inside us. One for them that always did and said good things about the Communist Government. The other was for our real life that never stopped wishing there would be some changes which made our lives look better in a brighter future. That is what I'm having now.
>
> After I read, Jack immediately commented, turning to Loi and telling him that he'd changed the opening so that it was "a lot smoother."

After response from groupmates, Loi's uncertainty gave way to pride:

> "I was so *surprised*!" he said. "I just sat down and wrote." He said that always before he had to think before writing every word—but that this time he just wrote "a whole page"—he held up his notebook to show us—a whole page without pausing to search for the next word or sentence. His surprise and pride were written on his face. He must've said "I was so *surprised*" at least three times.

Like Geri's log, Bonnie's shows groupmates confirming that Loi's risk taking paid off, and after they did, Loi first expressed confidence in his potential. Armed with new awareness that his work would improve with revising, Loi also revealed anxieties he'd hidden in the past:

> Our comments must have opened up some channel for Loi because he began talking about the writing process that he underwent to finish the piece. He told us that last Tuesday after he read [the earlier draft] he lost his "self-confidence." Loi said he realized that his opening was jumbled after Bob and Ferudin pointed it out, but that he wasn't sure about his ability to make it better.

Loi said that as he drove home last Tuesday he felt so proud because he'd started to revise and that it wasn't as difficult as he'd anticipated. Loi said that he felt scared about revision. I tend to forget how scary reading aloud is for the first time—especially for someone like Loi. I wanted to hug him for being honest; his face just radiated with pride.

All breakthroughs followed risk taking—in content, process, or technique—and the anxiety it produced was intensified by student ignorance of how vulnerable other writers feel. Once fear and ignorance came out of the closet, however, tutors could increase support at the point of need, reinforcing information students could not have grasped before. Before taking the risks that led to his breakthrough, for example, Loi had not understood what was meant by Bonnie's explanation that good writing requires risks. After the breakthrough, however, he understood from experience:

> I went back to his confession about losing his confidence, once again explaining how risky writing is. I said that's why the group support is so important, so we can take chances and learn from our mistakes. That's how the WTC works, I told him. It was brave of him to tell us, I think.

Though tutors like Bonnie intuitively helped students complete break-throughs, only after seeing many breakthroughs abort spontaneously did we learn to watch actively for breakthroughs-in-progress and devise ways of shepherding breakthrough students through to completion. Usually sudden changes—in interest, behavior, or writing—were what alerted tutors that risk taking had begun. After taking risks, students wrote more and asked more questions. Their behavior was also noticeably less dependent than before. And, as one might predict from the attitude/behavior/writing progression, risky writing grew longer, more vivid, and more interesting.

Not all breakthrough symptoms looked positive at first glance, however, for regressions also occurred when writers tried something new. Hesitating to read meant that writers felt unsure of their writing, and students who'd come to enjoy sharing their writing might now hang back, denouncing a new piece as "boring," "silly," "stupid," "too personal," "too mean," or "not very good." Few students valued their work as little as these comments suggested. Instead, they used negative comments to hide how much they cared and to preempt harsh criticism they felt unready for. So in the end, basic writers' derogatory statements served them well by alerting groupmates to the writers' vulnerability and to their need to be reassured of potential in their work.

So frequently did disparaging comments precede breakthrough readings that we came to view them as reliable breakthrough symptoms, as signs that, should the piece go unread, tutors would want to provide another chance for the student to read it later—to increase the odds that the breakthrough would be complete. So often did unread pieces turn into breakthroughs, in fact, that some teams scheduled "disaster workshops" midway through the term for the purpose of flushing breakthroughs-in-progress out of hiding.

"Tomorrow we'll have a disaster workshop for pieces you care a lot about but are having trouble with or think that they're no good. After you read them, we'll help you decide if they're worth working on," I heard Kai Wheatley, a novelist, tell her group near the end of the hour, setting students up for their most productive group session so far, even while offering them a way to save face if responses were poor. I'd found this technique some time before in a professional journal—though unfortunately I've now forgotten whose idea it was. Tutors and I express gratitude to the author, however, for it worked as well for graduate writers at the MFA level as it did with basic writers in the WTC.

These breakthrough symptoms showed tutors and groupmates what support students needed and again confirmed our surprise discovery that tutors' intuitions, informed by close observation, leapt ahead of the formal theories from the analysis and helped tutors focus instruction at the point of need long before they could put in words how they knew what they needed to do. Six years before the five-step breakthrough process emerged, in fact, the data show tutor-researchers recognizing breakthroughs-in-progress and helping naive and misinformed writers interpret them.

Serial Breakthroughs
and the Value of Secondhand Learning

It was doubly important that breakthroughs not be aborted, for not only did they increase student chances for certification, they caused outbreaks of breakthroughs to sweep through groups by providing process models for other groupmates, who then adopted breakthrough behaviors as well. In the interest of keeping our cast of characters manageable, let's take as an example a group we're familiar with, the group we studied when looking at interdependence in Chapter 3.

Ashley recorded a series of three rapid breakthroughs in her log. In early fall, Terry (see pp. 64ff.), the "all-American" student who had been uniquely "inhibited" at first, wrote a stiff, repetitive piece on driving in the mountains. Let me refresh your memory briefly on a few details that will be important to the current analysis. As you'll remember, Ashley described Terry and his piece this way:

> September 26:   He's correct, formal, nervous, inhibited, jumpy. He wrote six sentences in his tiny, neat handwriting. . . . He used "these roads" five times in those sentences.

At the next group session, Ashley noticed changes in Terry's behavior and writing and (correctly) predicted that a breakthrough might have begun:

> October 3:   I felt as if today were a breakthrough for Terry. He came in ready to write more about West Virginia. He said, "I've thought of more things to add." . . .
>
> He's been arriving first recently, and I'm glad. It gives us a chance to shoot the breeze, and I think maybe that helps him to relax. He wrote 2/3 of a page in his small neat handwriting. This work has the nicest flow yet.
>
> He began last week writing about driving in W. Va. . . . [Today's] piece (written on a separate sheet like a new piece) flows well and does a good job of visual description. An excerpt reads as follows:
>
> > If some night you are driving threw the coal mining sections of West Virginia you may see what looks like a whole mountain on fire. The mountain glows with red and blue colored flames which makes it seem as though a volcano has erupted.

After group response, awareness of potential increased, and soon Ashley would note that Terry seemed "so much more confident, both in his writing and in the group." Terry's shift from formality to relaxed joviality typified the more gradual breakthroughs of less resistant students who tried to apply what tutors offered in a timely fashion.

By contrast, the excerpts that follow show the more dramatic breakthrough Parvis had after writing the piece on his girlfriend's death. (See pp. 71ff. and 91ff.) Ashley, who saw Parvis as the group's most resistant student, had included numbers of log comments like these, some of which we've seen earlier:

> September 12:   Parvis . . . likes science and probably views this [program] as a real drag. Maybe I should get him to write about his feelings for WTC. If he does dislike it and writes honestly, maybe that would give me a chance to start a dialogue with him.
>
> When we freewrote, he was the first to stop. ("Time's up," he announced.) He looked at his watch several times. . . .
>
> *Lazy* and *lackadaisical* are the words which come to mind when I think about his behavior in [group]. ("My tutor says to write but nothing comes to mind. . . .") I know he isn't lazy, though—he gets up at five a.m., studies chemistry, and works as a cook.

As we've seen, on the day of the ill-fated mini-group experiment, Parvis again resisted participating in group:

> October 1:   You Chi worked with Parvis; he simply told her he'd give her an *A*. . . . I'm really disappointed (and a little irked) because I feel Parvis made so little effort to help. . . .
>
> When I wrote earlier in class that he appears *lackadaisical*, Marie wrote "Scared" [on my log]. I notice more and more how true that is on close

inspection—I see that his lip quivers. (This is the "laid back" kid who likes fast cars and discos.)

As had happened with Terry, behavior change foreshadowed Parvis's breakthrough:

I do think, however, that I have established some rapport with him. He stayed after group to show me his . . . research paper.

The bigger they are, the harder they fall, Ashley's team (Team 4) would later conclude, and Parvis was a student who illustrated that pattern. In fact, Ashley spotted a breakthrough-in-progress at the next session:

October 3:   Now I know what Marie means when she writes "WOW" on a paper. I've just read Parvis's first two-page piece of writing. Today was the first time he has ever failed to look at his watch. When I asked if group members wanted to share their writing (after 20 minutes or so), Parvis said, "I can't stop."

Before he wrote this piece, I can remember him closing his eyes. When he finished and gave it to me at the end of class, he said, "I didn't want to write it." On the top of the page, he wrote "A True Story—Why I want to be a doctor," and he went on to tell me (at least I think he was in part telling me) about the car accident he had in Iran in which his girlfriend was badly injured. They searched in the nearby villages for a doctor. The nearest doctor was 70 miles away, and the girl died before he could get her help.

I didn't lost a friend, I lost a sister, she was like a sister to me, and we knew each other for almost 10 years. I think you know how hard it is to lose a friend, a part of your body that you know for a long time. It is the reason that I want to be a doctor, to go back to my country, to go to small villages, and to help the people that need me.

Touched, Ashley realized that this seemingly blasé student might need more support than his breezy demeanor led her to suspect:

I feel like [Donald] Murray [who wrote about teaching writing]: "I have been instructed in others' lives." All semester long, I've teased [Parvis] about driving fast, etc., because he has written about it lightly or with bravado. His piece in the *Excerpts* [last week] was about his dad telling him he couldn't have a new car "because you might kill yourself." I asked, "Did your dad really say that?" Now I think over all of that, and I catch my breath.

Sensing even before our analysis emerged that this breakthrough was fragile or incomplete, Ashley kept close tabs on Parvis for a month or so:

October 10:   Because I was taking [my aunt] Juliet to the plane, I needed to leave early, [but] I stayed and introduced Kathy [Briggs]. . . . It was the first group session since Parvis's piece about his accident in Iran, and I felt the need at least to say "Hi."

At Ashley's request, Kathy suggested self-assessment thinkwrites to help groupmates select the pieces they wanted to work on next and transfer responsibility for their progress to them.

> I was anxious to read Parvis's self-evaluation (especially because this was his first time in group after his "breakthrough" about the automobile accident).

Self-assessments helped tutors know what kind of help students needed, and this one confirmed Ashley's hunch that the breakthrough was incomplete by showing Parvis's ambivalence about its significance:

> He evinces some ambivalence about his writing saying that "Sometimes I don't like to write about . . . something to personal" Yet by far the most personal piece by anyone in his group was his piece about the accident, and he says "When I wrote that essay last Wednesday, I felt so good and free."

Parvis's past resistance and his compelling topic combined to make him a likely candidate for a powerful breakthrough: Not surprisingly, given what we now know about breakthroughs, once he found a compelling topic and *experienced* his work's appeal to others, attitude and behavior changes showed up within the week: "I think I (would) like to continue this class for next semester."

Appreciation for Ashley's teaching was also growing: That same week she discovered, on a jotlist of possible topics, the words "My WTC Tutor" followed by a list of phrases that included "responsible," "humor," "step by step," and "no assignment." "The detail that touched me was 'kind'," Ashley wrote humbly in her log and, providing unwitting support for the "harder they fall" pattern, noted that Parvis had been "the most resistant group member initially." Weeks before he completed the breakthrough by sharing it in group, Ashley predicted this girlfriend piece might have an impact on him (but she never suspected the effect it would have on You Chi—the weakest struggling ESL student in the group):

> And this is the kid who acted so lackadaisical, who wouldn't commit himself. What will happen next? How will he be different for having written this? (How will *I* be different for having read it?)

Nor was Ashley mistaken in her "predictions." Over the next few days motivation increased rapidly, as evidenced by an increase in how much Parvis wrote. Even without group response, this breakthrough-in-progress made him take our noncredit program more seriously. Suddenly he was exploring other topics that held meaning for him, and the *amount* of writing he did had greatly increased:

> October 22: I looked in Parvis's folder [after group] and felt like I'd hit the jackpot. . . . There were two pieces (one of which he had read in group),

there was an extensive bit of mapping ("My Country") with approximately thirty subtopics branching out. . . . And there was also a reply to a question I'd written about his lab courses. For a kid who thought at the beginning of the semester he'd done his duty when he wrote two paragraphs, this is some change. . . .

What is important, and what I do feel unequivocally pleased about, is that Parvis's output tells one he is committed to writing. . . .

Already acting proactive, long before the end of the term, Parvis began working on his writing at home—even though tutors required no outside work:

> October 29: The changes in Parvis since that piece are remarkable. He wrote a piece at home this weekend and said to me today, "Three pages!"

Most tutors wisely refrained from pressuring students to read, especially pieces on topics that were painful or personal. But by reassuring students of their work's quality while offering praise and occasional chances to read, tutors increased the odds of having breakthrough pieces shared, thus ensuring completion of many breakthroughs-in-progress by helping writers get feedback on the impact their writing could have. When almost a month had passed since Parvis's breakthrough, Ashley (proactively) set up a chance for Parvis to "volunteer":

> Parvis provided us with our "Keynote"—our start. . . . I mentioned that he had done a fine personal piece. I had made reference to it before, saying that he hadn't felt like sharing it yet and that was fine. When I mentioned it today, I said, "By the way, if you feel like reading it sometime or if you want me to read it . . ." and before I finished the sentence, he handed it to me to read.

Breakthrough pieces often evoke so much feeling that they leave listeners speechless, touched, overwhelmed, unsure how to respond. Experienced writers learned to take speechlessness as a compliment, as vivid testimony to the power of their words. But beginning writers felt vulnerable in silence, so tutors often suggested written responses to help breakthrough writers discover what they'd done and to give speechless listeners a chance to recover their voices:

> After I read it, I said, "Let's write Parvis a response." Everybody did. Then they read them to him. I wrote Parvis a note on his paper later to say that I appreciated his sharing and that he had helped others by modeling writing about deep and difficult experiences.

"Sung Tae's honesty showed in his response," Ashley noted in closing: " 'If I say I understand, I am a liar,' he wrote."

Written responses to breakthroughs led to varied rewards. In addition to offering practice in writing to sensitive audiences, they gave more reticent groupmates an equal voice and allowed each one to respond in greater than normal detail. For authors, often too nervous to take in what everyone said, written notes provided records, for reading again and again, of the praise, suggestions, and support offered by friends. By letting Parvis see how his writing affected others, reading aloud confirmed potential he had only sensed and confirmed that his peers (and friends) empathized with him. As with Loi, this first risk seemed to open a channel for him, for at the next session he wrote and read—again with a disclaimer ("It's personal") but this time without delay—the piece (see p. 71) about how lonely he'd been since his girlfriend's death as a result of his pledge to her family "not to get another girlfriend."

Parvis's case shows writing and confidence expanding as he works through personal problems and finds the support he needs. And Ashley's handling of this sensitive situation shows the grace typical of thoughtful beginning teachers whose intuitions are informed by teacher-research. Though she offered Parvis repeated chances to complete the breakthrough, she leaned over backwards not to pressure him to write or read. Like most breakthrough students, however, Parvis seemed proud of what he had written, for despite its highly personal, even painful content, he chose this breakthrough piece for publication in the Center book.

> November 5:   He described the accident and her death. . . . After class, he lingered, telling me that he is working on this for the book. I want to make sure he isn't being pushed into doing it (by me, since I have told him, told the group, that I admired him for writing about a difficult and tragic experience, telling them that such experiences often make for good writing).

Parvis had his own motives for publishing this piece, and like many breakthrough students he did not feel it necessary to avoid his pain:

> I ask how he feels about doing this piece.
> "It's hard," he tells me, "I feel guilty." He tells me that "in 30 days, it will be three years" (since the accident). He talks about his affection for the girl, and I tell him to think of his piece as a memorial to her.
> "As a memorial to *me*," he says. (To his suffering, I hear.)

Tutors weren't the only ones to spot the value of breakthroughs. In fact, the chain reactions that took place in groups occurred when other students copied breakthrough students' risks. For example, the day Parvis read his breakthrough piece, You Chi, the group's weakest student, began to search for a powerful topic. Ashley responded to You Chi's search with sensitivity:

> You Chi said she hadn't yet written "the piece."
> I asked why not, and she said, "I don't think I put enough of my feelings in it."
> I wanted to shout "Yes! Yes—that's it exactly, You Chi," but I just nodded encouragingly and added, "What can you do about it?"

She suggested that she could write about her philosophy of life at CAU or about her relationship with her best friend.

I suggested that maybe she could focus on one incident.

Because thinkwriting helped students decide what to work on next, helped match instruction to needs, and put students in charge of their learning, skillful tutors suggested it regularly to increase the odds that the teaching they did took place at the point of need:

> October 29: "If you have piece you like, maybe you want to write about why you like it, and maybe pick out an area you want to strengthen," I suggested. "If you know you have some type of problem, mention that, too. Then go back and look at the piece, underlining anything you're not pleased with."
>
> "If you don't have a piece you like," I said, "write about that—about how you feel about your writing or what's missing or how you'd like it to be better or different."
>
> Then I paused and said, "If you don't have a piece, it's time to get motivated."

You Chi used the thinkwriting to search for a breakthrough topic:

> In my mind, there are a lot of things that I want to write. Those topics that stay in my mind must have very simple but (it wa) very strong. . . . The other topic I have interested in is described a relationship with my best friend. That is very special and different, I believe, from others.

Since Parvis's and Terry's breakthroughs, motivation had increased:

> After class she stayed (they keep on staying—I had to run them out . . .) to ask about focus. "I want to make sure I understand," she said. I was glad she stayed because I wanted to encourage her personally. . . .

It seems You Chi at last realized she too could improve if she tried, but she was surprised to find that Ashley thought her talented:

> I told You Chi that I thought she had special gifts for writing (and I really do, despite the fact that her English is decidedly the most limited of all my students). When she looked dubious, I reminded her of the award she had won for writing in Korea. "We just need to hear more of You Chi in your writing," I said, and she smiled.

Having noticed abrupt changes in attitude and behavior, Ashley predicted that a breakthrough might be near:

> October 31: You Chi's folder contains nothing from today, but I saw her writing. She's at a—what do I call it—transition point? At a *threshold*? She wants to do it; she's interested and motivated—she just needs a vehicle for her writing.

In You Chi's case, breaking through took persistent effort. She proactively tried personal topics without much result, so Ashley, who knew topics weren't the only route to success, suggested that another genre might offer a way in: "I asked her about poetry today and she told me she had written some Korean poems." You Chi took Ashley's advice, and adapted it to her needs—not by writing poetry, but by shifting attention from content to form. Apparently it had been structure, not content, that was blocking her:

> She asked me questions about the structure of writing today. She has a topic, "My Best Friend," in mind. She asked today if she could write "something about my precise feelings" and then give examples of specific incidents.

Well into the semester, You Chi searched for a breakthrough, and Ashley continued to expand her alternatives:

> "You Chi, have you ever thought of using conversation—dialogue—to show specifics?" I asked. She looked puzzled. I read her a couple of lines from my logs in which I discussed what we were doing or thinking about and then quoted from someone. I picked up a book from the shelf, found a page w/ dialogue, told her that if she was interested in knowing how to use quotes, she could read it. She took the book and began to read.

That night You Chi took a piece to work on at home:

> November 5: You Chi brings to class four stapled pages labeled "First draft" and "second draft." She had a jot list in her folder . . . with specifics about her best friend Faith. I compare the two drafts. . . . The second has rearranged the order of paragraphs and has only a few crossouts or insertions. I can see a few words in Hangul [the Korean alphabet] in the first draft, words which she has looked up in her dictionary, I think, [and] crossed out. . . .
> She began her piece,
> I have a best friend whose name is Faith. I believed that our relationship is very special and have many significance in our conversations.

Ashley studied this piece carefully, but despite much effort, You Chi's revisions weren't very successful. Even so, observing Terry's and Parvis's breakthroughs had helped her shift from anxiety to determination. Not until she finally broke through, however, would You Chi know the exhilaration breakthrough writers felt.

> I read the piece and worry about the ESL errors. On closer inspection, however, I realize that a great number of her sentences could be made correct by changing one word—one deletion, one addition, a different article or preposition, the tense of a verb. I consider whether the group will help. In some cases, I think they will not understand her well enough (because of her pronunciation).

Ashley correctly saw this piece as a move in the right direction, and You Chi's effort alone showed how much she cared, but the piece was still not a "breakthrough" in Ashley's eyes. You Chi had had a breakthrough in attitude and behavior, but the improved writing would apparently take awhile.

> I'm unsure about the writing. It is a serious document to her; I'm sure of that.
>
> We were totall different persons in phisically and and also characteristics. . . . During two very different persons hand around, characteristics are mixed and learned then formed between stages.
>
> She uses a lot of the language of love (it reminds me of Victorian correspondence). She quotes her friend: "If I can say surely meaning of love is implication of the transcendence of caring, thinking, accepting and understanding, I would say I love you." . . .
>
> Help, Marie! What do I do? I hope the group will really help her. . . . I don't know what to do here.

Just when Ashley felt like giving up, the problem of how to help You Chi resolved itself. This piece failed to live up to You Chi's rising standards as well as to Ashley's, so the now determined young woman revised her approach once again, and this time both she and Ashley recognized the difference, though You Chi herself was not quite sure what to make of it. At the next session (November 11), reluctance to read and negative comments suggested how uncertain You Chi felt about a new piece she had drafted at home. These behaviors told Ashley that a breakthrough might be in progress, alerting her to the fact that You Chi might need the group's help in evaluating the piece if the breakthrough were to be complete:

> You Chi issued a disclaimer before she read—"I don't like it"—and I wondered if this was going to be a breakthrough. She held back, reluctant to read it. "Let us see what we think," I cajoled. She began:
>
>> That day was drizzling rain and very darker than usual. That made me felt more depressed. That day was when my parents left to Korea without telling me and my brother stay in America. . . . I could hear . . . the rain hitting the windows . . . mayby that [rain] knows how each of our family feel so that it cried instead. . . ."
>
> Her mother slipped into her room and looked at You Chi:
>
>> Maybe she just want to put everything into her memory.
>
> She described hugging her mother:
>
>> My cheek touched Mom's neck. It was a unique softness.
>
> The bus came, and You Chi left for school:
>
>> I tried to catch them until the last sight when they are become smaller and disappeared.
>
> The group response was grand. "It's lovely," said Mouna immediately. "I hear some problems with grammar, but it touches the heart," said Sung

Tae. I wrote on her paper, "Your best piece yet. It has a nice feel of completeness. You've made my day."

By encouraging You Chi to read a breakthrough piece aloud, Ashley arranged for the feedback that would confirm its potential. Her group's response rewarded the effort You Chi had put out. But it was secondhand awareness of risk taking's rewards that originally nudged You Chi into higher orbit by motivating the effort and standards that would help her break through.

The Relationship between Personal Topics and Breakthrough Events

Contrary to what Center visitors sometimes assumed, the personal topics students so often chose were not required. In fact, tutors found no quicker way to inspire resistance than to suggest that students "ought to" write more personally. More successful tutors never pressed for personal writing. Instead, like Bonnie and Ashley, they leaned over backwards to prevent students from thinking they expected it. Our goal was to help student writing improve quickly, however, so tutors supported decisions likely to further that end. And because the logs showed that when writers cared more, their work improved faster, tutors encouraged students to write to please themselves, maintained sanctuary conditions so risk taking would feel safe, and demonstrated writing attitudes and writing behaviors that most frequently led to breakthrough levels of success. When students got blocked, their syntax "hopelessly" garbled like You Chi's, or when they had trouble motivating themselves to write, tutors never avoided sharing what the logs consistently showed about the role of involvement in writing development:

1. Most successful WTC students chose personal topics at first.
2. Those who wrote *with feeling* (as opposed to writing *about feelings*) wrote more and claimed to enjoy writing more.
3. Those who wrote *with feeling* had more breakthroughs than those who did not.
4. Breakthrough pieces tended to improve in many ways: grammar, diction, pacing, imagery, logic, idiom, organization, voice. . . .
5. Despite these improvements, students felt ambivalent about breakthrough pieces, for they were unsure how to interpret the experience until they received feedback from tutors and peers.
6. Groupmates paid more attention to essays that were personal and made more positive comments on them.
7. After breakthroughs, writers' topics and genres became more diverse.
8. As Chapters 7 and 8 will show, writing strategies practiced on highly personal essays transferred with little difficulty to academic prose.

Redefining "the Point of Need" as "the (Writer's) Point of Choice"

The breakthrough patterns that emerged when students wrote what they pleased confirmed Team 1's early finding that censoring content blocked writing development. Team 4 tutor and poet Yitna Firdyiwek expanded on that theme. Much of what college writers need to learn, he concluded, could be easily picked up from incidental instruction—instruction offered after students, given freedom of choice, learned to spot weaknesses in pieces they cared about. Like Team 1 tutors Linda, Kathy, and Andy, Yitna found that "the point of need" became a more stable target when he aimed his teaching at what students chose to learn. In other words, yet another tutor defined the workshop groups as *settings in which tutors as well as students need to learn*.

Dale's case (see pp. 36-37) illustrates the kinds of data from which Yitna's insights emerged. At the beginning of their tenure in the Center, Dale's and Yitna's behaviors were shaped by traditional expectations of what teaching and learning "ought to" be. Once aware of the potential in Dale's writing, however, both Yitna and Dale redefined their roles. During this process, like Bonnie and Ashley before him, Yitna intuitively spotted Dale's need for extra support in judging how he was doing. Dale's case fit the now familiar breakthrough pattern, though at the time we had not analyzed it:

> It took me a long time to see that my traditional views of what students were learning might not be correct. But once I understood this, I learned to redirect their attention to what they really needed to learn. Let me give an example of how this would happen in groups. When Dale wrote that angry piece about the calculus teacher whose English he couldn't understand, he resisted reading it—he thought it was "too mean." But when I pointed out that he had many sympathizers, that everyone in the group could understand his feelings, he accepted my prompt and read, though ambivalently.

Let me refresh your memory about that piece:

> Well right now I'm worrying about Calculus. I have a test tomorrow and Im not having the easiest of times. I can't understand how they can let a teacher teach, when he can hardly speak english. I should not even show up for the class. I go home and read the book that night to learn what is to be learned. . . . He writes the Theorems on the board, and does an example, which does not make sense, and then gives the homework. This I feel is not fair. Calculus is a hard class as it is. I paid a good deal of money to learn calculus and I can't even understand the teacher. I tryed to switch out of the class to another, and there is no more room in the other classes. I always like math, but know its just frustrating to go to class. Also the room is small & crowded and the air condition does not work. Plus they have construction workers outside the window. The smell of tar and the yelling of the workers add to the frustration. This situation could not be worse. . . . Calculus is not a breeze threw class, and it needs to be explained clearly. I don't mean to

be mean, he is a nice guy as a teacher but he can't explain what Im asking, and if he does, I can't understand him. . . .

Resistance melted when groupmates confirmed the work's potential, thereby resolving Dale's ambivalence about it:

> Because he saw his outburst as unchangeable and "too mean" (which taught me that he was already aware of its untempered honesty), Dale couldn't see how strong his writing was and was surprised when others praised its detail and honesty. This uncensored quality was *not* what he thought made good writing. In fact, it frightened him and blocked his ability to judge objectively, to get distance on the piece.

Appropriately, Dale and Yitna learned different things from this interaction, but both learned, at the point of need, what they'd not expected to learn. Like Loi, Dale *unlearned* instruction-induced misperceptions when groupmates convinced him he could revise private writing for public view. Likewise, by exposing Dale's ambivalence, group interactions taught Yitna that he too had missed the point, that what had earlier seemed a "deficiency" in Dale's writing was actually a regression that cloaked a writing strength:

> Dale's refusal to read grew from a strength he already had. So contrary to my expectation (and to his as well), his resistance was not a deficiency but a rational response to his *real* deficiency—lack of awareness of writing *strategies*, such as how to *revise*.

In other words, while Dale was learning about writers' choices, Yitna was learning how to discover students' learning needs. Apparently, for example, Dale had never realized that most experienced writers *choose* to do many drafts:

> Dale's attention was naturally drawn from his calculus frustrations and refocused, to his surprise, by the empathy of his group. It was their understanding of his uncensored feelings that made him reevaluate the potential of this piece, after which he quickly went back and toned down the personal "meanness" by adding a sentence or two to show some empathy for his teacher.
>
> Dale's concern for audience had been there all along: After all, he'd refused to read a piece that was "too mean." But what he was now aware of that he hadn't known before was that he *could* do something to make his writing better, that writers can *adapt* their work for an audience. Interestingly, once Dale became aware of this potential and adjusted the tone for a wider audience, his group encouraged him so much that he published his revision [in the *WTC Excerpts*].

During his extensive observations of groups, Yitna Firdyiwek, who taught more groups than any other tutor, followed the pattern I noted in Team 1 tutors as he reshaped his definition of how to teach. Transferring responsibility for content decisions to students, he relied increasingly on incidental teaching so that self-selected topics, genres, and goals could focus his attention at students' true points of need. As he put it:

> The shift in Dale's attention itself alleviated his concern by illustrating clearly that he had missed the primary focus. . . . The group refocused his attention by saying that rejection was not his only option, that an alternative was to make the piece more acceptable.

Just as WTC students who became self-directed picked up risky/successful breakthrough behaviors from peers, basic writers also took charge of helping each other, accepted teaching challenges, and practiced critical thinking skills. Yitna describes the role choice played in the development of critical thinking skills:

> Now, some students pick up on this alternative approach quickly. They welcome a challenge to see more in a piece than anyone else. They begin to say to each other, much as I have been saying to them, "But look here, what about *this*? Did you see *this* in your writing?" or "Had you thought of saying it *that* way instead . . .?" Or perhaps they'll say, "That's true too, but look what you've done over *here*. What about *this*? and *this*? and *this*?"

Resistance and the blocks it produced were complex and individual. Nor were they easily remedied by direct instruction. Instead, Yitna concluded, as have tutors before and since, that breakthroughs occurred spontaneously in the sanctuary where freedom of choice in matters of content, process, and form motivated behaviors he'd once thought he needed to teach. This freed time for Yitna to individualize instruction, addressing gaps in knowledge incidentally as they appeared and making learning more efficient in his groups:

> We can't force or mandate these breakthroughs in understanding. . . . We can't even pinpoint with certainty what understanding we need to provide for a particular student at a particular time. But we can provide a context in which better attitudes, behaviors, and products are nurtured, reinforced and supported.
>
> Krashen refers to this inability of teachers to know what content to provide when he talks about overcoming "affective filters" and providing appropriate "input." Because of this inability, he says, we shouldn't even attempt to control the "input" we give students. Instead, he suggests we offer a natural range of language exposure and motivations, and that is what I learned to do in the WTC.

Incidental Learning, on the Periphery

In her thesis, Team 2 tutor Jane Lofts Thomas (1988) describes "flexible and oblique approaches to teaching writing" that she and her Year 2 teammates learned to use in the WTC. Like Team 1 tutor Andy Cooper, Jane shows how WTC methods uncovered "hidden talents," while at the same showing students what they needed to learn.

Though Yitna Firdyiwek neither met Jane nor knew her work, he described the same phenomenon. What Jane termed "flexible and oblique approaches," Yitna called "incidental learning, on the periphery."

> This is an important point, I think, and one I want to emphasize: The most important things that happen in workshops occur on the periphery. They are not always those things the tutor (or student) is focusing on.

In other words, to both tutor and student surprise, *the awareness that triggered growth almost always emerged incidentally, from experience, in the process of looking at something else.* This, it appears, is one reason whole language instruction proved more effective than preventive/corrective drill—it offered multiple lessons simultaneously, and students could connect with whichever ones held meaning for them. Our data confirm what linguists have for some time believed, that language competence expands *not* when learners attend to rules but when they focus instead on whatever personal meaning a particular language activity holds for them.

My observations of tutors add substance to this view. In Chapters 7 and 8 I define incidental teaching—of conventions, attitudes, cognitive strategies, and behaviors—and show how tutors managed to do it successfully. I also show teaching incidentally, on the periphery of learner awareness, helping basic and ESL writers apply to academic assignments the repertoire of skills they'd practiced on self-selected work.

7

Applying Writing Strategies
Across the Curriculum

Learning Incidentally, at the Point of Need

Freshman composition papers like those Linda Blair's students wrote (see Chapter 5) weren't the only assignments to which basic and ESL writers applied stratgies picked up in the WTC. This chapter shows their writing improving across the disciplines. Focusing on three ways of teaching academic writing incidentally, it shows students transferring strategies practiced on self-selected pieces to a wide range of academic assignments. How well beginning tutors learned to teach at the point of need was a major factor affecting Center students' success, so the chapter also includes selections from various kinds of data that helped us figure out what students needed—logs, *Excerpts*, interviews with composition teachers, process writing, and student testimony. Using data from such sources, I offer evidence in support of our policy of teaching at the point of need—or, to operationalize the concept, evidence for *teaching at motivated writers' points of choice*.

Let's look first at what students said about incidental teaching to see how it affected academic success in courses from biology to creative writing, from Russian History to art criticism. Near midterm, Dianna Poodiack transcribed Farooq's views on how practice with self-sponsored writing had helped him succeed with biology and literature assignments:

> I felt improvement in two papers just this week. One is biology paper and [the other] a paper on *Troilus and Cressida*. On one, I wrote [only a] first draft, and first draft actually was good. . . . I knew I could do better, too. I just didn't have time.

Similar views showed up in the weekly *WTC Excerpts*. This freewritten comment by Carla, Yitna Firdyiwek's student, reports changes in attitude, behavior, grades, and the kinds of rewards her writing brought:

> When I first entered the WTC program I had many doubts as to the extent that [it] would help me. I now have a great deal of respect for these sessions. My largest amount of progress is in the confidence that has built up in myself in such a short time. Now when a paper is due I don't put it off till the last minute. Instead I jump in head first. The progress is portrayed in that my "C" papers have become "B" papers.

179

I have also learned to put emotion into my writing. . . . For the first time in my life I composed a poem that was worded well and meant a lot to me. Hopefully it will have meaning for someone else too.

My tutor has been a great inspiration to me and my writing. His teaching is done in such a way that I didn't realize I had been learning so much until I picked up a pen to start a poem explication that was required for another class. I am looking forward to learning more.

From Basic Writers to Writing Majors: The Story of Kamal

The Persistence of Confidence. Most student comments were volunteered, not solicited. The following exchange, for example, shows the extent to which motivation and confidence can outlive group membership. Imagine my surprise when a former returnee told me that he and two other WTC graduates had signed up independently for a 400-level fiction writing class. This caller—the once hostile Kamal, now a writing major—called to describe a breakthrough he'd had in a workshop with Dick Bausch, a well-known novelist teaching at CAU whose short stories appear regularly in the *Atlantic* and who has been twice nominated for the PEN/Faulkner award. This was the second 400-level fiction workshop Kamal had taken, and he'd made an *A* in a 300-level prerequisite. Freewriting his way through a stubborn writing block, Kamal said, he'd become blocked again when, with monitor turned low, ideas started flowing so fast he couldn't keep up. Kamal knew and feared this second kind of "block" well, for he'd been forced to take incompletes in some courses because of it. In the fiction workshop, however, he'd found a way to cope by adapting editing strategies learned in the WTC:

> KAMAL [on phone]: Hello, Marie? How are you? [voice rising] *I got to tell you what happen*! I just wrote a story using the WTC group methods, but with a little modification because I don't have many people around to help. . . .

At this point I asked and received permission to transcribe the call:

> My story I am writing is called the "WTC and I," and it's about all my problems studying writing in WTC. I'm trying to put my ideas about writing in short story form to be interesting for student who have problems with writing—like me. Actually, there's two things that makes me happy at this time. One is my ability to control my writing. The other is I find out I can use my tape recorder to improve.
>
> Let me give you an example. At first I was trying to write this story for my fiction workshop using my old procedures, writing sentence by sentence. I kept on working on the first paragraph a few times, but I could not

get it right. After some time, I remember the WTC method and start to freewrite, but then I get another problem—to decide what to write. I could write only one or two sentence because I got too many ideas.

Somewhere in the middle of freewriting a lot of ideas begins coming, and there is one point where I thought the story will grow too big so I stop and had a talk with my wife about how can I separate it. After this I took another piece of paper and outlined this burst of good ideas so I can work on them later. It work too, because after I make the outline, then suddenly my mind is tuned back to the first idea and I can *write* it again!

Kamal struggled with composing's two central problems—regulating the flow of ideas while getting them down on paper and improving structure and style once ideas are on the page. We've seen many examples of regression resulting when familiar problems crop up in unfamiliar settings. Kamal had dealt with these issues many times in the Center, where he'd learned to handle new challenges by leading from strength. Now he found himself using WTC strategies—asking for help from a peer and making jotlists of ideas—to overcome a recurrent writing block in a very different kind of writing class. In other words, his breakthrough resulted not so much from new learning but from new applications of what he already knew, from remembering that by leading from strength he could improve. At times, Kamal had dealt successfully with this problem. At others, however, he had coped less well with it. The breakthrough came with his awareness that he could adapt to academic writing a strategy he'd practiced many times on self-directed writing.

Awareness that he could adapt familiar strategies was only part of Kamal's exciting breakthrough, however. Unsuspected editing abilities also added to his developing sense of competence. Despite four years of practice separating and sequencing writing tasks, Kamal was still in the process of reintegrating these processes. His growing awareness that he was *still* improving gave his upward spiral an added boost:

> KAMAL: So, this way gives me a little bit more control in the sense [voice rising] that *the ideas* just kept on *flowing*, [voice rising further] and while they are flowing I can *pick out* the ones I want to put in the story.
>
> MARIE: You mean you're getting where you can monitor your selection of ideas *while* you write?
>
> KAMAL: Yeah. I can choose which ones to use and which ideas to leave out. Also, the other thing that make me happy, I can use a tape recorder to write.

Aware that tutors sometimes suggested taping ideas before writing, I asked whether Kamal had discovered that strategy on his own. Once again, I found, he had dealt with a challenge by adapting editing strategies learned in the WTC.

MARIE: Did you learn to use the tape recorder in the WTC?

KAMAL: No. But I did learned how to listen to good sentences and to sentences which have mistakes. I learned how to tell the difference when I read them out loud. So that is why I decided to use the tape.

Let me give you an example. After I finished the freewriting of my fiction, this is the modifications I made in it: First I read the story out loud, and then I tried to make the sentences smooth. Second I read it again and tape it into my tape recorder. Then I play back the tape to listen whether my sentences are smooth or not, and *I put a check at the places where I can hear my voice stumbles*.

After I mark them, I knew I couldn't fix the whole story at once, so I start working on paragraph by paragraph. Then I read the story aloud and tape my voice again to listen for the mistakes—this time just by paragraphs. I tape it at least *three times for each paragraph* until I completed the whole story. That take a long time—It's six pages, typed, double-spaced.

Like other writers we studied before and after, Kamal, who could no longer be called a "basic writer," had discovered an unsuspected cache of "hidden skills," and the increased efficiency they allowed added to his growing awareness of competence:

MARIE: What made you decide to call me to tell me about this?

KAMAL: Well, I worked *so-o-o hard* on it, and I didn't expect the amount of errors is minimal—but *for me* it is—and I get so excited I just call you.

Usually when I type other term papers, I found after typing it that I can see a lot of errors. But this time I can't find much . . . can't find *many*, I mean. I think I still need to work on it—maybe one or two more drafts. I will bring you all the copies, okay? Just so you can see all the errors I take out.

Nor did an honest look at the limits of his success seem to reduce the excitement Kamal felt. The fact that he was becoming increasingly independent made the hours invested in editing worthwhile:

MARIE: It is amazing, isn't it? How does all this make you *feel*?

KAMAL: I get very *excited* because I see that *to a certain level* I can be *independent* in my writing. . . . [Laughing] But I think I need a tape recorder to do it.

Though TAs and I were amazed at how far he had gone with his writing, Kamal was not entirely atypical, for two other WTC graduates showed up in that fiction workshop of fifteen. In other words, 20 percent of the students in Dick Bausch's course had been designated basic writers not long before. Kamal discovered this "coincidence" himself while reading classmates' written responses to "WTC and I." The piece was far from perfect—it still had ESL errors and digressed at points into exposition—but his fellow writers responded much like a WTC group, pointing out strengths before problems and offering support while alerting Kamal to features that weren't yet under control.

"I think there is some very good writing in this piece," wrote one, noting strengths and responding to content as well as form, just as he'd been taught to do in the WTC:

> I especially like some of the metaphors like in the first paragraph. ["My ideas struggled like a butterfly caught in a spider's web. . . . The flow of my ideas suffer from constant interruptions till it freezed like water turning into ice."] I also liked the sense of accomplishment you got from finishing the piece. I know how you felt because I went through the W.T.C. program for a semester myself. It's a good feeling when you finally finish something after several revisions.

The other WTC graduate confirmed Kamal's perceptions:

> I, myself, went through the same program, so I can relate to your story. I can truly understand the excitement of your [writing] discovery. It is obviously paying off.

For basic and ESL writers, we thought, it was an achievement to have come so far. Though we've never calculated the mathematical odds of finding three "basic writers" in a fiction workshop of fifteen, it seems worthy of comment that, among the 17,000 students then at CAU, three graduates of a small program serving 300 students a year independently signed up for the same fiction writing class. I don't know for certain that all three majored in writing (though *it was Kamal's third course in fiction, and at least the second for all*). Nor do I know how many other WTC graduates ended up in advanced writing courses after WTC, though I found many in my own courses over the years. What is clear is that three of fifteen classmates (screened for this course on the basis of submitted manuscripts) had not only attended the WTC but were succeeding with the assignments writing majors receive.

A Note on Kamal's Research and Its Role in Our Study

Soon after discovering that Kamal was researching our program, I began recording perceptions he volunteered as a double check on our analysis. This test should have been especially stringent because differences between his Malay and our (mostly) American backgrounds ensured that we brought widely different perspectives to the task. Although we interviewed Kamal a number of times, although he sat in on several tutor training sessions, and although he interviewed me and tutors about our program, I didn't discuss our analysis with him at the time so as not to contaminate his own analysis. Kamal's observations were so consistent with ours, however, and his understanding of program assumptions so astute (after five semesters in as many groups, Kamal understood the program better than many tutors who taught in it) that I agreed to direct an independent study in which he would use writing to pull together what he had learned.

Even though Kamal knew little about our emerging findings, he knew that his focus was similar to ours. Like us, he was studying what helps writers grow—and it was in this context that he had telephoned to inform me of the breakthrough he'd had. Kamal said breakthroughs like his were important to our analysis and he wanted to be sure our research team knew about them. In fact, at the end of the week he dropped by my house with the tape he'd made and brought copies of six drafts of "WTC and I"—"to prove," he said, how much he'd improved it by reading aloud on the tape.

Year 4 tutor Kai Wheatley, completing an MFA in fiction, was once Kamal's tutor and had become my research assistant. As an experienced writer, Kai confirmed the breakthrough's significance. In her critique of an earlier draft of this chapter, she commented on how independent Kamal had grown since he'd left her group and that his discovery resembled those of experienced writers:

> It's important, Marie, to make clear that he discovered all this himself. See how he's experimenting just like serious writers do? It's amazing how he was trying to be his own audience, so he could do for himself what groups do for each other in the WTC. But of course, that's what anyone who writes must learn to do.

Kai concluded her response to my draft of this chapter:

> Isn't it amazing how much we learn from our students? This breakthrough, for example, is really intersting to me—especially the section where he uses the tape to fix his sentences—because I've been planning to use a tape recorder to improve my novel. I can't believe Kamal discovered this before I did. Now I *know* I'm going to go home and try it too.

Risk taking had long been normal and breakthroughs common for Kamal, and this breakthrough exhibits several traits that distinguish successive breakthroughs from students' initial ones:

1. Increasing awareness that the student can be independent
2. Growing ability to diagnose writing problems
3. Flexible applications of writing strategies
4. Enough distance on their work to evaluate it accurately

It was different, however, in that we learned of it several years after this student had left the WTC.

Learning to Follow the Rules

It wasn't only hidden skills (see page 41) students had trouble transferring. They also had trouble applying conventions they'd studied for years. In her thesis, Jane Lofts Thomas (1988) quoted several students to this effect, concluding that teaching "the basics" in isolation from self-directed drafts had left students unprepared for academic writing, in the process alienating them from their own ideas. As one student put it:

> At school we had to write five paragraph essays. Once every quarter, or at least once every semester, you had to write paragraphs and make them perfect. You had to have a thesis statement and a topic sentence, the correct number of supporting sentences, and no misspelled words and so on. I got A's on them, but *as far as putting them in essays was concerned, I was confused* [italics mine]. I didn't know what to write. All I knew was that I was supposed to write in paragraphs. (p. 288)

Just as Kamal had had trouble using vocabulary when the words studied were isolated from meaningful use, Jane's students had trouble applying the grammar, spelling, and punctuation rules they had learned through drill isolated from purposeful writing experience:

> We had a lot of lessons on grammar, on how to punctuate, the parts of the sentence, and spelling rules. We did a lot of excercises. It was alright when you had the book in front of you with all the examples, but when you were faced with a blank piece of paper and told to write, suddenly all the rules didn't mean anything anymore. They wouldn't help me get my composition done. (p. 223)

Though another student had mastered grammar and other "basics," she too had found them hard to apply when she had to write:

> I know grammar because I was taught so much of it. I know how to say this is a prepositional phrase and explain what a noun and verb etc. are. I know all the basics and how to avoid dangling modifiers and run-on sentences. I could get A's on all that. And I know how to write a five-paragraph theme. But here I am—and I'm still having difficulty writing. (p. 234)

Because tutors heard comments like these repeatedly, they rarely structured lessons around exercises or drills. Instead, they let the focus and sequence of study emerge, watching to see what each writer needed to know to improve her draft and offering support with the problems students identified. In effect, tutors turned traditional syllabi inside out. Jane described her personal teaching approach like this:

> Thus, instead of teaching from external forms, I was teaching toward them, finding that many students mastered the various aspects of language usage indirectly. Here content, process and purpose took precedence over form, structure and correctness. Students were freed from negative responses, the constant evaluation of their "clerical skills" and their ability to conform to a structure.
>
> As a result, students were able to use language to think with and found that transcription and composition were no longer in constant conflict, but that they collaborated with and developed together. (p. 271)

These data show negative attitudes limiting writing and positive attitudes facilitating it. Jane concluded:

> Transcriptional skills are [traditionally] purchased at too high a price—at the cost of the ability and inclination to write anything in the first place—and . . . it is only when students' appetite for writing is whetted again that progress can be made. (p. 272)

It would be false to suggest that tutors didn't teach conventions just because they didn't design lessons around the same content for everyone. Following students' leads as often as leading, tutors like Jane offered support, rewards, strategies, impressions, structural tips, and information about print conventions *as they become aware of individual or group needs*. The more successful the tutor, the more consistently she helped basic writers articulate their own goals. And, as we saw in the chapter on attitude change, students reacted more positively to responsive teaching than they had formerly done to content-focused lecture and drill.

Incidental teaching offered another advantage—allowing tutors to deal with gaps in awareness, attitude, and behavior as well as with the gaps in the structure of what students wrote. The upshot of this (and its pertinence here) was that when given control of decisions about their work, basic and ESL writers almost always veered sharply away from assignment writing to practice the kinds of strategies they'd had less practice with. They justified this shift, as in the comments that follow, on the grounds that in the past, direct instruction had helped neither their writing, their attitudes, nor their grades:

> Every Wednesday our teacher gave us a title and an hour to write an essay which we would then be graded on. I wasn't helped to write.

> I hated being given a title and having to write an essay on it. Often, I would have no interest in the topic whatsoever. I would have to try and produce something off the top of my head and often just feigned an opinion or

adopted a style of writing which I thought would please the teacher and get me a good grade. I never took the writing seriously.

Teachers often give assignments on subjects which are not very interesting to think about. I just lose interest and get discouraged.

What does "writing" mean to me? Writing to me is associated with trying to beat the clock and writing about topics which mean nothing to me. I suppose it's quite challenging trying to write an essay on some of the obscure topics . . . but I don't feel I gain much from writing them. I don't really think about and explore the topic. I just want to get it done. (Lofts Thomas, 1988, p. 526)

Writing about topics they knew and cared about built confidence, which, as we shall see, helped with academic work.

Transferring Writing Abilities Picked Up at the Point of Need

After seeing how much self-directed practice improved the academic writing of their Carlas, Kamals, and Farooqs, tutors refocused data collection and analysis in an effort to understand how that transfer took place. A pattern that grew increasingly clear as the program evolved—and one I therefore allude to here and there throughout this book—was that *independence and confidence with assignment writing followed responsive teaching, offered on a need-to-know basis, the focus of which shifted as students and their writing grew.*

In *Flexible and Oblique Approaches*, Jane Lofts Thomas (1988) described incidental teaching at the point of need:

A prescriptive approach is abandoned, and instead of working one's way through a check-list of the rules and conventions to be covered, the students' writing becomes the guide, shedding light on what needs to be taught next. (p. 226)

Like the vocabulary that Kamal remembered better when he picked it up in the context of meaningful use, Jane's students had little trouble learning grammar when it was offered in the context of writing *they* chose to do:

I think I've learned a lot more here than in my grammar class. In this class you can find out what you have done wrong and why. I don't have to learn *a lot of rules that aren't meaningful to me*, but learn those things I *need* to know *as the need arises*. The grammar in a text book seems so unreal. *It is more meaningful to me when I have actually experienced the need to know the rule in order to get what I want to say across.* [italics mine] (p. 226)

The Less Is More Phenomenon

As we have seen in several earlier sections, students remembered grammar when studied in context better, took more responsibility when put in charge of their work, and began to discover hidden skills when the work became meaningful to them. As one of Jane's students reported:

> I have gained a lot from being helped to find my own mistakes and to locate and rewrite weak sections in my writing. In my English class we learned a lot of grammar, but I would usually just forget it. It didn't *mean* anything. But in the WTC my writing gives me somewhere to start. As I look through my work and try to put myself in the reader's place, I find I am increasingly able to make my own alterations and corrections. The grammar I thought I had forgotten often comes back to me—and when it doesn't, I can ask my teacher or my fellow writers. Then I get help, and *when I need to know something in my writing—or when I have a mistake pointed out by others—I remember what I am told*. [italics mine] It has meaning for me because my writing has meaning, and next time, I know what to do if I make the same mistake again.
>
> WTC has helped a lot towards helping me to write. For the first time someone gave me the help I needed, listened to my problems and believed in me. (p. 422)

Yitna's student Carla found that improvement in academic writing sneaked up on her when she hadn't expected it at all. Her words suggest that Frank Smith (1973, 1986) is right when he claims that language learners are rarely aware of what they learn. Notice how incidental teaching, at the point of need, recedes into the background of learners' awareness, giving them the perception that they have learned painlessly:

> My tutor has been a great inspiration to me and my writing. His teaching is done in such a way that I didn't realize I had been learning so much until I picked up a pen to start a poem explication that was required for another class. I am looking forward to learning more.

Carla's words confirm John Mayher's (1990) claim that "we can count on [people] to internalize unconsciously the useful distinctions of forms and functions as long as they have the opportunity to transact with them for real purposes" (p. 168). One of Jane's students made a similar point about how writing abilities improved unexpectedly:

> Grammar was always such a problem for me. When I had to consciously think about it, it would stop me from writing. Now I just write and write and get my ideas down, think things through. I can worry about the grammar and form later, and often I find that they have got better, as if on their own. (Lofts Thomas, p. 229)

As Andy Cooper and other Team 1 tutors had found (see Chapter 2), when students attended to what they *wanted* to learn, other traits in their writing improved as they uncovered "hidden skills." Focusing on this phenomenon in her thesis, Jane concluded with Yitna that "flexible and oblique ap-. proaches" that were unintrusive were more helpful than direct instruction:

> It was through both an exposure to and a *use* of language that students' awareness of [written language use] was increased. And the learning and development that occurred as a result were by far in excess of that which took place when students spent most of their time *learning about* language. (Lofts Thomas, p. 229)

Without ever meeting Jane or knowing her analysis (which was written up later, after she left to attend Oxford University), Yitna Firdyiwek reached similar conclusions about how writing skills develop holistically, through use. In addition, the most important things students learned, he agreed, very often emerged unexpectedly. Thus it was that tutors came to conclude that, when teaching writing, what appears to be *less* is *more*:

> The most important things that happen in workshops occur on the periphery. They are not always those things the tutor (or student) is focus-ing on. . . . [For this reason] we can't force or mandate breakthroughs in understanding. . . . We can't even pinpoint with certainty what under-standing we need to provide for a particular student at a particular time. But we can provide a context in which better attitudes, behaviors, and products are nurtured, reinforced and supported.

In *Uncommon Sense: Theoretical Practice in Language Education*, John Mayher (1990) echoes these themes. "Language is multi-layered," Mayher begins by asserting. Then:

> Trying to fit it into compartments denies the possibility that more than one thing is happening at once and focuses our attention on the wrong sorts of characteristics. Just as the traditional distinction between cognitive and affective domains of thought is vitiated by the recognition that every thought embeds a feeling and every feeling is entwined with a thought, so, too, making categorical distinctions can lead to . . . distortions. (p. 165)

Krashen's (1982) "ideal instructional level," the Britton team's (1975) "point of need," and Vygotsky's (1978) "zone of proximal development" all refer to a theoretical locale or range within which language development takes place. Providing instruction within this range had been our goal from the start, and teacher-research was our tool for measuring success. In the process we confirmed that three practices increased the odds of instruction falling within such a range or zone:

- Motivating students to want to practice and improve
- Giving students control of decisions about their work
- Limiting teaching to what students needed or wanted to learn

When students designed their writing projects and chose what risks to take, few had trouble remembering or using what they learned. *In other words, our data suggest, the terms "point of need," "ideal instructional level," and "zone of proximal development" all refer to a psycholinguistic "locale" that coincides with (or includes) the learner's point of choice.*

Incidental Teaching, at the Point of Need

Abstractions are notoriously hard to put into practice, so let's turn now to a concrete example, an excerpt from Dianna Poodiack's log, that shows a tutor teaching academic writing incidentally, providing information as students ask for it—after submitting their self-selected writing to the WTC book. Notice that by following intuitions about student needs—to the point of rejecting a "policy" a prior team had developed—Dianna provided contrastive data for her team. Notice also that this is a pattern in tutors' learning, for *as repeatedly happened during the study, exceptions made intuitively while "following the kid" foreshadowed needed change in Center policy.* (This was not always the case, of course, for risk taking also led in *unsuccessful* directions. Many of our most important findings, however, resulted from tutors' challenging what I'd taught them because of intuitions about individuals' learning needs.)

> Danny did some editing on an old piece, "Fork Union Military Academy." Jimmy edited "Apathy"—he worked primarily on the spelling errors, dictionary close at hand. Sunkyung had a history paper with her that she had questions about. First, she asked about the assignment: "Discuss the organization, style, use of reference, and thesis of the book." She only understood "thesis" and asked what the professor meant by the others.
>
> Although it is not our practice to work on assigned papers, Sunkyung had some very real concerns so we discussed her paper. First we talked about applying WTC techniques in our academic papers. Danny said you could brainstorm, freewrite, do a rough draft (adding that he had a friend who does at least four), and edit.
>
> Then I worked with Sunkyung, asking her to read for paragraphing and errors. She was clearly editing as we discussed the paper, and we did some revising together.

With academic writing as with self-selected work, vicarious learning played an important role. While Danny edited and Jimmy worked on spelling, they kept a close eye on Sunkyung as she studied the rhetorical vocabulary needed for a history assignment and applied Center strategies to a paper for that class. Without expensive tests or texts, with neither hardware nor software, students whom we trusted to choose what they would learn attracted instruction to the "ideal instructional level," that level just beyond their current abilities.

Three Teaching Conditions under Which Transfer Occurred

As we've seen, *questions asked at the point of choice attracted tutor attention to the point of need*, thus making possible peripheral learnings that fell within individual zones of readiness. Because only students themselves could identify those zones, writing developed more quickly when they took charge of their work. Weeks of practice at leading from strength in a sanctuary atmosphere provided an experiential base and willingness to take risks that let them extend and adapt for academic writing what they had practiced on self-directed work. Or, to use Vygotsky's (1978) terms, in groups students worked in the zone of proximal development, that zone in which they could do today, with a little help from friends, what tomorrow they would be able to do alone.

In addition to publishing process logs in the *WTC Excerpts*, posting successive drafts of papers on bulletin boards, and sharing their own struggles with assigned papers, tutors used three related approaches to help students transfer writing skills they'd developed on self-selected writing tasks to academic assignments in other disciplines:

1. **Planned Incidental Instruction in Academic Writing.** Planned incidental teaching was the same approach tutors used to help students with self-selected writing when several students had the same problem at the same time. The difference was that in this case the focus of instruction shifted from self-directed to assigned writing per se. In the pages below, excerpts from Kathy Briggs's logs show how tutors offered planned incidental instruction during the final two weeks of the term, a time when students often felt anxious about losing group support, particularly as essay exams and research paper deadlines drew near.

2. **Opportunistic Instruction in Academic Writing.** The story of Ned, from Louise Wynn's group, shows a beginning tutor seizing chances to teach assignment writing incidentally, on a need-to-know basis, without reducing students' control over their work. This was our second strategy for sequencing instruction, and it, too, was consistent with how we taught self-directed writing.

3. **Incidental Instruction in Strategies Useful for All Kinds of Writing.** Based on data collected by Dianna Poodiack, the long case study on Carmen explores (see Chapter 8 for details) tutors' main approach to preparing groups for assignment writing—letting students practice

whatever writing they chose and offering whatever help they wanted when they asked for it. Instead of practicing academic writing, Carmen chose topics she cared about, decided which aspects of her writing she would work on next, practiced strategies for succeeding with tasks she set herself, and applied these skills alone at home to academic work.

What is for me most striking about accounts like these three is how little traditional "content" had to be "covered" traditionally for WTC students to succeed at assignment writing. This effect was due, it seems, to incidental instruction and to the fact that students had memorized essay formats for years and been drilled repeatedly in grammar and mechanics. All most of them lacked was reduced anxiety and practice using written language for purposes of their own, for these hidden skills to become available and for new knowledge to attach itself firmly to old. Notice in the following excerpts how little direct instruction was needed for biology, history, and art history papers to improve. Kathy's group illustrates how less becomes more where academic writing is concerned.

1. Planned Incidental Instruction in Academic Writing: Kathy Briggs's Group

Tutors offered planned incidental instruction when they expected several students to have similar problems at once. Some planned incidental instruction had been with us from the start. For years I'd watched avoidance behaviors—"losing" assignments, blocking, cheating, procrastinating, plagiarizing—usually among students lacking in confidence. I'd therefore designed the program to avoid these problems by eliminating the pressures of homework, assignments, and grades; after all, insecure writers were our entire clientele. I also suggested tutors teach freewriting from day one, hypothesizing—correctly, it turns out—that students who overmonitored would enroll in the program in droves. Tutors developed other planned incidental strategies. When they saw how often resistance was rooted in fear, for example, they learned to present themselves as advocates, accepting hostile feelings and being careful not to take student anger personally.

Helping students confront fears of academic assignments while they still had regular access to group support was another plan for reducing avoidance behavior. Near the end of each term, seemingly independent students might panic when they realized that they'd "squandered" the whole semester doing personal writing, that they didn't know every format and rule they might need for future course assignments, and that if certified they'd lose access to group support. Term paper deadlines and essay exams also led to predictable regressions in confidence. In Kathy Briggs's 10:30 group, for example, anxiety focused on the WTC exit essay.

The exit essay counted relatively little toward certification, for it offered but one kind of data on student growth. When deciding who to certify, tutors looked at development—in attitudes, writing habits, and finished products—as well as at tests. Examining logs, portfolios, entry and exit essays, process writing, self-evaluations, and attitude inventories, tutors working in pairs consulted with me or with more experienced tutors when they felt unsure whether a student was ready or not. Independence, motivation, and confidence counted strongly, but the bottom line was whether students were proactive enough to seek out, after leaving the Center, whatever help they might need to succeed with academic writing at CAU.

Unlike other writing done in the Center, however, entry and exit essays retained the aura of a test—in part to provide data on how students wrote under pressure, in part to provide a measure of how test writing improved. Where this test was concerned, then, tutors did little to allay anxiety other than by helping students think through how to use what they'd learned.

After noting end-of-semester regressions in confidence, tutors set aside two weeks—while *The Drafted Writers* went "to press"—to study academic applications *if* groups so desired. The following excerpts from Kathy's log (with dialogue transcribed from tapes) illustrate planned instruction in academic writing that tutors typically offered the last two weeks of each term. Note that six members compose this oversized group on which we focused earlier in the (Chapter 3) section on group size:

Sandy: Female; 18 years old; American (white); WTC required—attending for the first time.

Jon: Male; 17 years old; Korean background; 11 years in U.S.; WTC required—attending for the first time.

Vo: Male; 19 years old; Vietnamese background; 4 years in U.S.; WTC required—attending for the first time.

Hun: Male; 18 years old; from Hong Kong; 3 years in U.S.; WTC required—attending for the first time.

Dean: Male; 18 years old; American (white); WTC required—attending for the first time.

Hosea: Male; 19 years old; American (black); WTC required—returnee attending for the third time. (*Did not show up in group at all until Week 5.*)

Once relieved of their struggle with revising and editing by the arrival of the book publication deadline, students often regressed in confidence when they suddenly remembered the dreaded exit essay:

Tuesday, November 20—Sandy, Dean, Jon, Hun, Vo: Absent: Hosea.

The pieces for the WTC book were due today. Everyone turned one in. Vo, Jon, Sandy, and Hun paid their $6.50 for a copy.

The group seemed anxious about the final essay that's required for certification. We've talked about it throughout the semester, and I've stressed that it's a final chance for them to strut their stuff! I've told them it's nothing to feel anxious about. They asked me what the essay question would be, and I told them they shouldn't worry, that it wasn't a subject they had to study for, that we weren't trying to *trick* them.

They looked skeptical anyway. Vo rolled his eyes and elbowed his buddy Jon. Hun looked a bit frightened the way his eyes darted around the room.

Increasing support for formal, academic writing *while affirming confidence in their abilities*, Kathy modeled a matter-of-fact attitude toward the test and got students brainstorming to solve their own problems. Notice how the answers that relieve anxiety emerge from no one person but from the pooled suggestions of the group. Notice also how needed vocabulary is taught by one student—along with concrete examples—at another student's expressed point of need.

KATHY: If you want, we can do what I did in another group—talk about how to attack an essay. You guys want to do that?

Vo: Yeah, that'd be good.

KATHY: This is something you can use in your other courses, too. If you see an essay question on a test, what's the first thing you need to do?

SANDY: Decide what to write.

DEAN: Figure out the answer.

Vo: What if you don't know the answer? [They all laughed.]

KATHY: Hey, that's a good point. What if you don't know?

SANDY: Pray. [Laughter]

DEAN: Well, if you start putting down junk, sometimes the answer comes out.

SANDY: But if the teacher hates bull answers, what then?

JON: You don't have to turn it all in. You could always scratch it out.

KATHY: Right. I think you're all on the right track. Use some kind of draft paper—it only takes a few minutes to organize things once they're on paper.

JON: Yes, you could freewrite or something and copy over the good parts.

SANDY: You've got to make it readable.

Vo: Need to structure it like an essay.

KATHY: Good suggestions. What kind of structure makes up an essay?

Vo: You know—introduction, paragraph, supporting sentences, transitional, umm, transitional . . .

SANDY: *Transitions*—like "meanwhile," "however," "on the other hand."

KATHY: Make sure your sentences are clear before you worry about organization. Then, things like transitions can help it flow.

As these were strategies students had practiced all semester long on self-selected topics, they felt pretty confident that they could use them again, and when Kathy asked what groupmates wanted to work on next, no one pursued the topic of academic writing. Apparently the desire to finish pieces they cared about had again grown stronger than fear of "failing" the exit exam: "This group has been pretty busy today. I asked if they wanted to talk more about this topic or write. Surprisingly, they wanted to write for the rest of the time!"

Though Kathy had set aside up to two weeks for academic writing, her students needed only reminding of what they'd practiced, and as little else was required to restore confidence, they returned to self-selected pieces they cared more about. Before the term was over, Kathy would check back twice, only to find these students acting more confident. Teaching incidentally, following student leads, helping them with problems they could recognize on their own, Kathy had little trouble individualizing instruction and students worked, for the most part, independently:

Tuesday, November 27—Sandy, Dean, Jon, Hun, Vo, Hosea

KATHY: Last Thursday we talked about how to handle essay questions and a few of you guys mentioned it would be good to have a practice session. Or, you can all go through your folders and work on a piece. We can do what you want. What do you think?

Only two-time returnee Hosea—who'd joined the group five weeks late and had missed the brainstorming session excerpted above—expressed any desire to practice essay writing. Adjusting was no problem for Kathy, however. Using incidental instruction, at the point of need, just as she had been doing all semester long, she individualized instruction for this group and one other. Notice how she helps Hosea build on what he knew, expanding his repertoire of uses for a strategy he chose to use:

Each person already had something in mind to work on. Vo wanted to go through and read things in his file. He was looking for something to edit. Hosea practiced developing an essay in fifty minutes. He seemed serious today. I went into the other room to work with another group whose tutor was out sick and came back in about 15 minutes.

KATHY: Hosea, how's it going with your practice essay?

HOSEA: Not so good.

KATHY: Why's that?

HOSEA: I wrote my topics down here on the side, but they're not flowing.

He showed me a jot list of the points he wanted in the essay.

KATHY: Have you tried going through and doing another jot list for each topic? Sometimes that's what I do. See where you've got "grades"

on your list? Next to "grades" jot down what it was about grades
that made the topic come to mind. Like, "went from an F to an
A." Then go on to the next topic on your jot list—"school"—how
does it feel to be at school?

Ask yourself some questions. Once you go through making
sublists like this, your ideas will be easier to sort.

Hosea nodded and turned to his writing. The rest of the group was still
writing.

Like more confident students, Hosea—the weakest, least motivated groupmate, who had frustrated Kathy with his slack attitude all semester—chose to
practice a strategy he had partially mastered, thus reducing the risk of failure
and the boredom of repetitive drill. By venturing only slightly beyond his
limits of confidence, Hosea selected a challenge he felt comfortable with.
Leading from strength by applying what he already knew, he activated a
framework into which new knowledge could be integrated. And because he
practiced a familiar strategy, he could practice essay writing independently,
thus increasing his confidence that he could do well. Consider, in fact, how
independently all Kathy's students acted: Only Hosea asked for help, and he
asked only once. Kathy concluded by noting the now well-recognized pattern
of interdependence giving way to independent work:

It wasn't a very talkative session today, but I think that's good. They've had
all semester to interact. These last few sessions are a chance for them to work
on finishing any loose ends in their folders.

2. Opportunistic Instruction in Academic Writing:
Learning from Ned and Louise

Kathy's logs show planned incidental teaching near the end of the term
convincing basic writers they could apply what they'd learned while writing
what they'd chosen to write to academic assignments. They don't show
students actually making that transition, however. By contrast, the following
excerpts, written by Louise Wynn, depict the successful transition of a student I've called Ned and illustrate the second method tutors used to teach
assignment writing in the WTC. Without reducing students' control over
how and what to write, Louise helped them see parallels between self-selected
writing and the formal, academic prose they needed to learn. Instead of
assigning academic topics and forms, that is, she taught assignment writing
using the same procedures she had used to help them with pieces they chose
themselves.

Benefits Talented Writers Received in Heterogeneous Groups. Louise's log documents yet another pattern—the benefits talented writers received in basic writing groups. Just a few weeks after Ned entered the WTC, an art history professor praised his gifted writing and critical thinking. When he entered the Center, however, Ned was unaware of these talents, for like other basic writers who were required to attend, he'd not tested well on mechanics or style, or on the entry essay. Past instruction had apparently forced him into a downward spiral, but his talents emerged rapidly in the sanctuary where strengths and potential were highlighted rather than weaknesses. Soon Ned was racing far ahead of his slower groupmates, earning outstanding grades and extravagant praise on art history critiques.

Ned's rapid upward spiral did not occur in a vacuum, however: He turned his downward spiral around in the sanctuary setting. Nor did he grow bored with the group once his successes began. Delightedly modeling breakthrough behaviors and attitudes for groupmates, he relied on their praise and support in order to take the risks that led to the *A*'s and *A*+'s he earned in art history class.

Assignment writing first showed up well into the term in a log Louise drafted on March 6. Following up on Ned's reference to an "A" on an art history paper, Louise suggested he bring it in to share with the group.

> March 6. Jamie got here early. Ned brought in his art history paper, which he'd gotten an "A" on, to share with us. (I had asked him to bring it in when he told me about it last week.) It was a review of the history of photography exhibit at a Smithsonian museum in D.C. I read the paper to myself, handed it around so everyone else could look at it, and said it looked like he'd used some techniques he'd learned in the WTC.

While arranging for Ned to get some much deserved prestige, Louise made his work both a process and a product model for others:

> Ned said, "Yeah, I kinda did. I remembered what you said about personal writing being more interesting so that's why I put in this part about when I was a little kid going to that museum display. And see . . . "—he opened up the paper and showed us the part he was talking about—"Here in my suggestions, I put in this part about making it more interesting for kids. But I left it kinda plain, you know, talking about one thing and then another, just in order."

Louise praised this orderly approach, building Ned's confidence while drawing others' attention to ways in which his paper typified a more formal academic style:

> I said, "But that's good. In a serious review, you don't want to jump around; you want the reader to see some order. You want it to be interesting, but you want him to understand first this thing, then that one, right?"

Ned seemed to appreciate this attention:

> He says, "Right" and smiles and nods, looking very pleased with himself.
> It really is a good paper, and I'm glad he's found some application for what
> he's been doing in here.

It wasn't only writing successes Louise took advantage of. When Ned had
problems later, she would highlight those as well. For now, however, she
praised the group, voiced pleasure at their progress, and reminded them that
two weeks near the end of the term were reserved for academic prose—*after*
they'd had more practice with self-selected writing:

> I talked a bit about applications, promising that with the progress they're
> all making, we should have lots of time to spend during the last two weeks
> of the semester thinking of and practicing ways to apply what they've
> learned to taking tests, writing papers for classes, and so on. Ned said, very
> emphatically, "Good!" Then I asked if Jamie would read his poem to us.

The issue of art history writing came up again a month later (April 3) when
Ned asked Louise for help with a troublesome piece. Instead of helping by
solving his problem herself, Louise submitted it to others in the group, giving
them practice with academic writing and again making Ned's work a process
and product model for them:

> All six students were here, Jamie, Ned and Willie (U.S.), Tranh and Mai
> (both from Vietnam), and Sofia (Bangladesh). Jamie brought in a piece he
> wrote over the weekend. Ned brought in a paper for his art history class. He
> asked if he could read it to me for some ideas for revision and then work on it
> in group. I said yes.

Time ran out, so Ned read his paper after group, with five of six groupmates staying late to work on the piece:

> Jamie had a class to get to. The others stayed and listened to Ned read a
> first draft of his new art history paper about the Vietnam Memorial in
> Washington. They all said they enjoyed it. I told them about my freshman
> art history paper on the student union building at Berkeley, "commonly
> known as ASUC" (which it was), and they all laughed. I said I got a C on it
> and that it was very boring.

Crediting "the way we're learning in here" with his success, Ned stayed to
work on his paper for still another hour. It had apparently become writing he
cared about:

> Ned said, "See, I'm using the way we're learning in here to write it, and I
> think it's making me a good writer." I said, "Yes, it really is." Ned stayed
> during Jan's 2:30 group to work on his paper some more.

Proactively seeking praise and support to bolster confidence, Ned later brought in a third art history paper. An "A+" was on this review of a Nicholas Nixon exhibit at the Corcoran, and this time the professor praised Ned's writing extravagantly. For a student who'd scored low on the TSWE and failed the WTC entry essay just weeks before, Ned was acting motivated, successful, confident, independent, and proud:

> April 5.   Ned comes in early (as usual), and this time he is grinning from ear to ear, and holds his hands up above his head in a victory clasp.
> "I did it! Look at this!" He has just come from his art history class, where the instructor has returned their latest papers. This particular paper he did not work on in the WTC or share with us, but did entirely on his own. He hands it to me. I look at it, and see the title—"Nicholas Nixon Review"—and the teacher's grade and comments on the front page:
> "A+   A superbly written, insightful and sensitive review of Nixon's work. Good discussion of specific images, as well as relating them to traditional black and white photographic trends.
> "The field could use your writing talents and sensitive eye!"

Louise looked over the paper, voicing her pleasure and pride:

> I congratulate Ned and sit down to read his essay, which is really good. He says, "I used all our WTC techniques. I wrote with my own personality and style, and it really worked!"

"Anything scarce is coveted—praise, for example." Those words were written by Zainoria, a Malaysian WTC student who took my introductory creative writing course, of changes she observed in herself and in fellow writers. Ned's case illustrates this pattern, also noted by tutors, of the power of honest praise to reward and motivate effort. (Thoughtless praise, by contrast, had the opposite effect.) Honest positive comments on strengths—from tutor, professor, and peers—let Ned know which parts of his writing were working well, strengthened his ability to critique his own work, and reduced the odds that he would revise the good parts out. The motivating power of well-deserved praise also showed up in Ned's plans for consoling himself should confidence regress:

> We talk some more about the exhibit which is still at the Corcoran, he thinks, and about his other papers in the art history class. At the end of the conversation, Ned says, "Well, anyway, I'm going to take it home and put it somewhere to remind myself that I really can write."

Ned had accepted the ebb-and-flow pace of regression and growth as natural and was developing strategies for coping with it—strategies without which few basic writers (few writers at all!) succeed.

Among continuing entries on Ned's self-sponsored work, on April 19 Louise made her last reference to art history writing:

> Jamie had typed up his final version of two poems for the book and had written another since Tuesday. . . . We discussed that for a while. . . . Meanwhile, Ned had brought in his art history paper on the new Vietnam Memorial. It's one he read to us a week or so ago when he was still writing it. Today he showed us the grade: 100/100. He was very pleased with himself.

Ned's groupmates also took pride in his success, pushed him to accomplish more, and took time from their own work on this busy book-deadline day, boosting his self-esteem as a result:

> Mai read the paper and said, "Can he put this one in the book, too?"
> I said, "Sure."
> Ned was blushing with pleasure and just a little bit of embarrassment. He said, "But no one will understand what it's about."
> Then Tranh said, "I understand it, and I've never even *seen* the memorial."
> Mai said, "I can type it right now."
> Ned agreed, so Ned and Mai went out into the office together so Mai could type it. She did it very quickly.

Ned's case shows how working in heterogeneous groups helps even better students stretch beyond what they could do on their own. Reciprocity characterized this group's interactions. Interdependent groupmates who deserved some credit for Ned's improvement shared his pride and excitement as well, reinforcing their own hopes for academic success. While they gave him suggestions, moral support, and appreciation, Ned modeled new applications for skills they were practicing, setting a rising standard to which each could aspire. This two-way collaboration occurred on many levels. Drawing on the strengths of all to help each one improve, groupmates at various levels of writing ability both drew on and contributed to a growing pool of writing knowledge, know-how, and support. Under Louise's guidance, they pulled themselves up by each other's bootstraps, building on the foundation of what each could already do by accepting offers to tap other's strengths. Repeatedly, then, we watched students like Ned learn to do today with group help what they would need tomorrow to be able to do alone.

One unexpected finding of this teacher-research study was that writing skills transferred far more than we'd ever expected. Once we shifted evaluation away from weaknesses, both our motivated Neds and our reluctant Hoseas reaped rewards by leading from strength whenever they tried something new. Strategies and writing techniques they felt confident with provided a framework into which they could fit new, assignment-related information. Ned's case shows the outcome—a rapid upward spiral—being transferred from self-selected to academic tasks. In other words, in the Center's small, writing-centered communities, the role of interdependence in writing development expanded naturally to include academic writing as well. One of Jane's Year 2 students described these changes in terms of their bottom line—growing confidence and success across the curriculum:

> Since the WTC I feel more comfortable writing papers and my grades have improved. For the first time in my life my papers are receiving B's. I feel so comfortable about my writing now that, instead of avoiding papers, I'm now looking for them. (Lofts Thomas, 1988, p. 188)

Inept structure had gotten most Center students labeled "remedial," but ignorance of sentence, paragraph, and text-level patterns was not the main "deficiency" that marred their work. In fact, "deficiencies" marred their work very little; what ruined it was taking what they'd been taught too seriously. Much as Mike Rose (1980) found in his study of writing blocks, our students were faithfully following past instructors' rigid rules. Even more ironically, perhaps, evaluation-induced error-avoidance strategies prevented students from using patterns and conventions they knew. The all-too-common practice of focusing evaluation on weaknesses left students anxious and confused about writing conventions they knew. These noisy negative feelings drowned out the subtle dissonance most writers feel when they use a word or feature they are unsure of, thus preventing students from catching errors they could have corrected.

In the supportive, positive, collaborative, ungraded Center atmosphere, noisy, counterproductive feelings began to subside, allowing students to engage their critical faculties. Once they learned to recognize strengths, separate and sequence tasks, and set aside evaluation anxiety, increasing distance on their writing helped them recognize which writing features they did not yet have under complete control and distinguish what in their work was strong from what was weak. When this happened, academic writing, though still not perfect, very often began to meet their teachers' standards, producing the independence we've seen in Kathy's group and in Ned.

Boosting the Spiral Orbit

A Natural Range of Rewards. Ned's case shows what happened when a wide range of naturally occurring rewards motivated writing practice, thus freeing grades to function for basic and ESL writers as they typically do for that select group of students at the upper end of the student hierarchy. Unlike the discouraging grades they had come to dread, intrinsic rewards for writing well boosted upward spirals, tempting students to work harder instead of threatening them. Ned reaped rewards in confidence, pride, and prestige and won praise for his substantial critical thinking skills. By taking charge of his own improvement, in other words, he achieved goals young adults typically struggle to reach—breaking free of authority and testing competence.

Nor was Ned alone in this breakthrough pattern. Offered in isolation from writing's natural rewards, traditional grading's stratification procedures and negative bias had left Center students anxious, worried about their futures, and fearful they would fail. Once grades no longer dominated their attention, they found parallels between self-selected and academic prose. Setting anxiety aside, they evaluated themselves, treating grades as but one of many useful kinds of response. Growing increasingly confident about academic assignments, they showed more concern for quality, in content and form, than for grades. Jane Lofts Thomas's students alluded repeatedly to this theme:

> I feel that my writing is continually getting better with each session. . . . When I realize that I can be creative, and I can write better than I had thought, it carries over to my studies. (Lofts Thomas, 1988, p. 530)

> I no longer fear writing and feel so much more self-confident now when I am given papers on particular topics. I can think more easily, am more organized, and find it much easier to put my thoughts down. (p. 188)

> When I have an assignment now, I go home and freewrite. When I've got all my thoughts down I have somewhere to start. (p. 322)

> My writing process has changed in that I think I am better organized than before. If I sit down and start writing and after I write, critique and shuffle the words around, I can write pretty well. Our freewriting has helped me with this. Now when I have a paper to write in English Literature, I freewrite for a while and get some ideas. Then I can write up a rough draft with further analysis and the outcome is a much better paper. (p. 371)

> When we are assigned topics to write papers on, a group of us often get together in the bar or the coffee room and talk about what we think, and what our views towards the subject are. A lot of ideas come out of these discussions. Not only do we more thoroughly examine our own thoughts and opinions, and understand them better, but we are also able to consider and question those of others. (pp. 178-179)

> I am able to find out what I think and feel about a subject through writing about it. It is so much harder when all your ideas are in your head, and they are all making so much noise you can't listen to any of them. And I believe that sometimes you don't even know what you think or feel until you write everything down. When I get an assignment now, the first thing I do is try to sort out my own ideas about it in writing. (p. 179)

Though their testimony suggests no lack of competence, in the past anxiety about negative evaluation had reduced these students' performance with critical thinking. Once Jane removed that threat, however, they began using writing as a way of learning, a way of discovering and clarifying what they knew, a serious medium for processing ideas.

The Common Grammar of Writing:
Understanding How Less Can Be More

Another unexpected conclusion suggesting that less can be more was that student writers didn't need to practice every kind of writing they might someday need to do. Though they wrote only in genres of their own choosing, Ned's groupmates learned that narrative, poetry, and expressive writing draw on a pool of strategies also useful for writing artistic reviews. More helpful than additional drill in academic formats, it seems, were hearing the drafts and struggles of peers and helping others solve problems. There were many structures, strategies, voices, techniques, and conventions that groups like Ned's knew of vaguely if at all. When they needed to write academic pieces, however, they knew how to ask for help when they could not solve problems alone. As Jane put it (Lofts Thomas, 1988), they "reached" for what they needed to make their writing improve. In other words, our basic writers learned what few had known before. *They learned that the grammar of writing includes not only linguistic components and structural patterns, as they'd been taught. They learned that fluent writers need operational strategies, too.*

We learned something comforting while watching our students develop: We did not have to feel overwhelmed by an expanding curriculum. Our students' development had not occurred arithmetically, we concluded, by adding discrete bits of knowledge, like pennies in a jar. If it had, students would have been competent when they came to us, for we found no lack of talent in WTC writers and most had been drilled on mechanics and grammar for many years. Fortunately, finding time for students to practice positive attitudes, brainstorming, collaboration, freewriting, thinkwriting, revising, editing, and critical thinking proved more easy than frustrating in the WTC. For when we focused instruction first on awareness and attitude change, desired behavior changes occurred incidentally, at the point of need. So did the study of rules concerning structure and formal conventions. And most students could learn what they needed in a single term.

In other words, teacher-research confirmed that, where writing development is concerned, at least, less is more. Once awareness developed and attitudes started to change, motivated practice with a small number of strategies built independence faster than had memorization and drill. Was it any wonder, then, that in Kathy's group, five of six students declined the offer of help (with assignment writing) she so dutifully made two weeks before the end of the term.

Incidental Instruction in Strategies
Useful for All Types of Writing

The freewritten, daily learning logs of Kathy and Louise show confidence expanding across the disciplines and document the kinds of successes many students achieved. The case study of Carmen, which follows in Chapter 8, confirms the finding that students could transfer strategies practiced on self-sponsored writing to academic assignments with little trouble and illustrates tutor's third strategy for teaching them how to do so: incidental instruction in strategies useful for all kinds of writing. A second contribution of the Carmen case study is that it delves more deeply than previous ones have done, tracing the roots of academic writing success to a period long before tutors could tell *any* learning was going on.

With Carmen we realized that slow students weren't very different from fast ones, that in fact Carmen fit the pattern Louise had documented in Ned: Relying on group support while writing strategies developed, she applied these to assignments for other courses on her own. Not that individual differences didn't occur, but between teacher-research and incidental teaching, we found that differences in attitudes, behavior, and writing revealed more about instruction-induced gaps in awareness than about lasting differences in how students felt, thought, or learned. Ned emerged early as a leader in his group, for example, while Carmen became a group leader during her *second* term—*after* being the *weakest* student in group the semester before.

A shaky transition phase that took place between semesters aside, Carmen's growth was a slow-motion replica of the process "better" or "faster" students like Ned went through, except that certification required not one semester but two. Once Carmen accepted her leadership role, however, she differed from Ned in a positive way as well, for she dealt with academic assignments *more independently*. Even more interesting to me is that at both extremes—in her slowest period and in her leadership role—Carmen differed from Ned in the *slope*, not the shape of her learning curve.

Ironically, the biggest difference between slower and faster students lay not in Center students themselves but in our perceptions of them, for we had to learn to wait for development to occur. While Ned's upward spiral was clear to Louise early on, Carmen was deemed a failure by two tutors after one term because she had not yet learned everything she needed to know to succeed. Had we known then what we know now about how attitudes shape writing progress through their impact on behavior, we would have been unlikely to label Carmen a failure, for she'd worked hard and wasted no time taking charge of her work. Like Chat, the student from Thailand, studied by Linda Blair (Chapter 5), she'd entered the Center with fewer strengths to build on, and her writing appeared weak compared to that of others. But a fine-grained analysis of her attitudes, behavior, and writing shows we need not have been discouraged by her papers' inadequacies. It also suggests that our negative views threatened Carmen's progress and would have threatened it even more had not teacher-research informed Dianna's intuitions and helped her guide Carmen through the shaky transition phase that our premature use of summative evaluation created.

Because of its length—and because Carmen taught us so much about other "negative cases"—Center students who did *not* improve miraculously—I have placed this case study in a chapter of its own. Don't forget, however, that it was initially chosen to illustrate *incidental instruction in strategies useful for all types of writing*, which was tutors' third way of teaching at the point of need.

8

Carmen, the Slowest of the Slow— Our Double Negative

For a directed study project in writing research, Dianna Poodiack kept daily logs on three of her four Center groups, documenting everything she noticed for several weeks while watching for themes, patterns, and categories that piqued her curiosity. Surprised by how much revising ESL writers were doing, Dianna focused more closely on Farooq's and Carmen's work (see the short case study on Farooq, pp. 109ff.). Making careful field notes on interactions in their groups, she transcribed audiotapes of sessions, had me videotape some, and began talking to students about the essays, drafts, process logs, and questionnaires in their folders.

Dianna's writeup on what she called Carmen's "breakthrough in revising" stands in sharp contrast to the concern shown by Maria Greig, who had been Carmen's tutor the term before. Unlike Dianna, who came to see Carmen as a breakthrough student with great potential, Maria had concluded that, though Carmen worked very hard, she was "one of our failures," one of "the slowest of the slow." Maria was in no way to blame for "misjudging" Carmen. Carmen was, in fact, among the weakest students we taught. Her later breakthrough confirms the success of Maria's work; in fact, without the data Maria collected and shared, the insights of this case study would not have been possible. Though she did not know at that time what we now know about slow students, Maria's careful study of Carmen's then undetectable progress obviously informed her intuitions well, for from the perspective of our current analyses, she offered exactly what Carmen needed in order to grow.

The Exception That Proves the Rule

The Carmen case study serves a dual function in this report. I chose it to illustrate our third way to teach academic writing—incidental instruction in strategies useful for all kinds of writing—because it also so clearly shows patterns typical of slow learners. Carmen was an example of what tutors called "our failures"—students who worked very hard but seemed not to improve much at all. As teachers we watched these writers progress slowly and felt discouraged. As teacher-researchers, however, we learned to rejoice in them, for although we rarely knew just how to help them at the time, we knew teacher-research would help us help them learn and that the insights we gleaned from it would help others who followed them. For such is the power of the negative case: It is the exception that explains the rule.

After failing to earn certification in a semester, many returnees grew hostile and resentful on their return, poisoning the trust tutors tried to establish in new groups. Others, like Hosea from Kathy Briggs's group, never got motivated again after being informed that they had to return for a second term. Carmen was different, however. She was more than a negative case, she was doubly negative. One of the constant percentage of hard-working students who did not earn certification within a semester, she became one of an even smaller number of returnees who did not develop negative attitudes on their return.

Our view of negative cases had not always been positive. At first we were tempted to see them as annoying exceptions that perversely insisted on undermining our research results. Gradually experience taught us otherwise, however, for they proved to be gold mines for analysis. Hidden in the data on every nagging exception, we found false assumptions that we'd accepted uncritically, and, packaged with them, data to help us revise those beliefs. Surprisingly, these discoveries rarely threatened existing analyses. Instead they helped us refine them and make them more accurate. Instead of debunking our upward-spiral theory, for example, Carmen's case helped us understand the anomalous downward spirals once-hardworking returnees so often fell into in their second terms.

Redefining the Term "Slow"

Once formulated, some "findings" seemed almost self-evident, but "self-evident" findings proved no less instructive than others. For example, a false assumption the Carmen study uncovered was our misperception about how "slow" students learn. Though we were using language commonly used to describe such students, language that taken literally described them accurately, we had uncritically accepted a nonliteral definition of *slow*, one that caused us to act as if students were *stupid*, not merely *behind*. Fortunately, anomalous data highlighted this widespread misperception that unexamined experience caused us to accept unconsciously. Reteaching and unteaching what we already knew at some level, negative data shed new light on our intuitive knowledge, making us question *how* what we'd assumed was true and *why*.

In *Women's Ways of Knowing*, Belenky and her colleagues (1986) call this unrecognized intuitive knowledge *fresh knowledge*—knowledge that is not new but has been "underground, unarticulated, intuited, or ignored" (pp. 19–20). Let me illustrate how fresh knowledge got brought to conscious attention, where it improved our success rate by making us realize that slow learners were simply that, *slow*, that they differed from quicker ones in timing but not in kind.

Some of our students were less than bright. A few acted disturbed. Others arrived with documented "disabilities." But these students were rarely the students with whom tutors struggled hardest. In fact, tutors seldom seemed to pay much special attention to them. Except for an occasional consultation (I remember three or four over a five-year span), tutors used methods developed with more typical groupmates to help such special students improve with scant input from me.

By contrast, two groups of students came frequently to my attention, usually just before or just after certification time. They were the resistant returnees I've alluded to and slow students who, though hard working, seemed not to improve much at all. In their second semesters, these groups overlapped almost entirely, thus making Carmen a doubly negative case—a hardworking student who seemed to make little progress her first term and a returning student who never acted resistant at all.

Though in the university's eyes all Center students were "slow," Carmen helped us realize that slowness was relative, that differences among students were more of degree than of kind. For example, though slower students took longer to certify, by the time they did improve, their spirals looked like those of more sprightly learners who had arrived in the Center with more strengths on which to build. For all students we found that when we offered rewards first, then taught by answering questions, all the while in a setting of trust, even the slowest learners began to think, feel, and act like writers well before dramatic improvement showed up on the page.

In the WTC's close-knit communities, where writing well quickly became a source of prestige, we tempted slower students with writing's natural rewards, pointed out emerging strengths (in attitude, behavior, and writing), relinquished control of content and form so they could take charge of their work, demonstrated writing behaviors, gave honest, supportive responses, and posted or published writing every chance we got. In the end, slow students taught us to trust that part of our theory which states that increased awareness, attitudes, and behavior are reliable predictors of writing improvement itself.

Evidence that we were right to wait for growth to occur confirmed our policy of postponing grading all semester and taught us to increase practice with self-assessment so that students could learn to decide when to have their work reviewed. In other words, slow students got less and less specialized treatment once we discovered that they responded the same way others did. Like the ESL writers we'd studied during Year 1, the slower slow students merely needed more practice, more support for writing well, and more time for their writing to develop naturally. And like other students with whom we worked in the WTC, these slower slow students also needed to take charge of their own growth.

Our experience learning to trust naturalistic teaching because it worked for slower learners as well as faster ones supported our conclusions on heterogeneous grouping (detailed in Chapter 3). Slow students neither looked nor acted like writers at first, but to our surprise, even minute improvements in attitude foreshadowed writing breakthroughs when we were patient and waited for them. Gradually we learned to trust strengths instead of fearing weaknesses—even when we had to search hard for strengths to trust. In other words, we came to expect slow learners to do well. Donald Murray (1978) once made a similar point about writers' potential:

> The writing teacher may not be able to locate the potential in the language on the page but may just hear a tone of voice, feel a sense of humor or a sense or rage, recognize a potential area of authority. It is good enough, in the beginning, to respond to that. (p. 58)

All slower students lacked, we discovered on close observation, was an adequate history of meaningful writing experience from which to develop and test their own ideas about how successful writing is done. When we let them do writing that was important to them, and gave them whatever time they needed to learn from experience, they fairly quickly overcame this handicap. And this included potentially talented students like Ned and the less talented but successful Carmens and Hoseas. The rest of this chapter traces the progress of Carmen, who was slow.

Coming from Behind

After a shaky transition due to "failing" WTC in the fall, Carmen spent several weeks that spring consolidating gains and doggedly practicing what she'd learned the semester before. Just before midterm, she had "an exciting breakthrough" followed by a second self-paced time of consolidation. This breakthrough boosted Carmen's learning curve to a steeper angle, at which time Dianna spotted the now-familiar upward spiral. (Carmen began accepting ambitious challenges and drilling herself repeatedly on what she'd most recently learned.) It was then that we realized, to our surprise, that Carmen's once-slower pattern had begun to fit the norm: Her alternating rhythms of consolidation and growth were now clearly punctuated at intervals by predictable regressions (in attitude, behavior, writing)—all associated with what she saw as risks.

Though Carmen appeared not to learn much during her first semester, it turned out that she was merely *behind*, not *slow*. She had further to go to build mental models for writing than most of her peers. From a teaching perspective, studying cases like Carmen's frustrated us, for we had to relive our worst failures to understand them. But from an analytic perspective, slower students' cases were rewarding, contributing disproportionately to the program's success by teaching us how to meet the needs of the students we'd failed the worst. Tracing their development was time-consuming, however, and the case study that follows is much longer than most, for it follows Carmen's growth across the two semesters that were required for her to be certified.

Some returnees gave tutors a lot of trouble, serving as powerful negative (resistant) influences in groups. By contrast, Carmen would develop into a leader, a positive model of writing behavior and attitudes whom other members of her second group would imitate. I got interested in her case after reading Dianna's research report because Carmen was so atypical, and I wanted to find out where the differences lay in hopes of solving the returnee problems tutors had. I therefore interviewed Maria about Carmen's first semester. Later, just before Dianna left for four years in Spain, she and I spent two full days studying Carmen's drafts, with Dianna answering dozens of my questions about Carmen's work. Without Maria's and Dianna's data, analyses, and cooperation, this case study would not have been possible.

I learned many lessons from Carmen, not the least of which was that, though she was "slow," her learning pattern was not atypical. Only at the surface level, the data informed us, did this negative case deviate from the norm. When we examined writing development across semesters, looking behind the surface structures of student writing and behavior to assess the awareness and attitude patterns that shaped Carmen's growth, her progress looked very similar to that of others. The same linguistic, psycholinguistic, and sociolinguistic factors determined what changes students went through and what structures they produced. Let me illustrate this finding in more detail.

Academic Writing: Carmen's Development

The bigger they are, the harder they fall, Team 4 tutors had found, and the Carmen case was another variant on this theme. Though Carmen was an ESL writer with a long way to go, her case study confirmed this chapter's central finding: that student-sponsored practice informed academic writing by attracting student and tutor attention to the point of need. Carmen spent no time in group writing academic assignments, but she practiced for two semesters the writing strategies that would earn her a "92" on a Russian History paper. As I've noted, her case was a lesson in definition. It showed us that we were wrong to equate "better" with "more rapid" growth, that "slow" students were neither "bad," nor "poor," nor "weak"—they were merely slow. Or, as Jane Lofts Thomas (1988) put it in her thesis, it confirmed that every student who tried could learn to write well:

> Indeed, I came to believe that the ability to write a good and powerful piece of writing was within *all* of my students. They could all learn to write well. I just had to help them tap their own potential. (p. 558)

> Murray believes that there "is potential even in the most unlikely student, and it may take a teacher all of ten minutes to tap it." . . . Although it often took me longer than ten minutes to tap the potential of some of my students, perseverance rarely went unrewarded. And I found that the difficulty in getting students to write often had nothing to do with their academic ability.
> Indeed, a significant finding of the research was that writing ability appeared to have far less to do with intelligence than it did with certain other factors. . . .
> Yet despite the fact that some students often seemed to do their best to convince me they lacked potential (sometimes, though rarely, by refusing at first to co-operate), all of them eventually achieved breakthroughs in their writing. I just had to dig deeper and try harder. (pp. 562–563)

The Carmen data show this pattern emerging, and while I would not suggest that clear-cut boundaries exist, I have broken her progress into several segments to illustrate the progression so many slow writers went through.

Segment 1: The Baseline Data

"Carmen Was One of Our Failures." Team 2 tutor Maria Greig viewed Carmen, a Puerto Rican of 25 who had been on the mainland for three years, as "one of our failures" because she progressed too slowly to be certified in one term. In fact, despite steady effort her writing improved so little that Maria concluded she hadn't helped Carmen much. After a full semester of persistent effort, Carmen's writing resembled that of weaker entering students. In December she was unable to organize or focus the only piece of writing she'd taken through more than two drafts. Nor did she have control of the simplest editing skills. Over a year later, when I called to ask about Carmen, Maria's sense of failure was still strong:

> I just couldn't seem to help her. I don't think I taught her much. I remember that her papers lacked organization and focus, but I couldn't get her to understand how to make them better. She wrote about a trip to Atlantic City, for example, and it was supposed to be her *pièce de résistance*, I suppose. But she could barely get us there she got so bogged down in

details. She kept going on about which gas station they stopped at, which road they took to Cape May. It was full of digressions like that. I just couldn't seem to help her.

I feel a little senstive about all the errors she made because I don't feel I helped her with corrections much at all, but she needed to learn to pull things together before we emphasized grammar, punctuation, spelling, or mechanics too much. I don't remember anymore just which errors she had, but I remember I postponed working on them much until she had a better draft. That was our WTC policy, and it was a good one, I think.

Ironically, though Carmen was weak compared to other WTC students, she made an *A* in Freshman Composition for Foreign Students:

One other thing I remember is that her English 100 teacher stopped me in the hall at the end of the semester. Carmen had apparently told him I hadn't certified her, and he couldn't understand why because he'd given her an "A." I remember feeling startled when he told me that. I was just a graduate student then, and I felt insecure that I had held her back in a tutorial program when an applied linguist had given her an "A" in Freshman Comp.

The English 100 professor, an ESL specialist, had focused classroom instruction on sentence-level practice and was therefore unaware of Carmen's problems with writing, for she could apply correctly on drills and tests rules she could not remember to use when she wrote or spoke. She also had other problems, Maria said:

When I explained, however, he understood. I said she needed to work further with organization, that her pieces rambled a lot and were very disorganized. Then he said "Oh-h-h," and I have the distinct impression that he was not puzzled after that. It seems that he had been focusing more on sentence structure and mechanics than on writing though I can't remember now exactly what he said. Anyway, once I told him about Carmen's problems with writing, he dismissed the incongruity between his evaluation and mine.

Being able to memorize and apply rules in isolation was a strength that would serve Carmen's writing well once she learned to develop ideas and revise until they were clear. Fall semester, however, it did her little good; for though she was fairly fluent, Carmen did not monitor. Because she had few of the structural inhibitions that marred the writing of so many entering students, she revealed a surface fluency. For a time tutors and I mistook fluency of this sort for a strength—or (more precisely) mistook it for *more* of a strength than it *was*. In the long run, however, students like Carmen progressed slowly, for, having had little practice finding their own mistakes, they had to learn from scratch how and when to correct their work. Many even had to become aware that they needed to. Certification could therefore take these students a long time. They simply did not have much writing experience on which to build.

To figure out how to teach future Carmens to lead from strength, we wanted to analyze just what this Carmen could do, so between us Dianna and I assessed her progress from several perspectives. In addition to that of the linguist Maria spoke to, we studied Maria's, Carmen's, Dianna's and the group's views and documented that of a history professor as well. A copy of Maria's final assessment was in Carmen's folder, where Maria had filed it after mailing Carmen a copy along with the formal notice of delayed certification. Beginning with the positive, Maria had noted strengths, then pointed out features on which Carmen might want to work when she returned:

> Carmen, you have good ideas for papers . . . but you need to organize them better. After you have written something, before you revise it, ask yourself "What is the main idea, the focus, of this paper?" Then take out whatever is irrelevant.

Dianna agreed that Carmen should not have been certified. In her case study on Carmen she wrote:

> In her folder I found seven freewrites on a variety of topics; two were taken to second drafts. I also found seven drafts of an episode in her "Literally [sic] Analysis" class. It had begun as a recounting of the class, but ended up as a dialogue among the students involved.

This excerpt typified Carmen's most developed piece:

> LISA: Hi! I lost my papers again.
> PROF: Here you go Lisa.
> LISA: Can I seat with you?
> ME: Yeah! Sure.
> PROF: Who can talk about the poem?
> LISA: This, I haven't read this, because my roommates took my papers.
> DOLORES: There's metaphors, similes, lots of adjective, etc.
> LISA: Ha! Ha! (laughing real loud)
> FRANK: Ha! Ha! (laughing real loud)
> LISA: What's she saying Frank?
> FRANK: Pay attention. You're always lost.
> LISA: No, that's not a metaphor. Becquer wrote . . .
> PROF: But, were not talking about Becquer. . . .

A former high-school teacher from a traditional teaching tradition who in the past had favored preventive/corrective instruction, Dianna was aghast at the surface-level problems that remained:

I felt at a loss how to help Carmen. This was the seventh draft of a piece she had worked on for seven weeks. . . . The errors of punctuation (''Here you go Lisa''), usage (*seat* for *sit*), and spelling (*literally* for *literary*) made me uncomfortable about where to begin.

Luckily, teacher-research helped Dianna reinterpret this ''failure'' by re-focusing her attention on strengths. Carmen had made progress—in awareness, attitude, and behavior—that (we know now as we did not then) could have helped us predict that the writing she was doing at the time would improve naturally. For example, she had begun to choose motivating topics and was assessing her own progress accurately. On the midterm self-evaluation done during the first semester, she'd noted the same strengths and weaknesses Maria would later note and then some, evidence that she had been able to critique her own work:

1. I can say that my strengths are to free write when I'm ask to. I can write as if I was talking to someone. I can get inspire easily about a subject.
2. My weaknesses as a writer can be so many, because I have English as a second language.
   a. The reason I say this is because when I write it might not sound quite well in English.
   b. I need a lot of time to revise and I would like to write for hours and hours.

Other strengths show up in a process log written on Carmen's first day in Dianna's group. Aware that she must learn to edit, Carmen also knew that she needed to balance attention to various tasks. And in-process revisions in this thinkwrite show that she has begun to monitor *while drafting*:

The WTC is harder ~~the~~ for me ^than^ getting a grade in a course . . . Whtting English was easy for me until I got here, I guess I didn't ~~worry~~ ^worry^ about mistakes! . . . My mistake for not being ~~certied~~ certified was: I wrote too much, ~~I~~ and edited just a little. . . .

Not only had Carmen taken responsibility for her progress, she had become aware of the rewards of group work:

I feel that I'm going to feel great this time, but just If I see any accomplishment on myself. It m gives me moral support Knowing that there are others like me.

While yearning for easy solutions, Carmen was realistic. She knew that attending to meaning was the key to improving her writing and that language abilities expand only gradually:

~~coming~~ I just would like to know the right formula for writting ~~En~~ in Engtsh; I guess there isn't any. I can say writing with sense is just a natural thing that comes with time maybe years.

In short, Carmen developed many strengths during fall semester, among which was a balanced and accurate view of her writing that would serve her well when she made decisions about her learning. Furthermore, while aware that she herself needed further help, she'd managed not to let groupmates' more rapid progress intimidate her, an accomplishment that was probably aided by the ungraded writing done in the WTC.

Segment 2: A Critical Transition

Was Carmen's Glass Half Empty or Half Full? Carmen fit a category that seems neither fish nor fowl—unless (like some students) we equate success with certification. Given what I'd been told of her progress fall semester, however, it seemed we'd been as much in error to conclude Carmen "failed" as we would have been had we certified her. A few days into spring semester, Carmen would rejoin the ranks of students who took part eagerly, demonstrated effective writing strategies for groupmates, and in the end succeeded with academic writing. Reentry into this category wasn't assured, however, and Carmen teetered for several days on the brink of a downward spiral, for the balanced view of her progress she'd held was hard to maintain in view of her recent "failure" to certify. Though she believed she'd grown as a writer, knew that she'd worked hard, and had heard her strengths confirmed by Maria and her first group, negative connotations associated with "repeating" weakened Carmen's already shaky confidence.

In other words, the end-of-semester summative evaluation process brought on the start of a brief but critical transition phase, for the positive attitudes on which progress depended relied in turn on Carmen's maintaining a balanced view of her work. This transition phase was similar to what breakthrough students went through. Whereas breakthrough students' initial shift to positive self-assessment depended on and was confirmed by others' positive views, the positive attitudes on which Carmen's continued progress depended relied in turn on her maintaining a balanced view of her work—even in the face of the "failure" she and others perceived.

Carmen was at a crossroad. As she said in a thinkwrite her first day in Dianna's group, she wavered between discouragement and thinking "in a positive way":

> I decided to start by asking Carmen to write about her feelings about returning for a second semester. In this way, I would have an idea of her attitude:
>
> > Coming back to the WTC see seems kind of discouraging. . . . So hard to come back and repeat the same thing. If I think in a positive way, coming back can be a challenge for what I didn't accomplished.

Carmen's ambivalence in this negative situation parallels the ambivalence of breakthrough students like Loi, Parvis, and Dale before tutors helped them see breakthroughs positively. In both cases, support for balanced self-assessment ensured the completion or continuation of upward spirals. Without support before and during *formative* evaluation by tutors and peers, however, potential breakthroughs remained incomplete because anxiety led to regressions in confidence. And, without even more support during *summative* evaluation, the upwardly spiraling progress of hardworking but "slow" students often aborted abruptly for the very same reason: Negative evaluation led to regressions in confidence that undermined students' faith in a balanced view of their work. In other words, when harsh or summative evaluation threatened the supportive, informal, formative assessment students felt safe with, it interrupted upward spiraling even when significant progress was being made.

In short, the negative bias in hierarchical summative assessment placed counterproductive pressures on basic writers. In fact, as Daniela found, whether teachers chose deficiency or growth models of evaluation determined for some whether they would improve or not. The pressures were exacerbated for our slowest students, however, for our growth model—as we had implemented it—did not adequately protect them when certification time arrived before they had reached the independent stage. Lock-step evaluation prevailed at CAU, so slower students were forced to face summative evaluation at the end of the term, often just a short time before they were ready for it.

Like all hierarchies, universities need negative evaluation to maintain their status as hierarchies by eliminating students (and faculty) at every level. It helps them maintain their competitive standing within the larger hierarchy of educational hierarchies and screen candidates for positions in other institutions within the hierarchy of hierarchies that makes up society. Despite pervasive pressures to maintain both negative grading and the lock-step evaluation schedules on which it relies, we found both traditions incompatible with our growth-oriented assessment approach because we saw our role as helping all students succeed rather than as guarding the gates of academe.

Hierarchical pressures intruded rudely at semester's end, however, when we had to certify students whether or not they were ready to handle university writing assignments on their own. While we were documenting the negative impact on learning of such summative evaluation, another evaluation-related variable emerged—the importance of self-assessment in fostering the awareness students need to maintain balanced views of their progress in the face of evaluation procedures designed at worst to discourage them, at best to alert the powers that be to their weaknesses.

Summative evaluation had a powerful impact on learning. Fulfilling the role for which hierarchies rely on it, it excluded slow students from ascending to the next level. And though we eliminated it within the program, failure to be certified by the end of the term led to the deepest regressions WTC students faced. Despite the progress they'd experienced all semester, "failing" convinced many returnees they couldn't succeed after all, leaving them bitter and angry at what they saw as a broken promise—the promise of success implicit in our balanced assessment approach. Unaware that needing more time did not invalidate their progress in any way, that they would not have to "repeat the same thing," to use Carmen's words, many returnees grew hard to motivate, and the logs show that disinterest, resistance, and absences interfered with the trust tutors were once again trying to build in the new groups.

Awareness was one condition that helped overcome these regressions. When tutors prepared students for summative evaluation, by clarifying how summative and formative assessment differ, helping them assess their progress accurately in advance so negative summative judgments would not take them by surprise, and providing support for maintaining a balanced view of their progress even in the face of negative results, returnees like Carmen were more likely to survive regressions. It did not occur to me or to the tutors, however, that the timing of summative evaluation was arbitrary and that we could have given our students control over it.

As we could now predict from the attitude/behavior/writing progression, more than confidence lagged during the transition phase. In the unfamiliar presence of a new tutor and group, risk-taking behavior and written products also regressed. On her second day in Dianna's group Carmen wrote three stiff, halting lines reminiscent of entry essays done under test conditions (like those described in Chapter 2):

> When I came ~~to~~ from Puerto Rico in 1981, I was a Secretary. I wanted ~~had more aspirations~~ to start ~~become~~ a ~~proffesional~~ start a better professional ~~f~~ career. I worked for the ~~f~~ Federal Government.

Fluency returned quickly, however, when Carmen recognized the familiar small group structure, and on the third and fourth days she found a likely topic during group discussion, tapping what would later prove a strong source of motivation. In the process, she demonstrated proactive behavior for first-time groupmates, dramatized the connection between revision and "making sense," and by taking off from a topic brought up by a new student, illustrated for the others that she expected to learn from them:

> It wasn't until the third session that she wrote something of some length. The piece grew out of a childhood memory discussion. We had talked as a group about various memories and got into writing easily from our discussion. Clarence had mentioned that he was a lifeguard, and, taking her ideas from his, Carmen wrote one and one-half pages about an experience of near drowning. In the next class session, she read this first draft to the group, saying "I'd like to tell [you] what is about in case it doesn't make sense."

Instead of forcing her to "repeat" what new students were doing, Dianna trusted Carmen to progress at her own rate—to pick up wherever she'd left off the semester before. In doing so she showed that she valued Carmen's experience by using her as a role model for others to imitate. Carmen responded positively to this encouragement, stopped writing of worries about failure and success, and settled down again, at last, to the task of improving her work. In fact, on a midterm self-assessment she would herself assert that during this time she'd "accomplished a period of transition."

Self-Assessment and the Desire to Persevere. Returnees fell into several categories according to whether or not ambivalence followed evaluation and according to how they dealt with it when it did.

1. Certified students who returned as volunteers and did *not* experience crises of confidence

2. Uncertified students who knew they needed more help, who had asked for assurance that they could return to the WTC, and who avoided crises of confidence because they were aware that they weren't ready to be certified

3. Uncertified students, required by tutors to return, who like Carmen felt ambivalent but managed to maintain a balanced view of their progress, demonstrated writing attitudes and behavior to others, influenced new groupmates to take writing seriously, and in the end succeeded with academic assignments

4. Uncertified students who (like Hosea, from Kathy's group) felt and acted discouraged, embarrassed, sullen, resistant, or noncommitted; stopped attending regularly or stopped attending at all; and, by demonstrating uncommitted behavior and attitudes, diluted commitment and bonding (and therefore progress) in their new groups

These categories reflect the impact of awareness, which tutors learned to encourage by letting students do more self-assessment, on basic writers' motivation to persevere even after "failing" to be certified. Students who were themselves aware that they needed further help rarely displayed negative feelings on their return. But for students less thoughtful or less secure in their self-assessments, being required to return to the Center threatened confidence and made them need extra support during the transition stage. When Carmen displayed her ambivalence about returning, for example, Dianna's positive response helped her resist further self-doubt. Had Carmen sensed Dianna's dismay at her problems, however, or had she been forced to "repeat the same thing," she might have followed the pattern of other returnees whose tentative upward spirals collapsed during the transition phase.

It's important to note that Dianna did not encourage Carmen by plan. Not only her logs but her research report and our long discussions confirmed that she felt overwhelmed by Carmen's problems at this point, but she controlled her negative responses in order to test our more positive approach. Teacher-research helped Dianna reinterpret signs she would once have viewed as negative and helped her recognize the balanced view Carmen had developed toward her writing the semester before. Without either pressuring Carmen or revealing her own dismay, Dianna waited calmly for the writing itself to improve, intuitively increasing support when confidence regressed and keeping her negative view of Carmen's abilities to herself.

Dianna's thoughtful self-control paid off handsomely for Carmen—just as Maria's had done the semester before. Soon the "breakthrough with revising" led to increased independence, and attitude and behavior changes begun the semester before began to affect the quality of Carmen's written work. Like Ned, Carmen began to influence those in her group, setting a high standard for the work groupmates did and dramatizing how what she'd learned at the point of choice transferred naturally to academic work.

Consider how like a powerful magnet teacher-research functioned, drawing Dianna to increase support intuitively even *before* she felt optimism about Carmen's work. As a result of Dianna's data-informed intuitions, Carmen was able to make it through the shaky transition stage and adopt the role of experienced writer for her new group. And she did so not by studying structures, patterns, and rules, but by practicing writing she herself had chosen to do.

Dianna's logs on Carmen show how exceptions account for the rule. By providing details that explained why one returnee succeeded, they led us to hypotheses about why other returnees failed. Revealing how Carmen survived a regression in confidence similar to those that derailed other returnees' upward spirals, the logs highlighted attitude shifts less-open returnees hid and showed the need to increase planned incidental support just before and after summative evaluation time. In the past we'd responded only *after* problems arose, attempting with infrequent success to rebuild returnees' trust, inviting returnees to resubmit portfolios at midterm, and bolstering self-esteem by using them as resources for others. Carmen's case suggests that basic writers needed preparation to survive the shift to summative evaluation, confirmed the similar problems tutors had in my seminar (Nelson, 1988), and suggested several possible remedies:

- Distinguishing the roles of summative and formative assessment
- Making clear from the start that success has no time limits
- Giving students experience with formative self-assessment
- Stepping students through summative self-assessment in preparation

- Assuring borderline students of how far they've come and of where they need work before they have to deal with a negative "grade"

It also convinced me to place returnees, when possible, with the tutors they'd worked with the semester before and to seek ways to balance their self-assessments during semester breaks.

The informal way in which Dianna came to support Carmen's learning was the process by which teacher-research helped all tutors change. Of course, the formal analyses I did for this book helped me clarify and understand how much I'd learned, and tutors' final research reports functioned for them the same way. But these written reports came *after* our teaching changed: They merely helped make explicit what we had earlier learned to do. Rather than the formal analysis that came later, it was the process of "keeping the records," our "follow the kid" stance, that taught us how to increase support at the point of need and nudge the program to evolve in more and more effective directions.

The process of basing teaching decisions on observation-informed intuitions also helped tutors become independent of me. Not unlike the think-writes in which basic writers assessed their own progress, deciding for themselves what directions they needed to move in next, observational logs served a metacognitive function, allowing tutors to monitor and assess their own work holistically and informing the intuitive awareness that led to growth.

Segment 3: The Long Slow Climb

Consolidating Gains in Confidence and Commitment. Carmen still had a long way to go to be certified spring semester, but once through the shaky transition phase she again worked hard, practicing writing strategies she'd learned the semester before and focusing her efforts on "making sense" in drafts—just as her past self-assessments suggested she knew how to do. Her focus on meaning proved an effective one. Looking back over her progress at the end of the term, Dianna noted the "important role" meaning making played in Carmen's development: "This desire to communicate would play an important role in the revising process later for Carmen."

Much as Kamal had done at home alone with a tape recorder, Carmen listened critically to her writing while reading aloud, comparing it to her memory of the English she heard every day and making changes when the two failed to correspond: "As she read, Carmen corrected some of her mistakes. For example, she crossed out *in* in 'It was in Illeana's house' and changed it to *at.* She had a hard time getting through it. Her English is very rough."

The following unedited excerpt from Draft 1 illustrates the kinds of problems Maria and Dianna saw:

> I went to this pool party, in which I almost drawn.
> It was in Ilcana's house. There was Teresa, Lizane, and Cindy raising from one corner of the pool to the other. I wasn't much of a swimer. So, I did go along swimming but just by the wall. I could hold my self from it and I would be safe., Later on I remember; Liazne, Cindy & I underneath a small plastic raft which it was turned up side down. Our heads were between the water & the top of the raft. . . . My knees are bent toword my chest, so I can't feel the floor. Time passed and I felt the Wind. All of a sudden I streched my legs, to my surprise We were in deep water, Luckily the raft had some hooks that I could hold onto. . . . and also Lizane swimmed us back. I new from Cindy later on that she was asthmatic.

By aurally scanning drafts they had written, slower students like Carmen, Chat, and Kamal detected and improved many features of their work— omitted words and word endings, misused prepositions, awkward idioms, sentence garbles, misused vocabulary, misplaced adverbials, and nonstandard article use. Reading aloud alerted them to more sweeping problems as well— like faulty logic, poor transitions, underdeveloped ideas, ambiguous phrases, repetition, redundancy, weak cohesion, and omitted details. When Carmen read this draft aloud, Dianna reported, she apologized for its weaknesses ("It's not finished yet") and orally added details needed for it to "make sense."

Aural scanning proved generative for so many students that tutors made a point of stepping them through the process, pointing out how well it worked, and rewarding surprised readers by making a big to-do when they did it spontaneously, as they often did. Almost all students stumbled at times while reading aloud, but unaware why they stumbled, few thought to make deliberate, conscious corrections as a result. Unaware that such stumbling almost always revealed a mismatch between what was on the page and what they'd expected to see (or between what was on the page and an emerging idea), many failed to stop as they read and improve what they'd written, until tutors pointed out that they'd stumbled because something didn't "sound right." Bringing dissonance to the conscious level helped students see the need to revise semantic, stylistic, or syntactic features; helped convince them of untapped "hidden skills"; and built confidence that their writing would grow naturally in the Center's sanctuary atmosphere. To facilitate learning, tutors learned to stay just one step ahead of groups. Assessing a wide range of factors that contribute to growth, they confirmed where progress was strong and modeled related concerns, helping students learn how to figure out what to focus on next. Cycling from proactive to interactive to reactive behavior, they directed feedback to the point of need. For example, as Carmen's group approached the interactive stage, Dianna withdrew leadership to examine student responses, focusing less on quantity than on appropriateness. As they had never received much positive response, most students entered the Center knowing how to give negative feedback, so Dianna was content to see them trying out positive comments and successfully avoiding harshly negative ones. Later she would expect more in the way of interaction, but as this was only the group's fourth session together, one positive comment matched to Carmen's confidence level seemed an adequate offering *for this point in the term:*

> Since this was a first freewrite, we did not talk about the areas that needed fixing. She had no paragraphs and there was a clear problem with organization, but we did not comment at this point. The group was still forming, and it was important to establish a trusting atmosphere. Only Mahmoud responded:
>
> > I liked the part where she looked very "fatigued." Most people use "tired." I'll have to remember that word. It meant more than just "tired."

Evidence of mutual benefit from heterogeneous grouping emerged early among this group's five natural language learners. Like tutors, whom they observed for cues about how to respond, students intuitively matched responses to the level of feedback other groupmates needed. Mahmoud's comment showed Carmen that he was learning from her and at the same time reinforced what was strong in her work:

> As I look back over this piece, I wonder if it wouldn't have been overwhelming for Carmen if the group had commented at this point. Her English is rough—she often leaves out subjects and her accent is thick. It was okay that they didn't respond further; she asked no more of the group at this time.

Though Carmen lacked confidence in her abilities, she was a fine role model for entering basic writers where motivation, independence, revising, and editing were concerned. Writing habits she had practiced doggedly for a semester set a standard for the others seated with her at the table and demonstrated a level of motivation and independence they would need to reach quickly to be certified in one term. Applying what she'd learned in Maria's group, Carmen voluntarily drilled herself on editing skills even while Dianna encouraged others to postpone such concerns. Starting to work immediately on a second draft, she added details as she read quietly to herself. Focusing on meaning, on whether or not her work "made sense," she worked independently for two sessions the following week, reporting that she was "adding to and revising" what she had. Carmen shows how returnees who avoided sliding downward modeled writing attitudes, strategies, and improvement; demonstrated the shifting scale of concerns to which writers attend; served as models of how to succeed for entering students; and helped groups get off to a faster start than they might have otherwise.

On February 20 (week 5 of spring semester), Dianna reported that Carmen had finished a revised draft but wanted to check for mistakes one more time before reading aloud: "She began to read her three pages, written on two different days, with pen in hand, correcting again as she read along."

An excerpt from Draft 2 of Carmen's "Drawning" piece reveals that many improvements still needed to show up on the page:

> My knees were bent toward my chest and I couldn't feel the floor. Time passed without noticing. ~~and Al~~ of a sudden, of a sudden, I streched my legs and I couldn't reach the floor. I got frightened being on the middle of the pool and unable to swim. Luckily, the raft had some hooks that I could hold onto. With the raft still over our heads, Lizane swimmed us back and we got off the water. . . .

As Carmen worked independently for several sessions, groupmates observed her separating and sequencing writing tasks. Soon others were also acting serious about writing, working past the time when group was scheduled to end:

> Everyone was still writing intently at 12:25. When I said it was past time to go, Carmen responded, "I sometimes hate to quit. It's hard to get back concentration." Reluctantly, she and the others left.

Carmen wasn't merely playing at editing. On February 22, Dianna asked if she wanted to read Draft 2, at which point Carmen started circling mistakes, saying "I'm not finished yet." Later, after reading aloud to herself, she reconsidered, musing about how different her oral and written versions seemed and complaining that her words often failed to "make sense" on the page. Discovering on her own how writing differs from speech written down, Carmen began to feel a need for the group's advice:

CARMEN: It makes sense when I *talk*. When I *read* it sounds funny. I can't follow.

DIANNA: Maybe you need to read it *aloud*. What do you want us to listen for?

CARMEN: Maybe for *everything*? Maybe if it makes *sense*. I don't know. I feel shy.

Shaken by growing awareness of problems in her work, Carmen seemed insecure about her many revisions. After all, this was her first substantial revising effort, for she had never done much monitoring before. Sensing her vulnerability, Dianna moved to increase support to make the risk manageable:

> I sensed her anxiety. The other group in the small room with us was discussing loudly, and I felt Carmen was uncomfortable. I also thought it might help her to hear her own piece read.

DIANNA: I'll read it—exactly *as it is*, though!

While trying to decide whether to read or not, Carmen sent subtle signals that suggested uncertainty. Dianna responded by increasing support, making it easier for Carmen to take the needed risk. In this interaction between Carmen and her tutor can be seen the beginnings of an ebb-and-flow pattern that characterized group interactions when tutors combined incidental teaching with teacher-research. Responding to (or anticipating) regressions of confidence that accompany new or risky writing behaviors, tutors increased structure, involvement, content, or support just enough for students to be able to succeed. Once the risk taking passed, they backed quickly away, leaving writers again in charge of decisions about their work.

Paradoxically, much of this seemingly proactive tutor behavior was in actuality reactive. While offering to read can be seen as proactive on Dianna's part, it also shows the reactive way in which tutors acted proactive, basing their proactive moves on subtle student cues. When reading aloud felt so risky that Carmen's confidence regressed enough for Dianna to sense it, then and only then did Dianna offer an alternative *in response to* the ambivalent gestures on Carmen's part. In other words, owning up to her shyness served a proactive function, the outcome being that Carmen negotiated a challenge for herself that matched the level of risk taking she felt ready for. Rather soon, now, we'll see Carmen growing more assertive, asking directly for help and volunteering her expertise. At this point, shortly after her shaky transition, however, Carmen was still acting as if she felt vulnerable and Dianna responded appropriately, getting Carmen the group response she needed to improve.

Regressions typically announce emerging strengths, and Carmen's loss of confidence about reading was no exception: It signaled an increase in her concern for quality as well as awareness of problems in her work. Carmen's shyness was not without cause, for on this, her first extended piece of revising, certain aspects of her writing had regressed. "Some of her revisions were not improvements," Dianna concluded, and the passage that follows confirms that view:

Later on, Cindy and I used the raft again up side down and started a conversation ~~again~~ ^again^ on the shallow area. This time without noticing we were on the deep area. Lizane wasn't there, and Cindy wasa an asmathic girl. For some reason I started to feel real scare. I knew I ~~wouldn't~~ wasn't going to be able to swim. I asked Cindy to swim us back, but all she did was ~~live~~ ^leave^ ^lev^ ^let^ me alone and swim just ~~to a corner of the pool.~~ ^to^ one of the pool's corners. I thought all along that she was going to swim me back, as ~~I did~~ we did before with Lizane. ̶Áll I know is that the time passed by until ~~I ran out of b~~ I couldn't breath. The edges of this small raff which were turn^ed^ up side down were stuck to the water, (just my head between the ~~top one~~ space from the top of the raft and the water). I had to ~~take~~ stick my head out. On a corner there was Cindy looking very exhausted while I was yelling for help. ~~I was~~ Obviously, I wasn't swimming, I was drawning.

This time Carmen's group, by now more confident, offered a few questions about sections they found unclear. During the discussion Dianna jotted these down, proactively helping the nervous Carmen remember useful ideas and demonstrating the value of saving responses to study later. Group questions and comments revealed some problems in Carmen's draft:

> JAMSED: When friends left, you were with Cindy. How it happened? Did she tell you she was going to leave?
>
> CARMEN: I thought she would come back.
>
> CLARENCE: I wanted to know what happened to the girl with asthma.

Carmen received advice on vocabulary and diction as well as these suggestions for additions, but Dianna made clear that final decisions were up to her:

> I suggested that Carmen think about our questions. Perhaps she needed to clarify some points. Then I commented that she hadn't used the word "fatigued" as she had in the first draft.
>
> MAHMOUD: Ultimate tired! (He had liked the word and had told her so last time she read it.)
>
> JAMSED: How do you express "drowning"—"Can't breathe"? "Flush water out of mouth"?
>
> KY: You didn't *yell*?
>
> CARMEN: My voice didn't come out.
>
> DIANNA: That would be a good detail to add!

I concluded by suggesting Carmen think about our questions and add details of her near drowning. Then Jamsed talked about a problem he was having with a writing assignment.

As Louise had done with Ned's art history paper, Dianna used Jamsed's problem to teach assignment writing incidentally. This excerpt therefore illustrates one kind of instruction that may have influenced Carmen's success in some way. After drafting a paper on "courtship" for freshman English, Jamsed claimed that the "paper for WTC help me write this [English] one." He'd run into some problems, however, one being confusion about the meaning of the term:

> JAMSED: "Courtship"? What's that? I had written about "culture" once before in WTC, but the thing that held me back on this paper was "courtship."

Reading over the freewrite done in group, Jamsed had found ideas to use in the English 100 essay. In just a few weeks he was bringing the monitor under control. Already, in-process revisions focused on meaning as much as correctness, and in-process structural monitoring was helping, not distorting, his prose:

> Custom, culture, Society and religion are biggest ^strongest^ factors involves in changing individuals ~~life~~ personnal life. Just by asking some one that where he is from what religion he believed on can ~~tell all about~~ give you a slight hint about his back ground. It might not be suitable, but what I have seen and experience in this country Some how ~~I have~~ ^made me^ ~~feeling~~ what ~~ever~~ I have said above is not appropriate for an average American.

Jamsed also found in his folder some freewriting on marriage customs that he could use to show differences between Pakistan and the United States:

> In the country where I came from . . . there have been lots of changes in the way of living. Peoples have become very modern they have change their living style but Some how deep Inside them they are still tide up with those old customs. ~~and~~ Their modern tyles of living havent change their mentality, still all the important decission are made by parents. Such as a marraige which completely ~~change~~ effects and changs every one ~~life~~ lives. But strange and weared thing about it that ~~a~~ Those decission are accepted by young peoples. They have been ~~aud.~~ learned and taught that ~~the bes~~ if any one can make a best decission in your favor that is your parents.

We cannot tell from these data whether this incident directly influenced Carmen's academic writing or not. Developing bits of personal writing into a formal essay was a different application than Carmen herself would need. By reading drafts of this essay in Carmen's presence, however, Jamsed demonstrated that strategies learned in the WTC could transfer successfully to academic work.

One week later, on February 16, Dianna commented on Carmen's increasing independence, her willingness to ask proactively for help, and the growing commitment of others in her group:

> Carmen read over her second draft and began a third:
>
> CARMEN: Should I make corrections on same paper?
>
> DIANNA: What kind of revisions are you're doing? If they're major, start an entirely new draft.
>
> Carmen began work. Jan's group left as usual at 12:20, but ours continued to write. I remembered Carmen's comment about breaking concentration from an early session. Once this group starts writing, they find it difficult to stop.

For the first third of spring semester Carmen practiced writing strategies she had learned to use the term before in Maria's group. The data suggest that during this time she practiced little new but she did survive a shaky transition phase and assigned herself regular drill on revising and editing. In other words,

Carmen spent five weeks of the second semester reviewing and practicing what she'd learned the term before.

Segment 4: Breaking Through

The Boost into Higher Orbit. After plateaus during which writing showed little change, even the slowest students often experienced breakthroughs that accelerated their upward spirals. These were triggered by the changes in attitude that followed increased awareness of how other writers work, and they led to risk taking, effort, and improved written products. These results confirmed the insights that produced them, fueling motivation and causing growth curves to veer upward, thus increasing the pace at which students became independent. Jane Lofts Thomas (1988) described this cycle, at one point referring to it as a "snowball effect":

> Memories, experiences, snippets of conversation, extraordinary sights and events are all stowed away in the memory, and I repeatedly found that if students could be helped to find the appropriate key which would unlock the doors and unleash them, and if they could be captured on paper before they escaped . . ., powerful writing frequently resulted. And the writing of a powerful piece often has a snowball effect, stimulating the desire to write and leading to the production of even more powerful pieces. (p. 544)

After several weeks of working on "Drowning," Carmen had a breakthrough that showed the snowball effect. Dianna reported the breakthrough in her research report:

> Carmen had an exciting breakthrough—an all night revising session—scissors cutting, pasting, and major reorganizing. The revisions she made brought "sense" to the piece, a sense she had earnestly sought. It seems that "outlining" *after* writing helped Carmen organize her piece. On March 5 she came in with the fourth draft of her "Drowning" piece. She had missed last Wednesday's session, but apparently had worked hard on this draft the night before, staying up until 2:00 am, then missing all her classes the next day until 1:30 pm.

Working hard at a task she'd assigned herself, Carmen became aware of her growing competence by solving, on her own, the very kinds of problems she and Maria had found troublesome the fall before:

> She seemed very pleased with the results and talked about her "revising process." She said, "I work a lot of hours on it. I cut a lot and pack it all up." She made a motion of cutting with scissors in her hands. "It was very confusing. For example, last time you ask me what happened to Cindy. I put that in and how I felt. I make an outline—but I didn't bring it today." Her outline turned out to be a brief list of what she discussed in her paper:

1. Told about a party that I went
2. Talking in the raft—~~Lizane~~
3. ~~All of a sud~~ Got trouble—Lizane took me back
4. Got Deep
5. Cindy took off—More panic—react
   Cindy's reaction
6. Panic & Trouble Sinking
   didn't dare leave the raft
7. Release when Cindy signals toward me and comes along
8. Got out of the pool
9. What Happen to Cindy

Finally Dianna began to see in Carmen's writing the rewards of a semester and a half of work:

> It was exciting to see how much she had invested in this piece and how well it had turned out, but it wasn't *completely* clear how she had done it until she explained further. She had cut out sentences (from her first two drafts) that were about her feelings or about Cindy. Then she taped them into a new draft from which she wrote draft four.
> "I really work so hard," she said.

This event illustrates several traits that accompany breakthroughs:

- The persistence generated by motivating topics
- The increased independence that accompanies motivation
- Writers' ability to improve their work *if they persevere*
- The excitement and confidence writers feel after solving problems
- The way conventions and strategies writers have studied but cannot apply are available when needed to improve writing they care about
- The way writers transfer strategies practiced on self-selected writing to note taking, term papers, and other academic assignments
- The desire of "breakthrough" students to share what they discover
- The way one breakthrough precipitates others in a group
- The tenacity of the upward tendency, at least for the duration of the "sanctuary," which offered temporary protection from premature evaluation

Dianna's log contained considerable evidence on these points. For example, while struggling with the logistics of copying cut-and-paste drafts, Carmen retrieved Maria's once-confusing advice from memory and used it to solve a problem with this piece. Only after perceiving the problem herself in a piece of her own work, she said, did Maria's suggestion make any sense to her. In other words, past learning became more meaningful in context, when the writer herself perceived a need for what she had learned. It was frequent recurrence of this pattern—in which ability to apply knowledge depended on personal experience of the need for it—that led us to an operational definition of the Britton team's (1975) concept of the *point of need*. When working with motivated students, we concluded, we recognize the point of need as the writer's point of choice:

> Carmen explained that last semester Maria had told her not to write on the back of her paper—that it would be easier to revise from one side of the page. She said the purpose for doing that had been unclear until she experienced the need to do so. She said, "Now I can see why it stopping you [to write on both sides] because if I have things written on the back, I can't cut it."

This passage shows the efficiency of offering instruction at the *motivated* writer's point of need. Writing only on the front of her papers was not an abstract concept that Carmen had failed to grasp but a concrete tip about arranging text on the page. Even so, what stopped Carmen from applying Maria's advice was lack of firsthand experience with cut-and-paste revising. As previous data had led us to suspect, this incident suggested that prior knowledge learned out of context can become accessible for a writer's use through motivated firsthand writing experience. Here a hands-on struggle to organize her work prompted Carmen to retrieve Maria's advice from memory and provided a context in which its meaning became clear. In other words, the log shows Carmen looking backward to salvage partial learnings from memory in order to apply them at the point of need. How much earlier, we wondered, might she have applied that tip had Carmen had more writing experience in the courses she took before coming to the WTC.

The log also shows Carmen looking forward as well as backward, anticipating future applications for new strategies: "She talked about a twelve-page paper due for her Russian history course: 'I'm going to do outline first.' " It shows her sharing insights—this time about repetition—anticipating that what she'd learned might help someone else:

> I asked, "Did you do outlines before you worked on 'Drowning'?" "Not really," she responded, "but on that piece I got confused myself. It seemed like it was repetition, like I said this same thing before so I cut all the pieces out and taped them." I asked Carmen to bring in her cut and taped drafts and to share her process with the group. She responded, "I think they will help someone else."

The log also shows Carmen's growing confidence in the quality of her work—quality measured against a meaning-related criterion. "She continued, by way of apology, 'The second draft was nicer [looking] than this one but more confusing. This fourth draft is *clear*.' She had made a lot of improvements, particularly in the first section."

Dianna continued to leave Carmen in control, encouraging her to figure out what help she needed next and suggesting she view her drafts as tentative until an audience confirmed their success:

> Finally Carmen was ready to read, so I asked what kind of advice she needed.
>
> She responded: "Questions. For example, *I'm* reading, and I know the story, but these things are inside my mind, so I don't notice if I leave one of them out. I need to know do you have any questions. Now I will read. If it doesn't answer your questions, you can tell me later on."

Afterwards Carmen edited systematically, using asterisks to mark prepositions she was unsure of and making in-process corrections while copying revisions from the cut-and-paste draft. The next excerpt is from Draft 4:

> One afternoon I went to this pool party in which ^where^ I almost drowned. It was a cloudy, windy day in* March, but it was very warm since it was in* Puerto Rico. Some girlfriends—Lizane, Cindy, and Teresa were swemming along with me from one corner of the pool to the other. Back then, I wasn't much of a swimmer. I swam by the wall only. I d had some kind of fear to of deep water, and the middle of the pool, at least wasn't for me, wasn't the safest place to be.

Here's another excerpt from Draft 4 with asterisks marking problems in the margins as well as within lines.

> *   After swimming for a few minutes, we all turned* a small raft
>   plastic raft upside down. We used it as if it were a hat. Our heads
> *   were in the hollow of the raft and* our bodies were in* the water
> *   while holding onto* the hooks connected to its edges. We all talked
>   for a while. I learned from our conversation that Cindy was asth-
>   matic, which became a problem for me later.

In her struggle to relate this experience, Carmen's underdeveloped monitor got some exercise. She had edited the whole piece again, in fact, making corrections (including a subjunctive form) on her own. Though Draft 4 was still far from perfect, Carmen's writing now revealed more accurately which written English conventions she needed to study. Thus it drew Dianna's advice to the point of need:

> *   She just took off* and left me along in the middle of that situa-
>   tion. Without Knowing what to expect for sure, I waited there as if
>   she was were coming back. I always thought that she was going to
>   help me get back to the shallow area. . . . Somehow, the edges of the
>   raft started to stick to the water. I realized just then that there was no
>   air for me to breathe breathe. The hollow in which my head was
> *   started to look small, since the water was right up* to my chin. I felt
>   helpless, scared, and trapped. I didn't know what to do. Among fear

* and confusion, I kept holding onto* the hooks, but was still unable
to breathe. I thought that the only way to reach for air was sticking
my head out and finally I did it. . . . There wasn't any balance, and
I started to sink.

Incorporating several pieces of group advice, Carmen had made two additions (see marginal notes below) to her next-to-final paragraph. Her drafts had
begun to resemble those of experienced writers, with the segment that follows
having been edited three times—once in pencil and once each in blue and red
ink:

> My fear of deep Water and what I was already experiencing made
> me very confused. I kept my body straight, jumping up and down,
> not daring to leave that awful raft, to keep me from drowning.* In a
> normal *situation, I would probably have acted normal—that is,
> getting to ~~swim~~ swim parallel with the water. All I tried to do was
> keep my head out of the water, to the point of exhaustion. I started
> yelling but ~~m~~ my ~~boi~~ voice didn't come out loud enough. (It
> sounded shaky and weird.)* My neck started hurting a lot, and I
> couldn't hear anything. Everything was bluRR, dark, and Cindy
> seemed ^to be^ miles and miles away from me. I felt weak, ~~thint~~
> thinking that I was going to die, and I prayed to God for help.

[+add #1]

[+add #2]

Attitude and behavior change preceded and followed the breakthrough,
with Carmen adopting a more proactive role in group and explaining her
editing process as if confident others could learn about writing from her.
There was nothing arrogant in her manner, however, and like the interdependent writers we studied in Chapter 3, she shared with groupmates the credit
for her success:

> After reading, Carmen pointed out places where she had made changes at
> the group's suggestion. For example, in the description of how she and the
> others held onto the raft, she wrote the simile, "We wore the raft like a hat."
> We talked about the "drowning" itself:

> CARMEN: I tried freewriting to remember more, but I didn't put in more
> about Cindy. I didn't think it was important what happened to
> her.

> I thought this was an accurate comment.

Carmen had not only organized and developed ideas, she'd omitted the
kinds of distracting details that had bothered Maria so much. With the help of
the group, Carmen's language also became more precise. Notice also that the
kinds of responses Dianna models remain just one step beyond what these
groupmates are able to do. After Ky shows that he can identify problems in
Carmen's draft and point them out without making harsh negative com-

ments, Dianna demonstrates more specific suggestions that give writers more concrete ideas about how to improve:

> Ky: It was a lot clearer, but I was confuse about part said "It seem so easy to get out of deep water." What you mean?
>
> CARMEN: Someone was near; I felt insecure. It was really something. You see the arm of a person, you grab it.
>
> DIANNA: Why not add that toward the end. Then tell how you felt about the arm being there.

I asked about a phrase she had used, "I probably would have acted normal in a normal situation." I said, "You used two 'normals' in one sentence. Read the sentence before and the other one after. Then we can decide what to do." Carmen read the sentence in context. Later she struck it out.

Later Carmen said, "I feel like if I could jump, I could swim." (This would have been good to add, but I didn't realize it at the time.)

Groupmates matched their responses to Dianna's example:

> Ky suggested using the wording "If I could get into *the position to swim.*"
> Carmen had said something about her fears adding to the panic, and I suggested a sentence: "You could add this: 'I realized that it was just my fear that kept me from swimming.' "
> Carmen added, "That panic—of being alone there . . ."
> I continued her sentence, " . . . had overwhelmed me. . . . "
> Finally I told Carmen how much better I thought the piece was. (The grammar had improved so!)

Though Carmen had been editing all semester, it was well after the breakthrough—after "Drowning" was clear and well-organized—that Dianna suggested Carmen needed to edit further and used this piece to demonstrate editing strategies for the others. An audiotape transcription captured this interaction:

> DIANNA: Now concentrate on editing it. Read this over *out loud* [to listen] for prepositions, and *ask me* if you have any questions.
>
> CARMEN: I already check for spelling and grammar as I read. And when I take notes for my classes, I realize that I make a lot of grammatical mistakes. Then I think of Spanish to write it in my own way. I write fast—later I have to fix the words.

Through her struggle to communicate with herself in writing, Carmen discovered that freewriting and revising could improve note taking—an academic writing skill.

Segment 5: The Rapid Upward Spiral
of Growing Confidence and Success

Breakthroughs were not limited to revising. Some happened when writers lowered the monitor. Others took place when they lowered the censor and wrote more honestly. Carmen, by contrast, had taken to freewriting with ease and had little trouble finding topics she cared about. Instead, her problem was that she'd never learned to monitor, so she was slower than most to develop revision and editing. After months of gradual increases in awareness, Carmen's breakthrough occurred when she grew motivated enough to struggle for hours with an organizational problem she'd discovered for herself. Then came a second period of consolidation, during which Carmen again took charge of drilling herself, extending and refining newly discovered strategies, and growing increasingly confident, independent, and motivated. This plateau differed from the earlier one, however, in the degree to which positive attitudes were intense, self-directed writing spilled into out-of-school hours, and noticeable improvement showed up in written drafts. It was as though the breakthrough had boosted Carmen into orbit. Certainly it had increased the angle of her learning curve.

Let's take a closer look at this second plateau, which we might once have seen as a regression, as a slowing down of the rapid progress Carmen had made. During it Carmen began to use the language of professional writers and publishers. On March 7 she brought a "revised edition" from home and offered groupmates further tips on revising. Confident that her experience would be useful to them, she identified a problem they had yet to encounter, a problem she had noticed herself—that she sometimes overrevised: "From third and fourth draft, I was confused. Once I start revising and start copying, I change too much."

Dianna praised Carmen's advice, suggested the others edit for those features they had the most problems with, and showed them how to separate and sequence editing tasks by reading drafts repeatedly for one feature at a time:

> I showed them the taped pieces and talked about how much more nicely her story flowed, with fewer grammatical errors. I asked Carmen to edit for prepositions again and suggested the others read their pieces for the type of error they make most—Mahmoud and Clarence for spelling, and Ky for past tense verbs.

In the reactive process of responding to basic writers' needs, Dianna acted proactively directive and supportive when helping them through transitions from one phase to another, but she backed away as soon as students grew comfortable. Her behavior reveals a pattern that permeates tutors' logs. Through the many overlapping and cyclic phases of writing—from finding ideas to drafting to revising to editing to feeling satisfaction when publication occurs—incidental instruction took on a tidelike rhythm, a predictable alternation between tutor and student initiative with tutors responding to fluctuations in writers' confidence. When (as during plateaus) consolidation predominated, tutors backed off, leaving students responsible for activities, acting as resources when students couldn't solve problems alone. By contrast, when risk-taking writers tested new strategies and had regressions, tutors moved in closer to demonstrate new coping skills and to offer the kinds of support they would soon expect groupmates to offer each other on their own.

Carmen wasn't the only one editing independently. Mahmoud joined her in sharing what he'd learned during editing. He'd tried WTC techniques on papers for other courses, he said, and had found two ways to get enough distance on his work to eliminate surface-level problems by himself. Mahmoud was now the third member of Carmen's group whose volunteering of strategies he'd found useful for academic writing was documented in Dianna's research log:

> Mahmoud talked about his "editing" process on a paper he just finished for a course. He'd found two ways of getting enough distance to find his own mistakes: "I read it three times at night, but when I woke up in the morning I still found six spelling mistakes. Then, when I got to school, I let my friend read it to me so I can hear it better because by then I memorized the piece so I can't find more mistakes by reading it myself." Advising the group, he continued, "Let your mother or brother read it *to* you. Then *you* find the mistakes."

Group discussions about what works frequently flowed back and forth between self-selected and assignment writing as if students saw little reason to separate the two. Not that they saw no differences in content, tone, and form, but they found they had similar problems with both kinds of writing and could solve those problems by using similar strategies. For example, familiarity kept Carmen from finding mistakes in her stories just as it kept Mahmoud from finding mistakes in teacher-assigned academic papers:

> Carmen agreed about the problem of "memorizing" pieces after several readings: "After a while, your own paper—you *know* it too well in your mind."

Dianna offered no direct instruction in assignment writing, but Carmen and her groupmates seemed to have little trouble transferring what they knew from self-selected pieces of writing to the constraints imposed by academic work.

At fairly regular intervals (or whenever writers got stuck), tutors encouraged the groupmates to thinkwrite for a few minutes to help them assess progress, clarify goals, and become aware of which strategies helped or hindered their work. In time we learned that suggesting a three-part self-assessment think-write helped produce insight (awareness) by focusing student attention

- First on strengths ("write about how your writing's improved")
- Then on weaknesses ("write about areas you think still need work")
- Then on the steps students might take to overcome weaknesses ("write about how you plan to improve in these areas")

Dianna suggested that groupmates write such self-assessments at midterm, and Carmen suggested how much can be learned from reading them. For example, more typical writers, who monitored and censored more, integrated these two functions with drafting only after they'd practiced separating and sequencing them for some time. By contrast, writers like Carmen, who'd neither monitored nor censored much in the past, needed time for monitoring and censoring skills to develop before they could hope to attend to content and form at once. Seven months building muscles she had lacked almost entirely brought new writing skills increasingly under Carmen's control, with Carmen herself noting in the self-assessment that she had learned to focus on content and form simultaneously. A close look at her writing supports this claim, for though in-process revisions were only partly correct, they neither inhibited fluency nor distorted her voice as they had done when she first joined Dianna's group:

> I gave directions for the self-evaluation, suggesting that they "think-write" about how their writing had changed and end it by saying what they need to work on next.
> Carmen told us that before coming to WTC she used to freewrite by letting whatever was in her mind about a subject flow onto paper. Now she still lets "things flow out of [her] mind," but is "trying to keep a definite purpose."
> I think what is what I want to say and be sure I ~~do~~ to don't ramble around. I'm more aware now when to make paragraphs. I think, that I've learned it on my own, but without the WTC, I would never ~~habe~~ have stopped to think about it. I always loved to write but in a lazy way, without worrying about any kind of punctuation.

Carmen was also learning, from Dianna's "oblique approaches" (Lofts Thomas, 1988), rhetorical lessons traditionally taught in more direct ways:

> Before I came here I thought that my writing ~~will always~~ would always made sense to everyone. I ~~learned that what is on my~~ I made myself rember since now or any time that I write, that what's it is ~~in~~ on my mind it isn't in the mind of anyone else. The readers or listeners aren't magicians, so, ~~thinking from~~ putting yourself in place of the reader is the best way to write.

The content of Carmen's thinkwriting reflects independent attitudes, while its structure reveals concurrent attention to content and form: Within one paragraph Carmen corrected a preposition, made diction more precise, improved a troublesome pronoun, inserted an omitted subject, and corrected a spelling mistake—all signs of monitoring that improved rather than marred the piece. And though she overgeneralized from her experience in two groups, the piece shows Carmen joining tutors and other students in the conclusion that anyone willing to work can learn to write well:

> I ~~think~~ I have accomplished ~~in~~ a period of transition that is to find out what one's own mistakes are. I have improved in revising and thinking for the correct forms of verbs, and I have learned that ~~every~~ ^any^ one could be a good writer. ^it^ is just a matter of making an outline! Putting one's thoughts together ~~in~~ ^on^ a ~~peace~~ ^piece^ of paper, for example, and follow that outline. As for free writing—just separate the different thoughts you have to make it clean and consistent.

Awareness that she *needed to improve* had motivated Carmen's attitude change.

> I really believe that WTC influences in the mind of any single student. [Last semester] I felt negative about it at the beginning, because I thought that I didn't needed. But now I think that even the most skillful writer needs advice from time to time.

Coinciding almost exactly with those of both of her tutors, Carmen's self-assessments had been balanced and realistic for a long time. In the fall she and Maria had concluded that, though fluent, Carmen needed more practice revising and editing. Now she and Dianna were also in agreement, both noting her upward spiral and (without always using these terms) commenting on changes in awareness, attitude, behavior, and writing. Both agreed that though she sometimes overmonitored, Carmen had developed substantial revising skill. At midterm, in fact, Dianna summarized the dramatic changes that had taken place in the three short weeks since Carmen's breakthrough: "Carmen, you certainly have improved. I am very excited about the kind of revising you are doing. Not only is it rewarding to see you doing it, but it also seems as rewarding to you."

As I've noted, our framework incorporates many perspectives, not all of which appear consistent at first glance. From Maria's fall-semester perspective, Carmen was "one of our failures," a student who showed little evidence of ability to succeed with academic assignments at CAU. From Dianna's spring-semester vantage point, by contrast, Carmen was a breakthrough case with great likelihood of success. From my analytic-clearinghouse perspective, Carmen was a negative case from whom we could learn how to help other returnees who caused tutors so many problems in groups. Given my longer and broader view of tutors' data—I studied ninety-odd logs on as many groups over the years—I could follow returnees' progress across semesters, from entry to certification, no matter how long that took. It was therefore I who discovered that Carmen's upward spiral, which to Dianna seemed to begin at the breakthrough point, had begun long before and had gone undetected for several months. That's how I realized that slow students weren't very different from faster ones.

Though this meta-analysis/metasynthesis made me question Maria's and Dianna's interpretations at points, it is entirely consistent with Carmen's own self-assessments. It shows her making steady progress throughout the fall semester, choosing to do exactly what she needed to do to improve. In other words, despite the outstanding quality of instruction that Maria and Dianna offered Carmen that year, Carmen herself was the one who most accurately assessed her progress. She "failed" only to the extent we projected "failure" because we acquiesced to the hierarchy's hunger for premature grades—or in this case for their substitute, which was getting certified.

In truth, it was not Carmen who failed that first semester. Though nothing in our backgrounds prepared us to do better, it was we who failed Carmen by failing to notice her progress and by relying too much on written products to detect signs of growth. Had we known then what we know now about patterns in writing development—breakthroughs, upward spirals, "the bigger they are, the harder they fall"—and how growth affects awareness, attitudes, and behavior—we might well have recognized Carmen's upward spiral and grouped her among our successes early in the fall term.

Though she worked harder than ever, taking drafts home to work on at night even though no homework was required, the rest of spring semester brought no further breakthrough for Carmen. For the time being, she abandoned taking risks in favor of consolidation and drill, applying the strategies she'd learned to various kinds of writing—exposition, note taking, research papers, and groupmates' work. And as had been true once before for Carmen, a period of self-imposed drill paid off for her.

Drilling themselves was one way students like Carmen stretched and grew when motivated by topics and genres of their own choosing. They also

- Adopted attitudes (confidence, motivation, persistence) that made it possible for them to produce well-written assignments
- Practiced a full complement of writing behaviors—brainstorming drafting, focusing, revising, "sleeping on it," editing, sharing responses, publishing—used by published writers, academic and otherwise
- Shaped their ideas to meet audience and contextual constraints
- Drew on structural knowledge acquired from reading, listening, and past instruction
- Used aural and visual scanning to tap language stored in memory

- Developed critical distance on their own and others' work through self-evaluations refined by audience response

Note how many of these strategies Carmen practiced during plateaus.

On March 26 Carmen brought in a new piece, done at home, in which revising and editing showed up much earlier than they had in the past. Working on "Dieting" for three hours in the Center, she reorganized and checked grammar again, this time at the draft-two stage. Like Kamal, Carmen had increased her efficiency, compressing various writing tasks into only two drafts, progress we would have missed had we looked only at her finished work. Another unexpected feature of this period was that Carmen treated her new piece as an exercise, using it to test strategies she'd discovered on the breakthrough piece. Her breakthrough topic motivated Carmen more strongly, however, and once convinced that strategies for reordering narratives could also be used to organize ideas for exposition, Carmen abandoned "Dieting" to work on "Drowning" again. Despite her short-term interest in the topic of dieting, Carmen showed no lack of commitment to practicing basic skills. Apparently it was not only writing strategies and rules but also positive attitudes, motivation, and commitment that Carmen learned to apply to expository work. One day, in fact, she arrived two hours early and stayed an hour late to work—for four hours altogether—on an organizing exercise she assigned herself:

> At 9:30 Carmen came in, brought a new piece about "Dieting" that she'd started at home, and worked on it for two hours until her group arrived. With it, she had an "outline" (of sorts). She said she had "just started writing without worrying about whether it made sense." She did the draft at home yesterday and said she was reading it over now, sorting it out as she had with her "Drowning" piece.
> The draft was in red ink, and Carmen had marked *in blue ink* near each paragraph's beginning to indicate which portions fit under each main topic. She had also bracketed certain sentences for possible relocation and said: "Since it's the second time working on topic, I trying to notice when I repeat." In the 11:30 group, Carmen worked for a third hour on this "Diet" piece.

Carmen was no longer "lazy" where writing was concerned: She was a serious writer who'd taken control of her work. The following excerpt, drawn from her three-page revision, shows the brackets and, in the margins, the organizational notes Carmen used for dividing freewritten material into subtopics. Notice how she stretched herself, using imagery to make her writing more vivid and reaching for precise diction (*impelling*), even when vocabulary was but partially under control (*regine*, *naturality*). By taking risks using words she barely knew, Carmen created chances to extend and refine her current knowledge of vocabulary and spelling at the point of need:

Body	. . . Your body is like an appartment, if you don't pay the rent you get kicked-out. [For that beautiful figure, you need more than good luck.] [Whether your petite or tall you need to exercise with body
Body	and mind, ~~y~~ that is, not move your body like the wind moves a leave, but, what ever you do ~~get~~ do it impelling energy.]. . . [To have a
Shape	beautiful shape you have to develop a regine that would last all your life. What works is useing a technique of patience, naturality, ac-
Diet	tivity, and never feel or be on a diet] [also never count Calories, is too
Diet	boring, and boring things are hard to keep.]

Carmen's work confirms a pattern we saw in Ned and Hosea—a pattern of students negotiating the level of help they need. In the sanctuary of three trusting workshop groups, students like these—one a standard, one a dialect, one an ESL speaker—worked close to the borders of their existing knowledge, practicing strategies and features they knew of but did not yet control. By moving into mistake-prone zones they'd previously avoided, they showed both their tutors and their groupmates what help they were ready for, thus ensuring that the help they got fell at the point of need. And when these three writers moved into that supercharged learning zone where new knowledge and know-how could build on existing knowledge, they found they could remember and apply rules and structural formats they had studied but had not been able to use in the past. Because they worked together, in interdependent groups, students learned to do today, with the help of tutor and friends, what tomorrow they would need to do independently.

At this point Carmen shows evidence of improvement with editing much like what I've documented in the case of Kamal. Jane's thesis (Lofts Thomas, 1988) offers similar examples, such as the quotes below, from students who claimed that receiving help at the point of need, in the context of writing they cared strongly about, helped them retain new material and apply what they already knew:

> Trying to correct my own work has been very helpful because it makes me more aware of why something is wrong, and if I can't find the mistake, it means more when it's pointed out to me and I remember it. (p. 422)

> I have gained a lot from being helped to find my own mistakes and to locate and rewrite weak sections in my writing. In my English class we learned a lot of grammar, but I would usually just forget it. It didn't mean anything. But in the WTC my writing gives me somewhere to start. As I look through my work and try to put myself in the reader's place, I find I am increasingly able to make my own alterations and corrections. The grammar I thought I had forgotten often comes back to me—and when it doesn't, I can ask my teacher or my group for help, and when I need to know something in my writing—or when I have a mistake pointed out by others—I remember what I am told. It has meaning for me because my writing has meaning, and the next time, I know what to do if I make the same mistake again. (p. 422)

Like these students, Carmen first learned to assess her weaknesses, then designed exercises and drills that helped her overcome them. Two days after reorganizing "Dieting," for example, she shifted from revising—at which she was now fairly fluent—to final, careful editing of the "Drowning" piece. Trusting Carmen's decision to abandon the exercise piece, Dianna took advantage of this shift in focus by making Carmen a process model for the step-by-step editing others in Carmen's group would be ready to practice soon:

> Carmen was working on her "Drowning" piece again. I held up her draft and talked about editing so the group would know how to begin. I emphasized the need to read for one pattern (such as past tense endings) at a time, then move on to another. I suggested she needed to check prepositions one last time.

After demonstrating how to separate and sequence editing tasks, Dianna backed away from overtly proactive behavior to interact more equally with students. As the dependence/interdependence/independence progression predicts, her increasingly independent groupmates responded proactively. Jamsed drew the quiet Mahmoud into group discussion, and Carmen, sharing strategies for locating errors, told groupmates she was now able to edit *during* drafting—evidence that she'd begun to internalize processes which, at the first of second semester, she'd barely understood. This proactive group was also independent enough not to act constrained by their tutor's agenda: Dianna's logs show them confidently ignoring her suggestions to pursue their own concerns about each others' work:

> As she worked, Carmen asked for help. From our session in which she had read the fourth draft [of "Drowning"], she had marked a few places to work on. We discussed the sentence "I started yelling but my voice didn't come out loud enough."
>
> Jamsed said, "Drowning voice that comes out is not normal voice." He turned to Mahmoud and asked, "What do you think?" Then he continued, "Voice could be 'shaky,' but that's when you go for speech."
>
> Carmen said, "No, couldn't be. When it happen, I can't think. It was kind of 'fear.' "
>
> Mahmoud said, "But did you *scream?*"
>
> I suggested Carmen brainstorm this section—think about what her scream might have felt or sounded like. I also suggested they use the *Thesaurus* she had brought in Monday. Mahmoud said, "I thought she couldn't yell."
>
> Jamsed asked, "Was there too much water?"
>
> Mahmoud said, "I was gonna suggest, say 'mute' because she couldn't talk, but maybe that's not right."
>
> I brought up Carmen's vague use of "weird" in "Her voice sounded 'weird.' "

After this discussion of connotation and usage, Ky consulted a reference, in search of the perfect word, thus illustrating how reference skills get practiced, in groups, at students' points of choice or need:

> Ky looked up "yell," "scream," and "shout" in the dictionary and read their definitions to Carmen.
> Finally we all went back to work—Carmen on "Drowning," Ky on "Swimming Pool," Mahmoud on "Pressures at School." Jamsed revised his long piece about witnessing his grandfather's death.

Carmen was not the only independent writer in group. Except for making announcements, in fact, Dianna had little to do:

> On April 4, Carmen told me before group that at home she had added two more parts to her "Drowning" piece but hadn't typed it yet. The group sat down to write. I talked about the Week 13 deadlines for the [WTC] book and handed out the typing guide for them to follow to help keep the format consistent.

Increasingly students themselves decided how group time should be spent, with Carmen acting consistently proactive by April 9, a pattern suggesting she might soon be able to be certified:

> I asked, "Who needs to do what?"
> Carmen had worked her "Drowning" piece, using notes from a group discussion, and wanted to read to the group. She had a separate page with two new parts and read a paragraph:
> My fear of deep water and what I was already experiencing made me very confused. I kept my body straight, jumping up and down, not daring to leave that awful raft, to keep me from drowning.
> Then she inserted this, from the separate page:
> A panic attack can be so powerful to be able to control your mind and body. Therefore, if I wouldn't have been scared, this probably would not have happened, because I did know how to swim.
> Carmen read the next problem area which she had worked on the week before, "I started yelling but my voice didn't come out loud enough," adding, "The sound of my voice and the feeling were as if someone were choking me."
> DOLORES [a Peruvian-American making up a session from my 10:30 group]: Was the water "strangling"? Try "I felt as though the water was *strangling* me."
> DIANNA: I think that sounds good.
> CARMEN: Yeah, it's a good way.
> JAMSED: I didn't like when you were gonna put . . .
> CARMEN [interrupting excitedly]: I think the thought is very original—"the water is *strangling*."

DOLORES: 'Cause it's all around you, no? I had that feeling of almost *drowning* you.

DIANNA: Don't forget you need to check on the prepositions.

CARMEN: Yes, I do.

DIANNA: Did you do it already? Do you have a question? Do you want us to listen to it with that in mind?

CARMEN: Well, I marked them all—the prepositions—to be sure they're right, but I *think* they're right.

There were, in fact, asterisks by almost every preposition and several that had once been misused were now correct.

Meanwhile, Dolores had noticed a discrepancy between how she and Carmen had formed the English subjunctive (see transcript above). During a chat about vocabulary in Ky's piece, Dolores sat silent, perusing a grammar text. The passage shows how writers became aware of grammatical issues, picking up standard forms from students with grammar no better than theirs:

> During the exchange with Ky, Dolores had been looking up the subjunctive in a grammar book in reference to the sentence she had suggested to Carmen earlier (She had offered ''I felt as though the water *was* strangling me,'' after Carmen had read, ''as though someone *were* choking me.'') She read to us what she found in the book about the subjunctive and we discussed it for a few minutes in the group.

Though increasingly independent, this group still practiced interactive strategies they could later use to improve personal, job-related, and academic writing. Carmen focused on editing for the rest of the term, but whenever the chance arose she also drilled herself on organizational strategies discovered during the breakthrough. Once, for example, when Jamsed read, Dianna noted: ''I didn't see the other [written responses], but when Carmen gave hers to Jamsed, she had outlined his reading for him.''

At semester's end, as publication deadlines grew near, groupmates worked alone or helped each other quietly, focusing largely on conventions of format and editing:

> I gave back Carmen's, Ky's and Mahmoud's pieces which they had rewritten as final drafts before typing to edit for the book. I worked with Carmen, asking Ky and Mahmoud to read over theirs to make corrections. I had made a few checks in their margins indicating something still needed editing at that line.
>
> Carmen really didn't need to do much more editing. We talked about the last paragraph since she expressed concern about the ending.
>
> Then I read over Ky's piece with him and after we fixed one or two verb tenses, I realized his piece ''My Overshoe'' was all one paragraph. We talked about paragraphing briefly, and I asked Carmen to move next to Ky so the two of them could discuss points where Ky could paragraph. They worked

quietly together for the rest of the session, deciding on five paragraphs (no relation to *the* five-paragraph essay!)

Even under pressure from the publication deadline, Dianna corrected no mistakes on student papers. Now did she try "to cover" rules students might someday need. Instead, she let them practice finding errors they knew they had made, focused their attention on more frequent, more stigmatized problems and emphasized whatever features each seemed most ready to learn. In the process, she "taught" generic editing strategies—how to find mistakes, learn from good writing, get help, and use references—that students could transfer to academic work. In other words, she taught grammar and mechanics incidentally, on a need-to-know basis, when students had problems with them.

Segment 6: Earning WTC Certification

Transferring Strategies Learned in the Center to Academic Writing. Unlike Kathy and Louise's somewhat more anxious students, this group made only passing references to outside assignments, and then only to share what they'd written or learned on their own. On April 18 (when Kathy's group was feeling anxiety), Carmen brought in a long research paper she'd done at home, and Dianna, spotting a need for further revision, recommended a reference to consult:

> Ky, Mahmoud, and Carmen brought in their papers all typed and ready for the book. I asked Ky and Mahmoud to proofread each other's while I worked with Carmen.
> She had brought in her History of Russia research paper—all 14 pages. (The assignment had been for a 12-page paper.) It was perfect timing, because now is the time for focusing on academic work.
> I read Carmen's term paper over briefly, and it seemed so logical, so organized! I did notice that her footnotes and bibliography were not in correct format, so I showed her Turabian's book as one example of correct form.

The fact that Dianna hadn't "taught" assignment writing directly did not mean Carmen hadn't gotten help when she needed it. Faced with this research paper, Carmen used Center approaches, solving problems at home and seeking support from peers, just as she had done with self-selected writing in group:

> Carmen started talking about this research paper and her writing in general. She said she had started discussing her work with her husband "like we do here." (I was excited and told her how my husband and I and my children have also begun to share ideas about our writing this year.)

I asked some questions about Carmen's revising process. She had written several sections at home on dieting and exercise—the same paper but different parts. She had done two drafts, one at home and one here. Now she was working on a third. I asked her if her revising process for "Dieting" was different from what she had done with "Drowning" (now titled "In the Pool"). Carmen said they were practically the same, explaining that she had "just started writing" and let whatever came out come.

Practicing what she'd learned on self-selected pieces, Carmen extended and refined writing abilities on her own. For example, though she didn't use textbook terminology, she began to distinguish *narrative* from *exposition*, demonstrating knowledge of their differing traits and goals. Her work helped convince us that, more than our own schooling had led us to believe, writing strategies practiced on narrative pieces could be used to meet the more abstract demands of expository prose:

> The pieces were different, she said, in that "Drowning" was *an event that happened* to her, but "Dieting" was *an overall experience*. She had read a lot about dieting so had "all sorts of ideas" to include as opposed to narrating an event chronologically as in "Drowning." Even though "Dieting" was different, Carmen said that what she learned revising the "drowning" story transferred to writing it.
>
> Carmen worked on another draft of "Dieting" that she had worked on at home. She had thought of some new ideas about dieting and instead of losing her thoughts had decided to write them down right away on a green piece of junk mail. Today she brought these thoughts in and worked them into her newest draft.

Soon it was time for end-of-semester routines—the final essay, two questionnaires, and a publication party to celebrate groupmates' appearance in *The Drafted Writers*, the photocopied collection of students' favorite pieces that the Center published (and sold at cost) at the end of each term:

> Jamie from the 10:30 group stayed late to do some more editing. Carmen did the final writing-process questionnaire today since she will be absent Wednesday. I hope to give her the exit essay on Monday. If we can't find a quiet place with the publication parties going on, she'll return on Thursday to write it.

Summative evaluation time was drawing near, but neither Diana nor Carmen seemed concerned. Though Dianna had once felt "at a loss how to help" Carmen's writing, since that time her view of Carmen's potential had changed. Following a naturally shifting scale of concerns (see Figure 5.1, p. 134), teacher-research had provided formative assessment—at the point of need—on the kinds of criteria listed in Figure 8.1. In addition to increasing practice with self-assessment, Carmen had received daily oral and/or written guidance from Dianna, along with increasingly skillful suggestions from her

amount of writing done
regularity of writing
development in writing attitudes
improvement in motivation
seriousness
took responsibility for own progress
changes in writing behaviors
diversity of things attempted
experiments/risk taking
  with topics
  with forms
thoughtfulness of response
responsibility to groupmates
insightful self-evaluations
asked for help when needed it
shared numerous drafts
discussed problems with group
large-group participation
maintained safe atmosphere

gave specific feedback
small-group work
partner work
used feedback effectively
style appropriate to projects
met scheduled deadlines
word processing
amount of revising
quality of revising
amount of work with editing
quality of editing
improved grammatical editing
improved spelling
improved punctuation
overall product quality
attentive to others' writing
attentive to instructions
drew out others
overall effort

Summary

truthfulness
thoughtfulness
thoroughness
timeliness
effort

product quality
improvement
independence (took responsibility
  for own success)
contributions to others
risk taking

Figure 8-1 **Illustrative Criteria for WTC Certification**

peers. All of these data consistently pointed to one conclusion—that Carmen was independent enough to be certified. Even without studying academic writing per se, Carmen had shown Dianna she could handle assignments alone:

> When certification time came, it wasn't difficult to make a decision. I knew how much Carmen had progressed by her dramatic breakthrough in revising. Although she had done some revising with Maria's group in the fall, it hadn't been as meaningful to her as what she learned this semester. For example, I remember the day this spring after she had come in with the cut-outs from her draft pasted together, when she spoke of Maria's suggestion to write on one side of the page. At the time it had been simply advice, with little meaning for Carmen, but this semester she had exclaimed, "Now I know *why* she told us to do that." Best of all, she had discovered cutting, pasting, and outlining on her own.
> After witnessing her process on the narrative "Drowning" piece, I saw Carmen use the same techniques on her expository piece about dieting. At

home she worked on a long research paper for her History of Russia class and talked about how she had made an outline and concentrated on organization. When she brought her final draft in, I was impressed by its tight, clear organization. She called my home a few weeks later to say she got a "92" on it.

I believe Carmen was prepared to handle writing in all her classes. She had become a strong, independent writer. I waited to read her final essay and to compare her pre- and post-WAT [Writing Apprehension Test] scores before giving final certification, but I knew she was ready.

Carmen's increasing confidence supported Dianna's conclusion: "Carmen called WTC in the summer session to tell me she was taking Advanced Composition (English 302) that summer."

Little was said in Dianna's log about writing across the disciplines, for Carmen's group expressed little desire for help in that area. Dianna therefore postponed such talk until the end of the term, but this group had few questions on the topic even then. As Yitna Firdyiwek put it after critiquing a draft of this chapter: "The 'postponed talk' you refer to, Marie, is just a safety net. The breakthrough students don't need it; in fact, *most students* don't need it, as Kathy's and Dianna's logs have shown."

Summary of Teaching Approaches Tutor-Researchers Used

Though to our knowledge she only once worked on an outside assignment in group, Carmen's academic writing hadn't improved by chance. Instead, strategies useful for all kinds of writing had grown strong in the sanctuary of a close-knit writing community. There a tutor learning to teach as her students learned to write had

- Successfully monitored her teaching success using teacher-research
- Relied on her personal writing experience as a guide
- Replicated the features of nonschool writing groups
- Provided diverse temptations—a smorgasbord of writing's rewards
- Modeled her own writing attitudes and strategies
- Carefully separated and sequenced writing tasks for students
- Put basic and ESL writers in charge of decisions about their work
- Transferred responsibility for the group's success to groupmates by shifting from proactive to interactive to reactive behaviors as appropriate
- Individualized instruction
- Watched for chances to teach incidentally, at the point of need
- Taught recursively, stepping students through a full complement of writing processes over and again as needed on piece after piece of writing

- Given basic writers practice critiquing each others' work
- Provided balanced, sequenced, and comprehensive evaluation
- Reinforced successes with honest praise, encouragement, and a focus on strengths
- Offered "sanctuary," minimized grades, and provided extra support during evaluation—all in order to make basic writers feel safer taking risks
- Encouraged students to talk and write about writing problems and processes
- Pointed out peer models (of process and product) for students to observe
- Shared her own experiences as a developing writer
- Taught conventions when needed to improve a particular piece
- Transferred responsibility for self-assessment to students
- Trusted student perceptions about what and how they needed to learn

Carmen's case confirms once again how relinquishing tutor control let WTC students practice strategies, forms, and conventions as they were needed; avoided the risk of boring them with repetitive drill; let them choose risks they felt comfortable with at the time; and avoided the sense of failure all had felt in the past. Freedom of choice made a difference by letting students lead from strength, allowing them to experiment with a few features at a time, and letting them practice tasks only slightly harder than what they had mastered, thus creating a balance between risk taking and control. *In sum, it was teaching at the point of motivated choice that prepared students like Carmen to write academic prose.*

An Independent Perspective on This Chapter's Analysis

When I first drafted this chapter (near the end of Year 5) Team 4 tutor Yitna Firdyiwek tested my analysis against his logs and his memories of four semesters spent working with groups. Yitna promised to read the chapter critically, watch for overgeneralizations from Dianna's Year 3 data and tell me if I'd neglected or misread any evidence. Yitna didn't think so, he said, and these were his reasons why:

Dianna's approach is the WTC standard, a standard motivated by tutors' experience, by recognizing patterns through our process of teacher-research. It comes from seeing that generally, *toward the end of each semester*, students "awaken" to the relevance of the group experience and apply it directly to academic situations. I believe this happens because of the third (and dominant) approach you describe—incidental teaching at the point of choice or need.

In short, Yitna said, instead of being separate approaches, all three of our incidental teaching strategies were the same:

> In other words, our three strategies for teaching academic writing are the same. "Planned incidental instruction" and "opportunistic teaching" are— *and this is the point I am making*—simply other examples of "teaching at the point of need." So that's what I mean when I say incidental teaching is the standard. *It isn't only the standard, it's the only approach we have—for academic writing, personal writing, essays, nonfiction, poetry and other creative genres. And— I suppose I should also include—for mechanics and grammar rules.*

Yitna's words confirmed a key linkage of our analysis—that the regressions in attitude that interrupted student progress, launching them on downward spirals of resistance, frustration, and failure, almost always resulted from "the threat of grades"—from summative evaluation students weren't quite ready for.

> The "postponed talk" you referred to in the last paragraph [p. 246] was our response to the pattern of collective anxiety, near the end of the term, that you've shown so clearly in Kathy Briggs' log. We confidently postpone talking about academic papers because we have learned to "predict" or anticipate these regressions—these anxious "demands" for "pep talks" on academic writing. We now recognize that these conditioned attitudinal measures reveal more about the threat of grades—about summative evaluation—than about what students need to learn to do well in school.

Yitna was not alone in highlighting the negative impact of grading. Jane Lofts Thomas (1988) dealt with it extensively in her thesis, and tutors' logs and research reports contain dozens of references. Frustration with grades had also been widespread among writers who teach (Nelson, 1982b). In addition to clear-cut patterns in most of the interviews, I'd observed writer/teachers in classrooms, in private and public schools, who postponed (or abandoned) grading with good results. Because in these classrooms the motivating power of writing's intrinsic rewards had been successfully substituted for that of grades, I'd eliminated grades from our program from the start, a decision tutor-researchers never questioned, perhaps because within a few weeks their data supported it.

What I had noticed but not fully understood, however, was how strongly negative evaluation thwarted success. Of course, I'd known that student writing improved when teachers first focused on strengths. And I'd known that anxiety scrambled prose and contorted ideas. I'd known enough to create and maintain sanctuary in the Center. But I'd never quite understood, until Year 8, as I was drafting what I hoped would be a conclusion for this book, that our choice of evaluation approach was the most fundamental decision affecting writers' success, and that it therefore functioned as a key linkage in this analysis. This decision illustrates a common trait of studies like this one— the degree to which learning (analysis) expands incrementally as researchers cycle through their data time and again, relying on writing to bring implicit connections to the conscious level. Though I've sketched broad outlines of this effect at points in the text, I have neither time nor space to elaborate further here, for details of this late-breaking finding remain to be specified. *Suffice it to say, however, that traditional evaluation had prevented basic and ESL writers from developing and that we reversed their success rates in the WTC by consciously reversing how we evaluated them.* As we have seen, however, despite our widespread success, summative evaluation, at the beginning and end of our program, dictated by the hierarchy within which we operated, repeatedly led to downward spirals among the writers we taught.

Timing and Development

In addition to making clear the problems caused by hierarchical evaluation, Carmen's case forced us to acknowledge how long development takes, to look at how and why developmental schedules differ so dramatically from one writer to the next:

1. We learned that we needed to broaden our definition of *learning to write* to include gaining awareness of writing's complexity.
2. We learned that this complex awareness, which triggers upward spirals, is broader and more holistic than we had realized in the past.
3. We learned that holistic awareness can take a long time to develop, depending on a student's past experience/awareness base.
4. We learned that some students require significant lag time between the point at which awareness brings attitude and behavior change and the point at which visible changes show up in the writing itself.
5. And we learned that lockstep evaluation sorted learners unfairly, that basic writers can judge their progress better than experts can, that they could tell when they were ready for summative evaluation, and that in grading as in every other aspect of teaching, WTC students did better when we withdrew to "follow the kid" and placed responsibility on the students themselves.

In other words, Carmen taught us about the role of time. She taught us that less experienced students needed more time to develop and that if we could accept this need nonjudgmentally, their writing would eventually improve, making them as successful as the quicker learners we'd taught. She taught us that students' past writing experience and the kind of teaching they'd known in other classes interacted with the frequency and timing of evaluation to produce different schedules for writing development. And she taught us that these different learning timelines are acceptable, that we need not lower expectations for students who are slow, and that we certainly do not need to punish them with bad grades.

9

The Next Ten Years

The CAU Writing Tutorial Center no longer exists, and tutors and I have since moved on to other challenges, but the learning that began there has continued. When I hear from former tutors, or from students like Kamal, they speak of new directions in their professional growth that result from adopting a teacher-researcher stance. I, of course, share my newest explorations with them as well, asking for feedback based on their recent experience.

From the start, Center experience affected the classes I taught, for WTC methods proved useful in many other contexts. For example, during the WTC's second semester, Team 1's preference for group tutorials convinced me to try using permanent five-member groups in all of my graduate and undergraduate classes. I started slowly, letting groups meet only four or five times that semester, but when at the end of each term I asked students how to improve the course further, the dominant theme in class after class was "We need more time for groups." In every writing course I teach, I now form permanent groups after modeling interactive approaches for three weeks or so, and from that point I allot about fifty percent of class time for group work.

The WTC project influenced tutors' and my teaching in other ways. For example, it forced us to redefine what we saw as "the basics." After seeing Carmen and others' progress with self-selected drill, I felt less pressure to assign exercises and drills. Students' problems applying rules teachers systematically "covered" also weakened whatever lingering inclination I had toward preventive/corrective instruction in grammar and mechanics, convincing me that teaching rules one to one, at the point of need, could be an effective approach in full-sized classes too. When working at the point of choice, writing what they preferred, practicing rules and techniques they knew they had trouble with on self-selected pieces, my writing students, like those in the WTC, began to view risk taking, revising, getting feedback from peers, and editing step by step as strategies they could transfer to assignments from other teachers. Gradually, then, as I gave students more and more freedom of choice, their motivation and commitment increased, and they directed their learning more effectively than I could do.

It's hard to write a conclusion to findings like these that won't stop emerging. This section is therefore as much a beginning as an end, a preview of insights still being gleaned from Center data, a rough map sketching where many loose ends appear to lead. Writing it brings to mind a comment made by Judith Goetz while I was a student of hers at the University of Georgia.

"You've got wonderful data," Jude said, referring to my earlier study of writers who teach. "But then, that's a benefit of this kind of research. Unlike those who do more deductive, quantitative studies, you'll be publishing from these data for at least ten years." I postponed extensive writing about that study's findings to test their validity in the WTC, but the work we did there confirms Jude's prediction, for after eight years of analysis, I have only begun to write. Our work also confirms the use of research by teacher/researchers for understanding individual students and how they learn, for insightful self-evaluation of classroom practices, for ferreting out unfounded assumptions about teaching and learning, and for program development, evaluation, and restructuring.

Even now, at the end of Year 8, the data we collected offer so many insights it's hard to decide which leads to follow. At least four unreported lines of inquiry have begun, two in response to questions asked by skeptical teachers, the third a Year 2 tutor's pursuit of a hunch of mine, and the fourth (which now seems to have produced a key linkage), an outgrowth of my struggle to draft a conclusion for this book. Let me sketch each of these lines of inquiry in turn.

1. And *Finally*—Back to the Basics

Early in the program widespread lack of familiarity with the workshop approaches of a new teaching paradigm forced us to gather evidence to fill in the gaps we found in the understanding of teachers attending the workshops we gave. Invariably, it seemed, some participants got the mistaken impression that WTC tutors and I resisted teaching "the basics." Though we explained that "postponing" such instruction did not mean that we abandoned it altogether, some teachers had trouble even conceiving of methods they'd never observed. Their honest misperceptions frustrated us at the time, but they helped us see where our presentations were incomplete and set us gathering evidence to fill in the gaps in what the teachers we talked with understood.

A paradigm shift had been reshaping writing instruction for several years (Emig, 1981; Hairston, 1982; Nelson, 1982b, 1983b; Young, 1978), and these problems of understanding were therefore to be expected. Making the shift from deficiency-focused, preventive-corrective instruction to growth-focused, experience-embedded learning required teachers to accept not only new teaching approaches but a theory that contradicted tenets of the theory that implicitly shaped their work. To *understand* (much less *adopt*) new-paradigm teaching approaches, they had to question dozens of "common-sense" beliefs (Mayher, 1990), including the assumptions that "writers are born, not made," that grammar and mechanics are "basics" writers must master before writing well, that negatively focused evaluation is "objective," that preventive/corrective instruction aids writing development, that writing development occurs arhetorically, and that instruction-induced "deficiencies" are the victim's fault.

This book offers data that shed new light on these issues, but as we've seen information is best acquired at the point of need. To address the questions workshop participants often came up with—on the assumption that readers might have similar concerns—Team 4 and I considered concluding this book with a chapter showing how tutors taught grammar and mechanics at the point of need. Though dozens of concrete examples are scattered throughout these pages, teammates felt that concluding with a collection of excerpts would help teachers who'd never experienced teaching at the point of need, especially if the excerpts were grouped under handbookish titles like these:

Vocabulary	Active and Passive Voice
Spelling	Usage
Punctuation	Transitions
Verb Agreement	Topic Sentences
Apostrophe Use	Outlining
Sentence Combining	Narrative Technique

We laughingly dubbed this prospective chapter "And *Finally*—Back to the Basics," but decided against including it after Bill Smith, a writing researcher at the University of Pittsburgh, posed a question that helped us clarify our central goal.

"Is your goal to write a methods textbook for teachers?" Bill asked. "Or is the central focus how you learned from teacher-research?" Though with teacher-research the two can be hard to distinguish at times, Team 4 at last decided against the former approach. Instead of prescribing methods that might or might not work in other settings, they felt, focusing on teacher-research as a problem-solving tool offered teachers a way to find out what methods would work for them and hope of improving whatever methods they currently used. Along the way it would help them discover any mistaken beliefs that might be interfering with their students' development. Since that point, the book veered away from a focus on methods, but teachers do need demonstrations of better ways to teach "the basics," and the logs contain many that we feel might be useful to them. If time permits, I would like to collect—from the tapes, videos, and logs—demonstrations of tutors teaching "the basics" at the point of need and of basic writers' positive responses to them.

2. Ruling Out the Hothouse Effect

Another response common among teachers exposed to our work was a pair of questions we were also asking ourselves: Could Center-tested methods succeed in other contexts? Or were they merely educational hothouse plants, requiring special conditions only the WTC could supply?

"I can tell that your approach works well in your situation. . . . " We heard this opener time and again from high school and college teachers—followed by assertions that it could never work for them, and always because of some contrast between our situation and theirs. These teachers' resistance echoed the pattern I'd seen in Team 1:

- You see, I don't teach college—I teach *elementary* school.
- My ESL students don't know enough English for this.
- I don't work with college students. I teach *eleventh grade*.
- I teach AP classes, and we can't *do* that in AP.

On and on went the litany of teacher's excuses, each based on some special case we had failed to address:

- Our basic writers are more basic than yours.
- My principal would *never* allow me to throw out grades.
- I can't teach like that. The counselor sends me the dyslexic kids.
- Our students are too *competitive*. They'd never follow "the rule."

At the beginning there was little we could say in response, for we were still testing the workshop approach in the Center. As the years passed, we had less trouble addressing such reservations. For though our central focus was basic and ESL college writers, we tested our theories under a widening range of conditions. After a year or two in the Center, tutors took other jobs, and as most of my own classes were for writing majors, whether at the graduate or undergraduate levels, we tested Center approaches with students of diverse abilities in a wide array of educational settings—from elementary to graduate school; in the United States, the United Kingdom, and Asia; with gifted, nongifted, dyslexic, disturbed, and retarded children. We used the methods in language institutes, in community colleges, with small groups of doctoral students, and in universities overseas—including one in the People's Republic of China and one in Korea. We used workshop approaches to teach creative writing, advanced composition, technical writing, advanced exposition, and in lower-level composition classes. We used them in business settings, at home and overseas, with unskilled employees and mid-level management. We even tested what we were learning in adult basic education courses offered for a large county school system's maintenance staff.

In private and public schools, in interdisciplinary settings, and with basic and gifted writers of all ages, tutors and I used now habitual teacher-research techniques to monitor and adapt the approach that evolved in the WTC. And whenever tutors continued to test their assumptions in the contexts where they taught, the workshop approach they'd grown comfortable with in the Tutorial Center expanded and/or adapted to meet their students' needs.

3. Recognizable Changes in Writing Development

A third focus of study that may be forthcoming sketches an emerging theory of phases in writing development—not discrete stages, perhaps, for boundaries are hard to define (and stages rarely describe nonlinear and recursive growth) but recognizable phases though which writers *tend* to pass. Through many discussions and written dialogues, tutor Judith Friedman and I informed each other's thinking until, as frequently happens in this kind of collaboration, we sometimes lost track of which ideas were whose. Focusing largely on qualitative shifts in student writing, we explored relationships between affect and cognition, between motivation and growth, between linguistic fluency and fluency of ideas. Judith and I have not yet fully formalized our thinking, but in the several years since we began this work, my classroom experience has consistently supported one of the central tenets of our work—that pursuing private associations on the page activates thinking processes that come naturally but that writers at all levels rarely tap otherwise.

4. Adopting a Bias That Allows Students to Learn

A fourth focus of study stems from my continuing efforts to integrate into the framework evaluation-related factors that lace all the data, not just those gathered within the WTC. These include the affective and motivational impact of grading as compared to the impact of the rewards writing brings, differences between formative and summative evaluation, and the role of student- rather than teacher-controlled assessment. I'm looking closely at negative bias in evaluations that have long been called "objective" and at the contrast between this bias and the less exclusive results of a more balanced, sequenced, and comprehensive approach.

Assessment-related factors that also seem to belong include the structural stratification of hierarchies, self-fulfilling prejudices against those the powers that be call "weak," and the characteristics of laterally structured, inclusive settings that use assessment as a tool to help all who work hard succeed (see Nelson, 1988, 1989, for preliminary development of these themes). The interactions among such factors are one current focus; another is their impact on writing development.

Gradually the "grading" analysis is coming together, and having immersed myself in the data for several months, I now believe that within this tangle of variables lurks the key linkage that could integrate everything we've learned. That's a tale for another time, as no framework has yet emerged; but when one does, it's sure to affect almost every page of this book. There is, after all, a ripple effect in emergent-design research.

The Ripple Effect in Qualitative Analyses

Because explorations like these are embedded in complex contexts, one new insight can affect everything that's been learned. In other words, an important finding, as part of a complex system, can lead to realignments among all of the system's parts, sometimes sending shock waves through an entire analysis. For example, each time I drafted a new chapter for this book, each preceding chapter demanded extensive revision to reconcile earlier findings with emerging ones. These secondary refinements in turn produced smaller ripples, requiring still further fine-tuning of sections of the text.

Such instability in one's knowledge can be disconcerting, especially as publication or graduation deadlines draw near. But instructional solutions, deeper understanding, increased classroom confidence, and greater student success were among the rewards that made this tedious process worthwhile. It takes time to bring "fresh knowledge" to the conscious level, but even before that happens teacher-research offers immediate classroom rewards to any teacher willing to follow her intuitions—as long as those intuitions are systematically informed. Team 1's breakthrough in attitude—the passing of their resistance to new approaches for ESL writers within a mere two weeks after this research project began—illustrates the immediacy of the insights available. Team 5 tutor Jody Bolcik (see Chapter 3) phrased it aptly, I think, when I suggested she cut log-keeping efforts from four groups to two:

> Hindsight/Insight/Foresight—that's what I get from my logs. . . . As I write what happened each day in my groups, I begin to figure out what my students need from me next. . . . So even though keeping two logs would take less time than four and I could focus data-collection on my research topic, I'm not willing to stop keeping logs on all my groups because it's from the logs that I'm learning how to teach.

Teacher Empowerment—Tutors' Ultimate Reward

The Writing Tutorial Center was dismantled three years ago, and I have since left CAU for another institution. I am therefore especially pleased to offer this account of the daring way in which five teams of beginning TAs used qualitative teacher-research to establish themselves as teachers. Like the basic and ESL writers with whom they worked, these mostly first-year teachers empowered themselves by relying on the interdependence available in small groups. Empowered by collaborative insights gleaned from teacher-research, they developed into skillful and independent professionals who were confident implementing an unfamiliar approach, were unafraid to confront mistaken assumptions affecting their work, were willing to examine their own strengths and weaknesses, were capable of helping every willing student improve, were able to motivate large numbers of unwilling ones, were competent to decide what help each student needed next, and, in retrospect, were seemingly destined to succeed. (See Nelson, 1988, for negative cases.)

The Development of Teaching Abilities

Learning to teach, like learning to write, is developmental. In addition, however, hierarchically structured schooling and the subtractive evaluation on which it relies make not only basic writers, but also those who teach them, feel insecure about taking the risks lasting growth requires (Nelson, 1988, 1989). Add to this the fact that one change always necessitates others, for changing one part of a system requires adaptations in other parts, and the position in which many teachers find themselves becomes clear. Working in rigidly structured systems that discourage change and penalize teachers for the loose ends their experiments produce, many teachers get trapped in evaluatory catch 22s not unlike the ones they have freed their students from. Given the fact that triangles are highly rigid structures, how appropriate that hierarchies are triangular in shape!

It would be nice if nonelitist, growth-oriented teaching did not require beginning teachers to struggle against odds like these, but hierarchies are justified by elaborate evaluations that interrupt and inhibit upward spirals of development. Given these realities, it's naive to expect teachers to try to alter existing conditions without assurance that such risk taking is safe. Unless we shift to formative evaluation of teachers, and offer them ways to understand and solve problems change entails, it is unfair to expect them to implement programs that others in their school communities don't understand.

The experience of the Center's first-year teaching assistants, however, leads me to suggest: 1. that collaborative teacher-research offers much to preservice education and 2. that it may help us streamline teacher education by providing a means by which teaching methods and theory can be taught incidentally, at the point of need. How else could groups of teachers with almost no prior training develop within a semester the expertise logs document:

1. The hindsight/insight/foresight teacher-research helped tutors develop
2. The personalized instruction teacher-research made possible

3. The solutions teacher-research helped tutors in crisis find
4. The growth-oriented self-assessments it helped tutors do
5. The confidence and success their students experienced as a result
6. The highly professional attitudes and behaviors tutors developed
7. The independence and confidence they therefore experienced

In other words, teacher-research empowered Center tutors by contributing to the kinds of conditions professionals seek—autonomy in making professional decisions, a method of gathering the data those decisions require, collegial support, a range of feedback on their efforts, and strategies for assessing and improving their own work. Teacher-research also offers teachers, should they need it, a body of evidence with which to defend the way they teach.

Works Cited

Allen, T. D. (1982). *Writing to create ourselves: New approaches for teachers, students, and writers*. Norman, OK: University of Oklahoma Press.

Becker, H. (1970). Problems of inference and proof in participant observation. In H. Becker, *Sociological work: Methods and substance* (pp. 25–38). New Brunswick, NJ: Transaction Books.

Belenky, M. F., Clinchy, B. M., Goldberger, N. R., & Tarule, J. M. (1986). *Women's ways of knowing: The development of self, voice, and mind*. New York: Basic Books.

Blumer, H. (1969). *Symbolic interactionism*. Englewood Cliffs, NJ: Prentice Hall.

Bogdan, R., & Biklen, S. K. (1982). *Qualitative research for education: An introduction to theory and methods*. Boston: Allyn and Bacon.

Britton, J., Burgess, T., Martin, N., McLeod, A., & Rosen, M. (1975). *The development of writing abilities (11–18)*. London: Macmillan Education.

Brown, R. (1973). *A first language: The early stages*. Cambridge, MA: Harvard University Press.

Dale, P. S. (1976). *Language development: Structure and function*, 2nd ed. New York: Holt, Rinehart and Winston.

DeVilliers, P., & DeVilliers, J. (1979). *Language acquisition*. Cambridge, MA: Harvard University Press.

Dulay, H., & Burt, M. (1978). From research to method in bilingual education. In James E. Alatis (Ed.), *Georgetown University roundtable on languages and linguistics*. Washington, DC: Georgetown University.

Elbow, P. (1973). *Writing without teachers*. New York: Oxford University Press.

Emig, J. (1977). Writing as a mode of learning. *College Composition and Communication, 28*, 122–128.

Emig, J. (1981). Inquiry paradigms and writing. *College Composition and Communication, 33*, 64–75.

Erickson, F. (1977). Some approaches to inquiry in school-community ethnography. *Anthropology & Education Quarterly, 8*, 58–69.

Erickson, F. (1986). Qualitative methods in research on teaching. In M. C. Wittrock (Ed.), *Handbook of research on teaching*, 3rd ed. (pp. 119–161). New York: Macmillan.

Erickson, F., & Mohatt, G. (1982). Cultural organization of participation structures in two classrooms of Indian students. In G. Spindler (Ed.), *Doing the ethnography of schooling: Educational anthropology in action* (pp. 132–174). New York: Holt, Rinehart and Winston.

Erickson, F., & Wilson, J. (1982). *Sights and sounds of life in schools: A resource guide to film and videotape for research and education* (Research Series No. 125). East Lansing, MI: College of Education, Institute for Research on Teaching.

Gardner, R., & Lambert, W. (1972). *Attitudes and motivation in second language learning*. Rowley, MA: Newbury House.

Gingras, R. C. (1978). Second-language acquisition and foreign language teaching. In R. C. Gingras (Ed.), *Second-language acquisition and foreign language teaching*. Washington, DC: Center for Applied Linguistics.

Glaser, B. G., & Strauss, A. (1967). *The discovery of grounded theory: Strategies for qualitative research*. New York: Aldine.

Goetz, J. P., & LeCompte, M. D. (1981). Ethnographic research and the problem of data reduction. *Anthropology and Education Quarterly, 12*(1), 51–70.

Goetz, J. P., & LeCompte, M. D. (1984). *Ethnography and qualitative design in educational research*. Orlando, FL: Academic Press.

Goldberg, N. (1986). *Writing down the bones: Feeling the writer within*. Boston: Shambhala Publications.

Gumperz, J. (1968). The speech community. In D. L. Sills (Ed.), *The international encyclopedia of the social sciences* (Vol. 9, pp. 381–386). New York: Macmillan & The Free Press.

Hairston, Maxine (1982). The winds of change: Thomas Kuhn and the revolution in the teaching of writing. *College Composition and Communication, 33,* 78–86.

Hearn, L. (1920). *Talks to writers*. New York: Dodd, Mead.

Hymes, D. (1972). Models of the interaction of language and social life. In J. J. Gumperz & D. Hymes (Eds.), *Directions in sociolinguistics: The ethnography of communication* (pp. 35–71). New York: Holt, Rinehart and Winston.

Hymes, D. (1974). *Foundations in sociolinguistics: An ethnographic approach*. Philadelphia: University of Pennsylvania Press.

Jacob, E. (1987). Qualitative research traditions: A review. *Review of Educational Research, 57,* 1–50.

Kirby, D., & Liner, T. (1981). *Inside out: Developmental strategies for teaching writing*. Postsmouth, NH: Boynton/Cook.

Krashen, S. D. (1978). The monitor model for second-language acquisition. In R. C. Gingras (Ed.), *Second language acquisition and foreign language teaching*. Washington, DC: Center for Applied Linguistics.

Krashen, S. D. (1981). *Second language acquisition and second language learning*. Oxford, England: Pergamon Press.

Krashen, S. D. (1982). *Principles and practice in second language acquisition*. New York: Pergamon Press.

Krashen, S. D. (1984). *Writing: Research, theory and applications*. New York: Pergamon Press.

Lofts Thomas, J. (1988). *Flexible and oblique approaches to teaching writing*. Unpublished master's thesis, George Mason University, Fairfax, VA.

Macrorie, K. (1968). *Writing to be read*. Rochelle Park, NJ: Hayden Book Company.

Macrorie, K. (1970). *Telling writing*. Rochelle Park, NJ: Hayden Book Company.

Martin, N., D'Arcy, P., Newton, B., & Parker, R. (1976). *Writing and learning across the curriculum 11–16*. London: Ward Lock Educational for the Schools Council.

Mayher, John S. (1990). *Uncommon sense: Theoretical practice in language education*. Portsmouth, NH: Boynton/Cook.

Meltzer, B. N., Petras, J. W., & Reynolds, L. T. (1975). *Symbolic interactionism: Genesis, varieties and criticism*. London: Routledge & Kegan Paul.

Murray, D. H. (1968). *A writer teaches writing: A practical method of teaching composition*. Boston: Houghton Mifflin.

Murray, D. H. (1978). Teach the motivating force of revision. *English Journal, 67*, 56–60.

Nelson, M. W. (1982a). Exploding all over the page: They can write better than they can. *Georgia English Counselor, 20*(2), 7–9, 18.

Nelson, M. W. (1982b). Writers who teach: A naturalistic investigation. *Dissertations Abstracts International, 42*, 3480A (University Microfilms No. 82-01, 569).

Nelson, M. W. (1983a). Trusting poetry to teach itself: A naturalistic approach to reading and writing poems. In C. R. Duke & S. A. Jacobsen (Eds.), *Reading and writing poetry: Successful approaches for the student and teacher* (pp. 59–67). Phoenix, AZ: The Oryx Press.

Nelson, M. W. (1983b). Bridging the paradigm gap—Adopting an expert-practitioner stance. *The English Record, 34*(4), 22–28.

Nelson, M. W. (1986). George Mason University required writing programs. In P. Connolly & T. Vilardii, (Eds.), *New methods in college writing pro-*

grams: Theories in practice (pp. 40–47). New York: Modern Language Association.

Nelson, M. W. (November, 1987). *Collaborative, cumulative analytic designs: A model for increasing the rigor of classroom teacher-research.* Paper presented at the meeting of the NCTE Research Assembly, Los Angeles.

Nelson, M. W. (1988). Women's ways: Interactive patterns in predominantly female research teams. In B. Bate & A. Taylor (Eds.), *Women communicating: Studies of women's talk* (pp. 199–232). Norwood, NJ: Ablex Publishing Company.

Nelson, M. W. (November 1989). Patriarchical elitism vs. inclusive women's ways: How deficiency and growth models of assessment affect university-level learning. Paper presented at the Conference on Gender in Academe, Tampa, FL.

Orage, A. R. (1930). *Psychological exercises.* New York: Samuel Weiser.

Phillips, S. U. (1983). *The invisible culture: Communication in classroom and community on the Warm Springs Indian Reservation.* New York: Longman.

Rose, M. (1980). Rigid rules, inflexible plans, and the stifling of language: A cognitivist analysis of writer's block. *College Composition and Communication, 31,* 389–401.

Schatzman, L., & Strauss, A. L. (1973). *Field research: Strategies for a natural sociology.* Englewood Cliffs, NJ: Prentice Hall.

Schumann, J. H. (1978). The acculturation model for second-language acquisition. In R. C. Gingras (Ed.), *Second-language acquisition and foreign language teaching* (pp. 27–50). Washington, DC: Center for Applied Linguistics.

Skinner, B. F. (1956). A case history in scientific method. *The American Psychologist, 11,* 221–233.

Slobin, D. I. (1971). *Psycholinguistics.* Glenview, IL: Scott, Foresman.

Smith, F. (1973). *Psycholinguistics and reading.* New York: Holt, Rinehart and Winston.

Smith, F. (1986). *Insult to intelligence.* New York: Arbor House.

Stake, R. E. (1988). Case study methods in educational research: Seeking sweet water. In R. M. Jaegar (Ed.), *Complementary methods for research in education* (pp. 253–265). Washington, DC: American Educational Research Association.

Stevick, E. W. (1980). *Teaching languages: A way and ways.* Rowley, MA: Newbury House.

Taylor, B. P. (1974). Toward a theory of language acquisition. *Language Learning, 24*(1), 23–35.

Taylor, B. P. (1981). Content and written form: A two-way street. *TESOL Quarterly, 15,* 5–13.

Terrell, T. D. (November, 1977). A natural approach to second language acquisition and learning. *Modern Language Journal, 61,* 325–337.

Vygotsky, L. S. (1962). *Thought and language.* Cambridge, MA: MIT Press.

Vygotsky, L. S. (1978). *Mind in society.* Cambridge, MA: Harvard University Press.

Welsh, T. K. (1988). *An integrated framework for the acquisition of second language and written proficiency.* Unpublished D.A.Ed. project, George Mason University, Fairfax, VA.

Wolcott, H. E. (1988). Ethnographic research in education. In R. M. Jaegar (Ed.), *Complementary methods for research in education* (pp. 187–206). Washington, DC: American Educational Research Association.

Worsham, S. E. (1980). *A naturalistic study of a basic writing program.* Unpublished Educational Specialist project, University of Georgia, Athens, GA.

Wotring, A. M. (1981). Writing to think about high school chemistry. In G. Camp (Series Ed.), *Two studies of writing in high school science.* Berkeley, CA: Bay Area Writing Project Classroom Research Series.

Young, R. (1978). Paradigms and problems: Needed research in rhetorical invention. In C. R. Cooper & L. Odell (Eds.), *Research on composing: Points of departure* (pp. 29–48). Urbana, IL: National Council of Teachers of English.

Zamel, V. (1976). Teaching composition in the ESL classroom: What we can learn from research in the teaching of English. *TESOL Quarterly, 10,* 67–76.

Zamel, V. (1982). Writing: The process of discovering meaning. *TESOL Quarterly, 16,* 195–209.

Zamel, V. (1983). The composing processes of advanced ESL students: Six case studies. *TESOL Quarterly, 17,* 165–187.

Index